# MODERNITY
# AND ITS
# DISCONTENTS

# MODERNITY
# AND ITS
# DISCONTENTS

*edited by*
JAMES L. MARSH, JOHN D. CAPUTO,
*and* MEROLD WESTPHAL

FORDHAM UNIVERSITY PRESS
New York
1992

Copyright © 1992 by Fordham University
All rights reserved
LC 91–46765
ISBN 0–8232–1344–7 (cloth)
0–8232–1345–5 (paper)

Library of Congress Cataloging-in-Publication Data

Modernity and its discontents / edited by James L. Marsh, John D.
  Caputo, and Merold Westphal.
    p.   cm.
  Based on a symposium at Fordham University in March, 1989.
  Includes bibliographical references and index.
  ISBN 0-8232-1344-7 : $32.50. — ISBN 0-8232-1345-5 (pbk). : $19.95
  1. Postmodernism—Congresses.   2. Philosophy, Modern—Congresses.
I. Marsh, James L.   II. Caputo, John D.   III. Westphal, Merold.
B831.2.M63   1992
190'.9'04—dc20                                                91-46765
                                                                   CIP

Printed in the United States of America

# Contents

# Abbreviations

PCM      James L. Marsh, *Post-Cartesian Meditations: An Essay in Dialectical Phenomenology* (New York: Fordham University Press, 1988).

RH        John D. Caputo, *Radical Hermeneutics: Repetition, Deconstruction and the Hermeneutic Project* (Bloomington: Indiana University Press, 1987).

# Preface

## *Merold Westphal*

Two books, two visions of philosophy, two friends and sometime colleagues. Do we not have the makings of an exciting philosophical dialogue? Not quite. The crucial ingredient, as the Socrates of the *Gorgias* reminds us, is the willingness to enter into conversation, to abjure the making of speeches and to engage in open and honest question and answer without precondition. In this volume two contemporary philosophical postures, which, for the sake of convenience, can be labeled critical modernism and postmodernism, have been incarnated in persons who embody that crucial willingness to converse. While neither can be accused of passing up all opportunities to score rhetorical points, both have shown themselves passionately unwilling to reduce dialogue to playing games or to allow jargon to compromise the search for understanding.

This particular incarnation of the dialogue between critical modernism and postmodernism has a second remarkable asset. Readers of this volume and of the two books that lie behind it, *Radical Hermeneutics* and *Post-Cartesian Meditations,* will note with gratitude that Jack Caputo does not write like Derrida and Jim Marsh does not write like Habermas. Both have resisted the temptation to identify obscurity with profundity and have rather put in the service of their readers their ability to write lucid prose.

In seeking to make sense out of this debate it is important to keep in mind the political and philosophical common ground on which it is fought. Politically speaking, it takes place well to the left of center. Neither Caputo nor Marsh is willing to let the evils of state socialism or its collapse in eastern Europe blind him to the sufferings and injustices created and therefore tolerated by American society.

But the philosophical proximity that accounts for much of the heat generated by the disagreements that come to the fore is, if anything, more important. The shared presupposition of the present debate is the failure, to date at least, of the Enlightenment project. In an oft-quoted footnote to the First Edition Preface to the *Critique of Pure Reason,* Kant defines the key element of that project even better, perhaps, than in his famous essay, "What is Enlightenment?":

> Our age is, in especial degree, the age of criticism, and to criticism, everything must submit. Religion through its sanctity, and lawgiving through its majesty may seek to exempt themselves from it. But then they awaken just suspicion, and cannot claim the sincere respect which reason accords only to that which has been able to sustain the test of free and open examination. [A xii]

It was the Enlightenment's intention to subject the prevailing social order to critical examination, and, in the process, to examine the theories, including theological theories, that provided its ideological justification. Thus, for example, John Locke directs a critique both at the political institution of absolute monarchy and at the divine right of kings theory that was often used to legitimate the former. The goal was a utopian one, as expressed in the title of Becker's classic, *The Heavenly City of the Eighteenth-Century Philosophers*, and in Hegel's summary of the Enlightenment dream, "The two worlds are reconciled and heaven is transplanted to earth below."

That sentence from Hegel's *Phenomenology of Spirit* is the immediate introduction to his analysis of the French Revolution, entitled "Absolute Freedom and Terror" (VI, B, III). In it he argues that the Terror initiated by Robespierre revealed the intellectual bankruptcy of the Enlightenment in spite of its noble aspirations.

If critical modernism and postmodernism agree in a more general way with Hegel that the Enlightenment project has been unable to achieve its goals, it is not because they wish to return to precritical postures toward social structures and the theories that legitimate them. On the contrary, their goal is to preserve critique by rescuing it from those who gave it modern birth. Each seeks, in its own way, to reenact the Socratic union of radical critique, passionate commitment to reason, and epistemological humility.

For the two conflicting strategies embodied in this volume agree that the failure of the Enlightenment lies not in its critical goals but in an uncritical, arrogant view of reason that leaves it with pretensions to clarity and certainty that it cannot support. It was not that the Enlightenment thought there could be a critique of society without a corresponding critique of reason. The overwhelmingly epistemological character of modern philosophy bears witness to the fact that the Enlightenment was first and foremost a whole series of critiques of reason.

These critiques, from Descartes to Husserl and from Locke to logical positivism, were uncritical because they occurred in a historical context that specified a priori what the outcome must be. If reason was to stand in judgment on traditions and texts, institutions and practices that claimed for themselves the authority of the sacred, it would have to be sacred itself. It would have to be Reason, not merely reason. It would have to embody an Absolute Knowledge so completely unconditioned as to be, in the apt words of Thomas Nagel, "the view from nowhere."

Under this self-imposed pressure, the admission that it did not possess the whole of truth all at once was the extent of the humility possible to the Enlightenment. But it had to claim that it had access to pieces of the truth that were utterly clear and certain. This is the essence of the philosophical strategies now known as foundationalism. It is not the innocent claim that some of our beliefs rest on others, which play a foundational role in relation to the former. It is the stronger claim that some of our foundational beliefs can be final truths, pure pieces of cognitive gold, bits of Absolute Knowledge.

Critical modernism and postmodernism agree that all forms of foundationalism have failed, be they rationalist, empiricist, phenomenological, positivist, or whatever, and this in two senses. First, at the theoretical level, they cannot be defended. In the face of the many ways in which human knowledge is conditioned, the claims of this or that "piece" of knowledge to be unconditioned is at best unconvincing and at worst ludicrous. Second, at the practical level all forms of foundationalism embody the hubris that turns progress into pathology and liberation into terror. The adage of Lord Acton that "absolute power corrupts absolutely" is joined here by its corollary, "Absolute Knowledge corrupts absolutely."

So it is not surprising that Caputo begins his work by drawing heavily on Kierkegaard and Heidegger, while Marsh does the same with Merleau-Ponty. For these thinkers are among the most forceful of the many critics of foundationalism and its claims to Absolute Knowledge.

Thus, beyond the agreement that we live in a society badly in need of critique, the critical modernism and postmodernism presented here agree that while foundationalism cannot ground critique because it is itself uncritical, philosophy must nevertheless be critique. The disagreement comes over the nature of postfoundationalist critique. Or perhaps it would be more precise to say that it is over the diagnosis of where foundationalism went wrong, since conflicting diagnoses underlie the competing attempts to redefine critique and thus to show how philosophical reflection can help us find the way to a better world.

Following Habermas, critical modernism finds the pathologies of modernity in the monological conception of reason that is its trademark. Beginning with Descartes, the subject has been conceived as seeking to penetrate and expose the object quite without essential relation to other subjects. The slogan "Think for yourself" came to mean "Think by yourself," and autonomy became inseparable from atomism.

Accordingly, critical modernism begins not with a theory of society (in the case of Marsh, a phenomenological Marxism) but with a theory of reason as dialogical. By seeking to specify (counterfactually) the conditions under which discourse about behavioral and institutional norms would be free of the distortion brought about by domination, it seeks to preserve a working concept of critical reason without having to claim possession of any final knowledge.

In spite of the just-mentioned disclaimer, postmodernism finds all this to be too optimistic about the power of human reason. Modernism appears as chastened in critical modernism, but insufficiently so. For by locating the problem in a monological concept of reason, it suggests that while I may not be able to grasp the Truth that Enlightenment opposed to tradition, We may not face the same obstacles that I do. There may be no intrinsic barrier between us and the Truth. The voice of the people may be in principle the voice of God.

For Derrida (as for Kierkegaard before him), the radical finitude of human understanding is not affected by shifting focus from the I to the We. Both the monological schemes of modernity and the dialogical strategies of critical modernism are insufficiently attentive to the systematic interdependence of absence and presence in any mode of awareness. Among the terms he uses to point to this structural feature of human understanding is *différance*. Part of the meaning of this strange word is that if intentions can never be completely fulfilled by means of the total presence of the intended, fullness of meaning must always be deferred to a future that will never become a present.

This may sound very much like Habermas, for whom the conditions of fully rational discourse always remain counterfactual, meaning that no actual understanding can be fixed or final, but is always subject to revision. Without doubt Habermasian dialogue and Derridean *différance* agree in pointing to the finitude of reason, the permanent impossibility of Absolute Knowledge. The challenge before the reader of this book is to sort out the difference between *différance* and dialogue and to find out what difference it makes.

While it is not the task of this preface to relieve the reader of that task before she has even had the chance to try it for herself, one clue may not be inappropriate. While the critical modernist concept of dialogue is prescriptive, the postmodern concept of *différance* is descriptive. The one tells us what we can do to be more nearly rational, while the other tells us about a condition from which we cannot escape, individually or collectively. Not surprisingly, critical modernism will seem to postmodernism to be so nearly as optimistic as modernism as to represent little more than repackaging of the Enlightenment; and postmodernism will seem to critical modernism so pessimistic as to have thrown out the baby of reason with the bath of Absolute Knowledge.

It is important to remember that much more is at stake than might at first be apparent in the sometimes abstract epistemological wrangling over such questions as whether the words ''The truth is that there is no truth'' represent important philosophical insight or the unpardonable philosophical sin. The modernity whose self-assurance is challenged throughout this volume includes Marxism-Leninism-Stalinism on the one hand and Adam Smith, John Locke, Thomas Jefferson, and James Madison on the other. While the Leninism of the Warsaw Pact nations is disintegrating in the face of economic failure, there is no shortage of opportunistic politicians and pundits in the West who are willing to gloat, more or less overtly, about this ''vindication'' of liberal society with its democratic and capitalistic institutions. But if modernity is mistaken when it holds the truths that legitimate liberal society to be self-evident, liberalism (in the classical sense of the term) may be as lacking in adequate foundations as Leninist society. If the Damoclean sword of Third World debt, the resurgence of racism, and the stubborn persistence of poverty, drugs, crime, and homelessness are taken as signs of an all too present crisis in the West, the problem of finding a cogent theoretical rationale for liberal society may seem a bit less "theoretical" than even philosophers are in the habit of thinking.

The basic question of this book, I believe, is what role critical reason can play in shaping and supporting a truly humane society. Even if in the heat of debate we sometimes forget it, it is the passion of that question that unites all of the contributors to this volume. We hope it will find readers who share that passion, who will benefit from our discussion, and who will make their own contributions to an ongoing conversation whose bearing on life in the "real world" may well be more direct than we suspect.

A word, finally, about chronology. This volume had its origin in a symposium held at Fordham University in March of 1989. The papers given by Marsh and Caputo, the responses by De Nys and Yount respectively, and some of the discussion that followed are included in this volume. These materials are preceded by Marsh's review of *Radical Hermeneutics*, which was written before the symposium, and by Caputo's review of *Post-Cartesian Meditations*, which was written later. In August of 1989, Caputo, Marsh, and I got together for the informal three-way conversation that appropriately follows the materials of the Fordham symposium in this volume. It was after that conversation that Caputo wrote his review of Marsh's book and I wrote my own response to the Fordham symposium, with reference to Cratylus. The final two items in this volume are the responses of Marsh and Caputo to this essay, dashing my hopes of having the last word.

Those of us who have engaged in this conversation have had more fun than philosophers should ever be permitted. But there has been a lot of hard work as well. We would especially like to thank Nemesio Que, s.j., Kathryn Shaughnessy, Cynthia Cruz, and Bruce Harasty for their expert help in transcribing taped material and in preparing the final manuscript. We would also like to thank the *International Philosophical Quarterly* for permission to reprint the reviews with which this volume begins.

# MODERNITY
# AND ITS
# DISCONTENTS

# Postmodernism/Critical Modernism[1]

*POST-CARTESIAN MEDITATIONS* is an attempt to formulate what James L. Marsh describes as a "critical modernism," that is, a philosophical standpoint which remains faithful to the essential tendencies of modern philosophy from Descartes to Kant and Hegel, while tempering the claims of modernism in the light of the critique of modernity which has taken shape in twentieth-century continental philosophy. Critical modernism is conceived in contradistinction to postmodernism, which Marsh takes to be an excessive, illegitimate, and, as he has no hesitations claiming, irrational rejection of modernity. Postmodernism is antimodernism and irrationalism, the outright rejection of reason (x–xi, 254–55). Critical modernism is the correction and perfection of modernism, its secret longing, its truest friend and *Aufhebung*. Marsh's "post" is post-Cartesian, not postmodern.

PCM is a challenging, intelligent, and clearly written volume, a comprehensive assessment of the state of philosophical art in the late twentieth century. Marsh does not fear to take a stand; he does not hide behind continentalist cant. His work is clear, forceful, and out-in-the-open. He uses a consciously non-sexist prose and he invites debate and discussion. There is much to agree with in Marsh's study and, as I hope to show, much to disagree with. But one is, in either case, grateful to the author for this vigorous, readable work which makes an energetic defense of modernist thought, which is not afraid of being understood, and which takes on the postmoderns with gusto.

In what follows I will present the main argument of PCM, tossing in a friendly word of support here and there, but perhaps a bit more often—as a sometime postmodern myself—making some trouble for PCM by pushing the "post" in post-Cartesian. PCM is an essay in "dialectical phenomenology," a discipline with three phases: an eidetic-descriptive phase deriving mainly from phenomenologies of Husserl and Merleau-Ponty; a hermeneutic phase deriving from Gadamer and Ricoeur; a critical-suspicious stage deriving from Marx and Freud. The first phase is temporally keyed to the present; the second to the past (the tradition); the third to the future, a new, perhaps utopian world (xi, 17–80). But before taking up the eidetic phenomenology, Marsh offers us a "historical reduction" which positions PCM relative to the debate in progress in the late twentieth century about the meaning of "modernity."

For Marsh, Descartes is the father of all us moderns and we should not be out to kill our progenitor but only to chasten, temper, or reform him. (Marsh prefers revolution to reform in politics, but reform to revolution in epistemology and metaphysics. He wants to be a moderate in philosophy but a radical on the streets.) Descartes set things going in the right direction but he went too far. He put philosophy on a methodical, critical, and reflexive path (6); he gave us all our philosophical bearings by making it clear that hereafter philosophers should proceed by questioning prejudices and presuppositions and producing evidence for their beliefs. The Cartesian project came to grief only because of its excesses. We who have read Heidegger and Merleau-Ponty, Gadamer and Ricoeur, have since learned the limits of any possible *epoché*. Descartes is guilty of a prejudice against prejudice, for it is impossible to be absolutely presuppositionless. Likewise the Cartesian desire for clarity and distinctness is misplaced, for it lays conditions befitting mathematics upon philosophy at large. Marsh thus sides with the arguments of a "hermeneutic phenomenology" against Cartesian dualism, but he remains attached to the spirit of the Cartesian inauguration of the modernist project. That is the tension of the book, and the question is whether PCM can master that tension.

Marsh is moving closer to Husserl than to Descartes. For Husserl continues the Cartesian undertaking in the manner of transcendental phenomenology, according to which "evidential rationality" (xi)—a linchpin word for Marsh which sets his heart aflame—comes to mean the clarity of phenomenal experience rather than the limpidity of logical deduction. But Husserl's own Cartesianism is "exploded" (23) by his return to the life world in the *Crisis*. Once the life world is affirmed as the uncircumventable matrix of all higher-order operations, philosophy finds itself unavoidably caught up in historicity, liguisticality, and ambiguity, and the claims of pure transcendental reason are thrown into question. With the discovery of the life-world comes what Marsh calls, following Merleau-Ponty, the "triumph of ambiguity" (23ff). Hereafter critical modernism must not only be post-Cartesian but post-Husserlian.

This is for me the pivot on which the success of PCM turns. Marsh is saying right at the beginning that dialectical phenomenology wants to take full stock of ambiguity, which includes for him historicality, linguisticality, embodiment, sociality, and intersubjectivity. He wants to concede, to embrace, what Heidegger calls "facticity," the factical situatedness of what modernity calls transcendental consciousness. One might say, to make things simple—and Marsh is not adverse to making things simple—that there are two ways to deal with ambiguity. The first tack, the one taken by Marsh, is to fess up to the difficulty but to try to contain the damage. That is what he means by critical modernism. Ambiguity muddies the waters of the philosophy of transcendental consciousness but it does not altogether sink its ship. Ambiguity is a negative moment in the total life of reason, not a mortal wound. This strategy, whose modernist prototype is clearly Hegel, has been carried out in an exemplary way by Paul Ricoeur. For years now Ricoeur has been judiciously balancing and dialectically mediating mythos and logos, freedom and necessity, Hegel and Freud, truth and method, explanation and understanding, structuralism and humanism, Habermas and Gadamer, analytic philosophy and hermeneutics, sense and reference, and whatever can be cast in the form of dialectical contrariety. Ricoeur is the not so secret hero of PCM: it is Ricoeur's philosophical style, his neo-Hegelian negotiating between modernist aspirations and the existential phenomenological-hermeneutic critique of modernity, which provides Marsh with his philosophical paradigm. Like Ricoeur, PCM wants to range over a lot of positions and literally put them in their place, situate them within a comprehensive dialectical scheme. Like Ricoeur, Marsh thinks you can " both/and" these disputes into submission, taking the side of the angels while giving the devil his due. He wants to defend what modernists call "reason"—this entitles one to speak in the name of reason itself, a formidable advantage which gives one the right to declare one's opponent irrational—while agreeing that reason is marked with finitude and ambiguity. The head of (critical) modernist reason is bloodied but unbowed.

The other strategy—and this is the one I myself pursue, the one that Marsh thinks is *verrückt* (literally: it is irrational and self-contradictory, according to him)—is the more "postmodern" option, which takes its lead from late Heidegger and Derrida, not Ricoeur. The postmodern idea is to stay with the ambiguity, to follow it out, and to renounce the claim that one can gain a transcendental high ground from which one attempts to "situate" ambiguity in the first place. What the postmodernist has against the critical modernist is that the very claim to be able to deal with ambiguity judiciously, to balance out its rightful claims against the claims of reason, is not in the end to give ambiguity its due and hence it is not even very balanced. After all, once one claims to have put ambiguity in its place, one has already effectively transcended it, localized it, and removed oneself from its influence. The very attempt to *mediate* between reason and ambiguity, between transcendental rationality and factical situatedness, the very claim to be able to oversee this dispute, has already taken the side of transcendental reason, has already laid claim to a higher, transcendental-dialectical vantage point, has already staked out a position above the tidal waters of ambiguity from which it surveys the whole, both sides, both/and. The dialectical desire to mediate between transcendental reason and ambiguity is already an act of transcendental mediation, already committed to transcendental reason. That is why from my perspective PCM fails to be a truly "radical" hermeneutic—because it fails to take ambiguity or facticity completely seriously. It thinks itself already on the other side of ambiguity, able to survey and mark off and so to contain the extent of its influence.

For the postmodernists dialectical mediation comes to the bargaining table of philosophical discussion with a set of transcendental non-negotiables. Mediation does not stay "between" reason and ambiguity but moves "beyond," becomes transcendence and *Aufhebung*. Postmodernism, at least of the sort that I admire, remains *in medias res,* in the midst of the dispute going on within the things themselves, stuck between, tossed to and fro, in a position of "undecidability." On my account, mediation fails to stay "between" while undecidability adheres more rigorously to the inter-mediacy of the human condition. The effect of this in Marsh's text is that the triumph *of* ambiguity is relentlessly transmuted into a triumph *over* ambiguity, into an outright intellectualism which is deeply marked by Habermas and Lonergan and which, in my view, all but subverts the factical-hermeneutical element in PCM. I admire the sweep of this text and its effort to come to grips with ambiguity, but I am convinced that in the end facticity and ambiguity are swept under the rug.

Consider the discussion of Merleau-Ponty, the great philosopher of ambiguity. After an illuminating comparison of Wittgenstein and Merleau-Ponty on the rejection of an ideal language, Marsh goes on to claim that Merleau-Ponty was always a philosopher of essence. This is in some sense true of *Phenomenology of Perception* but it is not a credible claim to make about *The Visible and the Invisible*. It tells us more about Marsh than about Merleau-Ponty. Marsh is not going to let go of the idea of an "eidetic" phenomenology in some strong sense—even though he wants to admit that any such "essences" as he finds are steeped in language and history.

Let us now turn to this eidetic phenomenology, which is the first phase of PCM, in which Marsh takes up the classic questions of "existential phenomenology"—perception, objectification, freedom, and intersubjectivity.

In the manner of Hegel's *Phenomenology,* Marsh's dialectical phenomenology wants to start out from perception and work its way up to the higher levels of the spirit (beyond description to interpretation and then to critique). He wants to defend a version of Husserl's thesis that perception is the founding stratum of experience, that expression is founded upon perception, and that reflection is founded upon expression, the higher stratum being related to the lower as the explicit to the implicit. However, Marsh also wants to hold that there are no unmediated perceptual data, that the perceptual world is mediated to us by language and history. But these two theses are at odds with each other: the one says that language expresses and explicates perception, the other that it actually constitutes it in some non-trivial way, that language does not simply unfold the implicit contents of perception but shapes it. You can see the trouble it makes for speaking of an eidetic reduction. Husserl thinks that he has achieved an essence when he reaches a perceptual invariant, something which cannot even be imaginatively varied away. But someone who has taken a linguistic turn ($x$) would simply suggest that what Husserl has run up against is not an essence but the limits of his language. What is lingering behind Marsh's approach is the implication that he somehow knows what lies on the other side of language, that he has some kind of access to a pure nonlinguistic real or prelinguistic perceptual essence. It is this privileged access which enables him to oversee the relation between perception and language, to look so judicious, and so to say with serene balance that language is just the expression of the perceptual.

Dialectical phenomenology also wants a theory of objectivity, which it thinks has been rashly jettisoned by Kierkegaard, Nietzsche, and the postmodernists. Such rashness can be avoided by distinguishing among eight different senses of objectivity, an account of which Marsh happily supplies. The upshot is that not all objectification is alienation, and that even critiques of objectification—like Kierkegaard's critique of objective truth and Heidegger's critique of presence at hand—presuppose and make use of objectification in another sense, inasmuch as Kierkegaard and Heidegger produce careful descriptions of matters which they have explicitly thematized. There is some truth to that and I do not think that a more sensitive reading of Heidegger, for which Marsh is not famous, would deny that. But one is impressed with the enormous resistance of PCM to any troubling of "objectivity" at all. One wonders about all this anxiety about a loss or even a diminishing of our objectifying powers. What does PCM will, want, desire? What is it afraid of?

The chapter on freedom argues for a conditioned liberty, not an unconditioned, Sartrean freedom. To disagree with dialectical phenomenology on this point is to fall into self-contradiction. (This is a fate which *consistently* befalls those who dissent from PCM. If I have counted right, every single position which differs from PCM is declared self-referentially inconsistent and hence logically absurd.) For to deny freedom is to discredit one's own claim to be offering considered evidence for one's claim (since one can hardly offer any other view), while to affirm absolute freedom is to undermine the possibility that one determinate view is to be preferred to another. A suggestion by a sensitive Sartrean commentator (Thomas Busch) that Sartre might be more complicated than this (i.e., that Sartre's text is more involuted, more textual, that it admits of other readings) is just waved off with the remark that that would only show that Sartre is even more self-contradictory than Marsh thought (158–59, note 28). It is astonishing how little ambiguity Marsh actually finds either in philosophers or in the things themselves.

Furthermore, this free, existential self is not a solitary but an intersubjective being. Intersubjectivity is to be explained not by means of Husserl's transcendental apperception, but by invoking the dynamics

of embodiment as presented by Merleau-Ponty. Others are given in
their bodily presence, in their gestures and movements; they are not
somehow hidden behind bodily appearances. This is I think an extremely sound move. But a great deal of the good that Marsh's hermeneutic phenomenology does for him is undone by the Habermasian
account of intersubjective communication in terms of the distinction
between coercion and appeal. Appeal is a free, rational, undistorted,
unprejudiced communication (which acquires such elevated status by
meeting Habermas's four conditions for validity claims), a communication which does not violate or distort. Appeal is never contaminated
with coercion; it is virgin pure and Cartesian clean. Yet how, one might
ask, can that possibly be if intersubjective communication occurs between impassioned, embodied, interested, free, existential subjects
who always operate under language and history, prejudice and presupposition? The distinction is dualistic and Cartesian, a straightforwardly
metaphysical distinction which succeeds not in escaping Cartesianism
but only in extending it from the subjective to the intersubjective level.
This is the sort of trouble that I think PCM is always getting into.

   In introducing the ''hermeneutical turn'' which PCM wants to take,
Marsh stresses the limits this imposes on us: that there is more than one
way to read a text, the non-definitiveness of any reading, that all one
can say is that some readings are better or more probable than others
(164, 167–69). The reader—this reader, anyway—has to catch his
breath at this point. Because Marsh's very sensible commitment to hermeneutics at this juncture in the text has been preceded by a series of
chapters in which every position which differs with PCM is reduced to
absurdity—quite literally—by being shown to be in performative contradiction with itself. Far from making its opponents stronger in the
hermeneutic fashion, PCM makes them look ridiculous so that one
wonders how such foolishness ever found its way into print. Such excessive intellectualism does not permit hermeneutic flexibility, any
more than it was prepared to admit phenomenological ambiguity. It
aims at wiping out its opponents with a mortal blow pointed at the very
coherence of those who differ from it. Whatever lip service PCM pays
to hermeneutics in theory, its real working practice is a black and white
logic in which positions are either rational or irrational, fully legitimized or self-contradictory, without ambiguity, shading, or alternate
interpretations. Texts do not admit of second readings; to differ from
PCM is to become absurdly self-contradictory. PCM wants to do her-

meneutics but it has sold its soul to Lonergan and Habermas. (Were it not for the fact that I consider the argument from performative contradiction to be for the most part completely barren,[2] I would suggest that PCM is in performative contradiction with its own commitment to phenomenological ambiguity and hermeneutic plurality.)

Following Ricoeur's adjudication of the Gadamer-Habermas debate, Marsh goes on to argue that his hermeneutic commitment to the tradition requires also—in dialectical balance—critical distance from it, although one must also recognize—more balance—that one cannot carry out absolute, total critique because one lacks the absolute standpoint (1973). This completes the triumvirate that Marsh wants to establish: his "transcendental method" includes a descriptive eidetics, an interpretative hermeneutics, and a critique. It is interesting that Marsh is happy to say that PCM practices a transcendental method (179), because he elsewhere denies the distinction between the embodied and the transcendental subject (128) and claims that he breaks with Husserl's transcendental subject "completely" (205). But what is the transcendental subject other than a subject capable of performing transcendental acts, and what else is the deployment of a transcendental method other than a transcendental act?

Of Ricoeur's three masters of suspicion, only Freud and Marx merit special chapters. Nietzsche evidently has been contaminated by postmodernism; his is too much of a break with modernism; he does not even pretend to be delivering science and apodictic truth. Nietzsche is excess; PCM cannot appropriate him. Be that as it may, there follows a nice presentation of the Freudian unconscious which is, of course, integrated with conscious and intentional life after the manner of Ricoeur's *Freud and Philosophy.* That is followed by a discussion of the "social unconscious," which is where Marsh finally gets brazen. Now the talk is no longer of "reform" but of "radicality." Now we are told to seek not a capitalism which has been mediated with Marxist critique but Marxism itself, albeit one purged (by an eidetic and hermeneutic phenomenology) of its reductionistic tendencies. Here we move beyond Ricoeur, who may have been guide enough in matters metaphysical and epistemological but who must now give way to critical theory. There follows an interesting attempt, which makes use of the work of Roslyn Bologh, to integrate phenomenology and Marxism. Phenomenology has a built-in critical function inasmuch as its account of the life world functions as a critique of scientism and technocracy, even as ideology critique is itself a phenomenology of a life itself shaped by capital, a life which itself is a form of reification and positivism. I am largely in agreement with this Marxist streak in PCM, not because I am a Marxist, but because I agree that Marxism does have phenomenological cash value, as Marsh and Bologh argue. Marxism offers us a good phenomenology of an alienated life and it is an excellent tool for making trouble for the bourgeoisie.

Still, I have three complaints with this phase of PCM. First, it is an illusion that one requires a transcendental apparatus to make such a critique when good phenomenology of those who are being ground under by the system will be just fine. Secondly, Marsh seems to pin technology and techologism to capitalism in such a way as to suggest that socialism is less committed in theory or practice to more and better technology. My own view is that the powerful sweep of technology has both the capitalist and the socialist world in its grip and indeed, as Albert Borgmann suggests, tends to erode the difference between them, provided that socialism survives at all.[3]

Thirdly, and most importantly, it is disingenuous simply to note—as Marsh does (205)—and then to proceed to ignore the fact that one could also make an equally scintillating critique of state socialism. The capacity of capitalism to exploit and oppress is at the very least matched by the capacity of state socialism for terror and murder. Nothing is innocent. What PCM requires here is an even healthier suspicion, an even wider range of critique, of all power/knowledge, of everything that tries to pass itself off as the science of human affairs, as holding the meaning of history, as history's chosen instrument for revolutionary change. It is just at that moment when thinking desires closure, when it wants to totalize, that it is the most dangerous to the rest of us who are just trying to make it through the day.

That is why I am so troubled about the last chapter of PCM which amounts to an apocalyptic announcement of the "emergence of dialectical phenomenology." I single out a highly symptomatic passage, not at all untypical of the philosophical tenor of this text, which I wish to reproduce here with a few pointed Derridean jabs—in order to make a point.

*"What I have done in this book is to show how phenomenology, and by its implication the whole of modern Western philosophy"*—that is a tall order, a large totality: not just phenomenologists but everybody from Decartes to the present—*"can and should lead to"*—this is

going to be teleological, we are going to get the *telos* of everybody from Thales to the present—*"dialectical phenomenology"*—PCM is what we have all been waiting for, our secret longing; philosophy will become Marsh—*"if it is faithful to itself"*—but philosophy will become Marsh only if it is true, authentic, self-present.

There is more: *"Only with . . . "*—this is the only way, no hermeneutic plurality here—*"the final step into critical social theory"*—critical theory is the *final* step, the *finis* and *telos,* the end of philosophy, the end of us all—*"does one achieve full rationality,"*—everything will be rational and the rational will fill everything, this will be the fullness of presence, of reason, everything we always wanted, in all its fullness—*"do full justice to the phenomena,"*—the phenomena will have been saved, one and all, they will have been fully rationalized, made fully transparent; no more ambiguity here, no more need of alternate interpretations—*"and reconcile theory and practice fully."*—this is really full of it, of fullness, that is.

*"Short of this move into critical social theory"*—this sounds like a warning—*"we have not asked crucial questions and not explained crucial contradictions."*—we will be living in contradiction, inauthentically, lacking presence—*"The dilemma for phenomenology then, is this: either it moves into critical theory or not"*—you notice all the ambiguity here, the hermeneutic flexibility, the shifting contextuality—*"If it does, then it is fully self-conscious and faithful to itself"*—and this from a philosopher who says he has broken with the Cartesian subject and pure transparency—*"If it does not, then it remains obscurantist,"*—Habermas and Lonergan of course will show us all how to be clear—*"dishonest"*—PCM evidently knows what lies in the heart of man—*"and less than fully comprehensive."*—which one would have thought PCM conceded was the fate of us all once it admitted our finitude, fallibility, and ambiguity.

Go then and sin no more.

In sum, PCM is a forceful and robust presentation of some of the best work in contemporary continental thought which makes a sustained effort to take into account the critique of modernity which has been underway for the last century or so. In the end, it is my judgment that it succumbs to its own worst intellectualistic, scholasticizing tendencies and turns hermeneutic phenomenology into something other than it is. To use the argument that it loves to use on everyone else, PCM is itself one long performative contradiction. While it pays lip service to phenomenological ambiguity and hermeneutic plurality, it treats everything as black and white, good or bad, rational or irrational, and tries to leave a crater wherever it finds an opponent. Just where we need rich phenomenological description, it gives us Lonerganian *reductio ad absurdum*; instead of a conflict of interpretations, it offers the annihilation of dissent.

Now let me try to practice some of this Ricoeurian hermeneutic balance on PCM. Despite my disagreements with this text, it is light years removed from the lisping, limping nonsense that sometimes passes itself off as postmodernist thought; it undertakes a phenomenological and hermeneutic delimitation of the modernist project; its ethico-sociopolitical heart is in the right place; and it invites a good argument by its clear and forceful prose. My one wish for Marsh, as he now turns to a promised (threatened?) sequel to PCM, is that the son of PCM not inherit all the bad habits of its father.

## MARSH READS CAPUTO: IN DEFENSE OF MODERNIST RATIONALITY

*Radical Hermeneutics* is an important book: original, critical, creative, dangerous in the best sense of the word. While rigorously and seriously responsible to the highest standards of academic, scholarly inquiry, Caputo roots philosophy in the flux of real life, personal, political, religious, where, he argues, real thinking begins and flourishes.

For those such as myself in the tradition of western, continental philosophy, the book plays the role of "shaking us up," much as Rorty did to and for the analytic community a few years ago. With this book Caputo takes his place firmly as the foremost American continental postmodernist, continuing a line of inquiry extending from Nietzsche and Kierkegaard on through late Heidegger, Derrida, and Foucault. Such a line of inquiry questions the legitimacy of metaphysical reason—evidential, conceptual, scientific, serious—and argues for a postmetaphysical notion of rationality: preconceptual, asystematic, questioning, playful.

In such an undertaking, in which the risks of obfuscation and jargon and mystification are great, Caputo's language is eminently clear and forceful and concrete; the literary quality of the writing is unusually high. In Caputo's voice, continental philosophy speaks a vigorous, eastern seaboard, Philadelphia prose that makes the book not only intellectually stimulating and enlightening but emotionally intense and moving in a way that is sustained throughout the book. Consider as examples: "Radical hermeneutics operates a shuttle between Paris and the Black forest, a delivery service whose function is not to insure an accurate and faithful delivery of messages" (5); or "Apocalyptics presupposes hermeneutics, deep hermeneutics, with a hotline to the gods" (166).

Rhetoric never substitutes for argument here, but the unity of rhetoric and argument operates forcefully on the reader, urging her to an intellectual and emotional conversion away from the reign of western *ratio* and toward radical hermeneutics as a way of thinking and living. Almost in spite of oneself, the reader sees Caputo's alternative as tempting and compelling. Almost in spite of oneself, the reader begins to think. In this respect the text practices what it preaches—the performance of the text is deconstructive, insinuative, disseminative. Radical hermeneutics shows as much as it explains, plays as much as it argues, seduces as much as it demonstrates, conceals as much as it reveals. The Socratic gadfly in the twentieth century becomes a Derridean *stylus*. The playful, deconstructive pen is mightier than the metaphysical, rational sword.

Caputo's main line of argument in his book moves from Kierkegaard to Husserl to Heidegger to Derrida. Although Nietzsche is not explicitly treated in a systematic and exhaustive manner, he functions in the background as a genial, playful presence. Caputo shows convincingly how his own radical hermeneutics emerges from a problematic internal to phenomenology. In the last part of the book, he considers the implications of radical hermeneutics for a theory of rationality, ethics, and religious belief.

"Living in the flux" is the central controlling concept of the book. Deconstructive, radical hermeneutical thinking is characterized by its willingness to think the flux while living in it. Metaphysics extending from Plato up through Gadamer tends to freeze the flux, fix it, falsify it, control it. This concept between metaphysical thinking and radical hermeneutics is the central contrast in the book: metaphysics devoted to fixity, conceptualization, truth; radical hermeneutics to change, questioning, the play of untruth. "The truth is that there is no truth" (156). Truth is a woman, and woman lies.

For Caputo, the origin of radical hermeneutics lies in Kierkegaard. Kierkegaard's critique of Hegel is the first thoroughgoing, modern critique of metaphysics. Kierkegaard's opposition to the Hegelian system, his insistence on the incomplete, changeable existing individual, his notion of repetition as an active, creative taking up and choosing existential possibilities rooted in one's past are all motifs that continue to resound and reverberate in twentieth-century continental philosophy.

Caputo next contrasts Kierkegaard's and Husserl's accounts of repetition. Kierkegaard is concerned with the existential subject, Husserl with the knowing subject. "Two philosophies of life and becoming: existential life and becoming on the one hand, intentional life and genesis on the other" (37). To the extent that Husserl presents human intentionality as interpretive and anticipatory, he contributes to the development of hermeneutics. To the extent that he tries to arrest the flux by recourse to unchangeable, apodictic, eidetic unities, he remains captive to metaphysics.

Martin Heidegger in *Being and Time* takes up this Husserlian emphasis on anticipation and interpretation and integrates it with Kierkegaard's existential subject. Because *Being and Time,* however, is still grounding metaphysics rather than overcoming it and because it is still centered too much on the projective, existential subject, Heidegger has to move away from this stance. Grounding metaphysics gives way to overcoming metaphysics.

Hermeneutics after early Heidegger has a center: late Heidegger himself, as described above; a right wing: Gadamer; and a left wing: Derrida. Gadamer's *Truth and Method* has a valid critique of enlightenment disinterestedness, draws out the implications of *Being and Time* for a theory of the sciences, and develops early Heidegger's account of historicity. Gadamer remains for Caputo too Hegelian, too metaphysical, too uncritical of tradition. "He never asks to what extent the play of tradition itself is a power play and its unity something that has to be enforced by the powers that be" (112). Caputo's critique is on the money here; it is similar in some respects to Ricoeur's and Habermas's critiques of Gadamer from within the western, modern philosophical tradition.

With Derrida, finally, we reach home ground. He brings to fruition the overcoming of metaphysics that began with Kierkegaard. Although late Heidegger is devoted to overcoming metaphysics and its commitment to presence, he still finally remains caught up in the nostalgia for presence. In contrast to late Heidegger's reverent, serious, obedient listening to Being, Derrida's critique is irreverent, playful, disobedient.

Caputo does not simply reject late Heidegger here; in a manner similar to Ricoeur's blending of a hermeneutics of disclosure and a hermeneutics of suspicion, we must keep the play between tradition and deconstruction open.

> Just when thinking is lost in solemn stillness, when it is beginning to take itself seriously, dissemination bursts upon the scene with its disruptive laughter. Even so thinking follows dissemination home, after the singing and dancing is over, through the city streets, to see if it ever takes off its mask. [206]

In the last part of his book, Caputo considers the implications of radical hermeneutics for a theory of rationality, ethics, and religious belief and practice. Some of his best, most insightful, most moving pages are here. Rather than conceding the charges of irrationality directed at radical hermeneutics, he argues for postmetaphysical rationality, playful, questioning, Socratic, preconceptual. Rather than conceding that radical hermeneutics cannot have an ethics, he argues for an ethic of fair play that keeps all voices in the conversation and refuses to marginalize. Rather than conceding that deconstruction is necessarily irreligious and atheistic, he argues that openness to mystery, to the suffering, marginalized other, and to a God identified with the oppressed enhances and completes radical hermeneutics. Conversely, radical hermeneutics liberates us from false, one-sided, authoritarian metaphysical forms of rationality, ethics, and religious praxis. Christianity is a religion of freedom.

There is much that is attractive, compelling, and true here; Caputo reveals himself to be a postmodern, post-Marxist, anarchist religious leftist. One of the big achievements of his book is to have put the issue of politics at the center of philosophical discussion; Caputo *politicizes* reason. To the extent that reason remains apolitical, purely contemplative, purely disinterested, merely in the ivory tower, reason is irrational. Some of Caputo's best pages illustrating and proving this point are his discussion of the modern university: the way its definitions of reason often serve to marginalize other definitions and groups (witness the recent politics of the Eastern Division of the American Philosophical Association); the way reason as technique has infiltrated the university, too often turning it into a servant of the corporation and the state; the way the utilitarian definition and use of reason limits the free play of reason. Making it to Greenwich becomes more important than making it out of the cave; the soft rustle of money in the pocket becomes more important than the sting of the gadfly. Socrates is domesticated or fired. Instead of putting him on trial, we deny him promotion or tenure.

At this point, doing justice to the book requires that I engage it critically. Taking the book as seriously as it deserves to be taken means dealing seriously and playfully with the issues it raises, even at the risk of possible disagreement with some of its theses. That I think the book has much positive merit should already be evident: its Socratic provocativeness, its questioning of the nefarious political uses to which rationality is often put, many of its individual insights and arguments, its insistence on the limits of rationality, and its very clear articulation of the radical deconstructive turn in continental philosophy.

While agreeing or sympathizing with many of Caputo's individual claims, however, I do not go along with his general turn, powerful and compelling as that is, toward a postmetaphysical rationality. My own conviction is that insight and conceptualization, question and answer, freedom and rule, play and seriousness operate together in any adequate conception and practice of rationality. What he thinks he has to leave metaphysical rationality to find is actually, as the Prodigal Son discovered, already at home.

My own stance of disagreement is that of a critical modernism linking evidential, conceptual rationality and critique. Critique without such rationality, I think, becomes self-contradictory, arbitrary, one-sidedly totalizing, descriptively inadequate, oblivious to the difference among different kinds of · rationality, politically pessimistic. Caputo, to the extent that he does sever such rationality from critique in favor of a postmetaphysical rationality, may fall into such difficulties. Of course, my stance is not innocent either, any more than Caputo's. If his main sources of insight and inspiration are Kierkegaard and Nietzsche, Husserl and Heidegger, Derrida and Foucault, mine are Marx and Hegel, Ricoeur and Tracy, Lonergan and Habermas. Like Caputo, I have metaphysical and postmetaphysical blood on my hands.

In keeping with the spirit of Caputo's book, however, my aim here is less to come to definitive conclusions about the issues raised—I have done that elsewhere—than to engage in a Socratic, playful questioning and testing of his book. In doing so, the value of Caputo's book even to a dedicated critical modernist like myself should become apparent.

A logical place to start questioning lies in considering Caputo's central concept of "living in the flux." Here I ask the following: assuming that such a state is desirable, what does it mean to live in the flux? Is the flux pure flux or is it a unity of flux and permanence, identity and difference, presence and absence? Now much of the philosophical tradition from Plato to Aristotle on up to the present has argued for the latter position. Aristotle argues, for example, that without some kind of permanence underlying change in the object, we have mere substitution, not change. Thinkers such as Kant, Husserl, and Lonergan argue that without some kind of underlying unity and permanence in the knower, there is mere atomistic succession or substitution, not a unified object or change in such an object. Husserl argues that, in addition to constituted or constructed unities, there is also the eidetically permanent "how" of different levels of conscious experience: perception is essentially perspectival, reflection is oriented to the universal rather than the sensible particular, imagination in contrast to perception is active and creative.

If these accounts are correct, then permanence and flux, identity and difference, presence and absence are equiprimordial; one does not have priority over the other. Good philosophy has to give an account of the unity and the interplay between such opposites, not simply opt for one over the other. Rather than Caputo's two alternatives, metaphysics and radical hermeneutics, we have three: good metaphysics that tries to do justice to the unity between such opposites as flux and permanence, bad metaphysics that tries to escape the flux, and radical hermeneutics that simply gives itself over to the flux.

We can ask, therefore, playfully, turning Caputo's question against him, "Has he made it too easy on himself?" In identifying all metaphysics with bad metaphysics, has he not simply constructed a caricature, easily refuted and rejected? Is there not in the metaphysical tradition itself a critique of naïve presence to which his own account does scant justice? Consider late Plato's critique of his own earlier account of the forms, Aristotle's critique of Plato on the reality of the sensible particular, Kant's critique of Leibniz's pure reason, Merleau-Ponty's critique of Husserl's complete reduction.

In opting for pure flux, has not Caputo simply sunk into another form of bad metaphysics, the opposite of a metaphysics of pure presence and permanence, but wedded to that negatively? In so doing, has he not made it too easy on himself intellectually, existentially, politically? New York City, after all, and any American city, is filled with adepts at living in pure flux: alcoholics, drug addicts, sexually promiscuous persons, hedonists. Is not the more difficult and more authentic task—intellectually, ethically, politically, religiously—thinking and living in the tension between flux and permanence, identity and difference, presence and absence?

A second difficulty concerns the possibility of saying anything true. If reality is basically pure flux, with no fundamental, only constructed, permanence, then all truth claims are imposed arbitrarily. However, reflection on experience discloses the falsity of this implication. I sense the arbitrariness in describing as rectilinear what is really circular. A certain figure may be ambiguous in that I may see it in both a duck and a rabbit; it is more difficult to see it in an elephant or a lion. If experience is not structured at all in a fundamental sense, are not such truth claims about experience impossible?

Now to his credit Caputo realizes this implication of his position; for this reason there is a questioning or denial of truth. "The truth is that there is no truth" (156). Aside from self-referential difficulties here, to be taken up later (Is it true that there is no truth?), we return to our point above about the violence done to our own experience by such an account. Caputo does admit, following Nietzsche, that there are necessary, useful, healthy fictions as opposed to unnecessary, useless, sick fictions. But then we are tempted to ask, "Are such fictions really necessary, useful, and healthy?" The basic difficulty is pushed back another level, but is not solved.

Third, we may question, in a manner hinted at earlier, the descriptive adequacy of Caputo's own account. I sense at times a tendency in his work to juxtapose a bad conceptual, explanatory, serious, formalized account of reason to one that is preconceptual, questioning, playful, free. "I resist the notion that the life of reason can be formalized, reduced to a rule of law" (226). Caputo is at his best and most eloquent in making this point. My own conviction is, however, that both his and the purely formalized account are one-sided. Reason, as Lonergan, among others, has argued in the first chapter of *Insight,* is both preconceptual and conceptual, questioning and rule-governed, playful and serious, free and bound. "If reason itself . . . cannot be understood apart from the play" (226), is not the opposite also true? Can the play itself be understood apart from rules, concepts, judgments, evidence, systematicity? If thinking begins in question and insight, does not it complete itself in definition and judgment?

Fourth, related to the question of descriptive adequacy is that of hermeneutical adequacy toward the philosophical tradition itself. Is the tradition merely metaphysical in the bad sense, or is it a contradictory unity of good and bad metaphysics, attempts to think the flux and attempts to escape it? In addition to the examples already given that might support the latter option, we can think of Ricoeur's hermeneutics of suspicion, Habermas's critical theory, and Hartshorne's metaphysics that criticizes, in a manner reminiscent of Derrida, the classical metaphysical preference for permanence over change, necessity over contingency, omniscience over fallibility. Does Caputo's account do justice to this critique of presence within the tradition itself?

Fifth, there is the issue of consistency—logical, self-referential, textual. Caputo is aware of such issues, but he may too easily dismiss or evade them. For example, is the claim ''The truth is that there is no truth'' self-referentially consistent? Or again, is the claim that there is no preference to be given to one epoch over another or one position over another compatible with the argument for radical hermeneutics? Does Caputo not mean us to take this account as preferable to earlier versions—Kierkegaard's, Husserl's, Gadamer's, Heidegger's? If so, is his account somehow not truer, more adequate, more comprehensive (Husserl does not interpret adequately the flux in experience, whereas I do) than these other versions? If so, is there not a version of truth implied? If so, then Caputo is giving us a version of his metaphysics. If not, then why should we not simply continue to prefer the old metaphysics?

My own guess is that there may be in Caputo's work a contradiction between the deconstruction of truth—all truth claims show themselves to be contradictory, divided impositions on the flux—and the truth of deconstruction. If we opt for the former, then deconstruction is not any truer than any other version of reality, and we are entitled and quite justified in continuing to do metaphysics. If the latter, then the content of deconstruction contradicts the performance of affirming deconstruction as true.

Or again, is Caputo's denial of teleology compatible with an apparent progression in his own account from Kierkegaard to Husserl to Heidegger to Derrida to himself? If this interpretation is a useful fiction only, then why not prefer other fictions, and what is the criterion of ''useful?'' As fictions, does one have any more weight than the other? Are we not simply left, again, with our own aesthetic preferences here?

Seventh, I am bothered by the question of criteria for critique. If ''fair play'' is the basic criterion for a postmetaphysical ethics, then why should we prefer this to another criterion? Caputo may be caught here in a dilemma of self-contradiction versus arbitrariness. If I argue for fair play as criterion, then am I using the *ratio* I am claiming to reject? If I merely assert fair play as the criterion, then what is arbitrarily asserted can be rationally questioned or denied.

Again, why prefer the marginalized, the poor, the dispossessed as Caputo, influenced by Derrida and Foucault, does? Why not opt for the center of power and privilege and wealth? Life at the center is certainly easier and subject to less affliction than life at the margin. Here I am not quarreling with Caputo's choices; they are also mine. The question, though, for any postmodernist leftist is whether these choices can be justified as choices. Are not Caputo's preferences arbitrary in a fundamental sense? To dramatize this point we might imagine disenfranchised racists, male chauvinists, and capitalists, shoved to the margin in a fully liberated society, using deconstruction as a way of justifying themselves ethically and improving their lot—George Wallace and Ross Barnett reading and using *Writing and Difference* or *Grammatology*. Why, on strictly postmodernist grounds, is their stance less justified than those of King or Steinem?

There is something too formal about postmodernism here; it does not have the tools to make good on its political, ethical, and religious claims. The intuitive plausibility of Derrida's or Caputo's preference for the marginalized lies, I suspect, in their implicit and, at times, explicit reliance on ethical and political argument in the tradition, natural law theory, Kant, Hegel, Mill, Marx, Rawls, Dworkin—"Racism is unjust, sexism is unjust, capitalist exploitation is unjust in fact or in principle." For this reason, the kind of marginalization experienced by a black is different from that of a white racist. One is unjust, the other just. Caputo's postmodernism, as far as I can tell, has no way of making or arguing for this distinction. For this reason, radical hermeneutics could be used by Barnett or Wallace to make a comeback.

Now the "lack of a criterion" is a common complaint against postmodernists, and they do have a response. The standard reply is that developments in twentieth-century philosophy, such as the critique of foundationalism, have shown the impossibility of any transcendental criterion. This reply is cogent, however, only if one forgets the distinction I drew earlier between good and bad metaphysics. If there is a third way between the Scylla of postmodernism and the Charybdis of a strict Cartesian foundationalism, then that third way could offer a criterion. Rawls's principles of justice rooted in the original condition and Habermas's ideal speech situation are two non-foundationalist attempts to ground "fair play" as a norm. We might expect a hermeneutical injustice in lumping these attempts together with "foundationalism" or "logocentrism" or "metaphysics" in the bad sense.

I wish to avoid giving the wrong impression here. Caputo is quite correct to warn against defenders of the metaphysical tradition, such as myself, appropriating the mantle of rationality for themselves. In this way, as in many others, he chastens, enlightens, teaches us. Caputo's insistence is that his idea of rationality is preferable to that of the tradition. "We do not destroy the idea of reason with the talk of the play; we just tell a more reasonable story about it" (222). However, again, the nagging question arises: what is the criterion for "more reasonable"? Here the operative, perhaps transcendentally functioning one seems to be "more comprehensive, more faithful to experience, less partial, less one-sided." If so, that criterion operates in any number of "metaphysical" thinkers from Husserl through Habermas. In contrast to Caputo, however, these thinkers attempt to justify their use of this criterion; they do not just assume it in an apparently arbitrary manner.

We are faced, then, with a choice between two competing versions of rationality: a critical modernist alternative as I have sketched it and Caputo's postmodernist alternative. How do we choose between them? One way would be simply to opt arbitrarily for one over the other, with no argument. The other way would be to argue, define, give reasons in a context of discussion, as philosophers from Plato have done. Is there not a *prima facie* superiority to a position that can, in a performatively consistent way, do that—argue, define, and give reasons—and one that cannot? Once again the dilemma of self-contradiction versus arbitrariness seems to afflict the postmodernist position.

Other questions arise in choosing the most reasonable version of reason. Using Caputo's own criterion of comprehensiveness and phenomenological fidelity to lived experience, we might ask which is more comprehensive: a version of rationality stressing the question, the freedom, the preconceptual, the play, or one insisting on unity between question and answer, freedom and norm, preconceptual and conceptual, playfulness and seriousness. Which version of rationality gives a more comprehensive, nuanced, differentiated account of the philosophical tradition: an account which sees a progressive growth in domination and withdrawal of being since Plato or one that sees the tradition as a growing, complex, dialectical interplay between light and darkness, truth and falsity, liberation and domination? Without arbitrarily taking the mantle of "rational" upon herself, the critical modernist may have resources, using the criteria of self-referential consistency, descriptive adequacy to experience, and hermeneutical adequacy to tradition, for answering the postmodernist.

In any event, these are some of the issues raised by Caputo's rich, provocative, "outrageous" book. As I have indicated, while finding much that is suggestful, insightful, and true, much that I would wish to incorporate into a more straightforward philosophical account of human experience, I disagree strongly and sharply with some of its major theses. Nonetheless, the book is so productively outrageous—I learn so much from it—that I prefer it to other books with which I agree more. Not the least of its virtues is that in attempting to take a standpoint outside of the philosophical tradition as a whole, Caputo allows us to thematize that tradition, question it, ferret out its weak and strong points in ways that are philosophically fruitful. In doing so, not only do we increase and deepen our understanding of what rationality is, but we become aware of its limits in the postrational, transrational, transmetaphysical other. "All that I have written seems like straw."

## Notes

1. The two sections of this initial part first appeared as reviews in *International Philosophical Quarterly* in December 1989, pp. 101–107, and December 1988, pp. 459–65, respectively.

2. As Gadamer shows, following Plato's *Seventh Letter,* this would not refute it materially; one could be determined to say that determinism is true even while it is true. It could be that all Megarians really are liars. The objection is formalistic and vacuous and is about as much help in getting to the bottom of things as the scholastics who refused to look through Galileo's telescope on the grounds that it was formally incoherent that the principle of light could have dark spots. Cf. *Truth and Method,* ed. J. Cumming and G. Barden (New York: Seabury Press, 1975), pp. 308–10.

3. Albert Borgmann, *Technology and the Character of Contemporary Life.* (Chicago: University of Chicago Press, 1985), pp. 82–85. Technology creates a system which cuts deeper than either capitalism or socialism.

# Uncapitalizing on
# *Radical Hermeneutics*

## *Mark Yount*

THIS VOLUME WAS ENGENDERED by two books and the difference between them: *Radical Hermeneutics* and *Post-Cartesian Meditations*.
These titles could also serve as labels for more general strategies of
thought; indeed, each title reflects what each author thinks philosophy
stands in need of. Caputo Derridizes Heidegger, Marsh Habermases
Husserl,[1] and both authors urge us to rethink their continental sources
so that what they find most profound can be turned to the ends of liberation. Can't we have our philosophical cake and feed others too?
Both authors insist that a "both/and" is the only choice that effectively
serves either alternative, truth or liberation.

Perhaps the most important difference between these two texts is the
logic of that "both/and." Radical hermeneutics finds its logic along
the slash in a Derridean double gesture. Marsh's post-Cartesian meditation aspires to the encompassing quotation marks of Hegelian synthesis. That is the contended point, the *punctum*: Is it the punctuation
of Derrida or of Hegel we should observe as our words grope for a
more liberating truth? That is the difference I will explore here, without claiming to be objective (except as one claims the use of a convention, almost in inverted commas).[2] This essay is partisan, affiliated
both to the texts and to the philosophical inclinations of radical
hermeneutics. My most evident task is to offer a selective précis of
Caputo's published text and to highlight especially those points most
contended by Marsh's reading of Caputo (and of Derrida, and of
"postmodernism" generally). I hope this essay also practices radical
hermeneutics in an uncapitalized form, evoking possibilities suggested
by the title work but not contained in its volume. Not only a title, radical hermeneutics names an event field as yet undetermined, not entirely prescribed by the capital form of the book.

Consider the irony of "THE CONCLUSION OF THE BOOK":

> This book is an illusion. It pretends to have a definite beginning and a
> distinct conclusion and to show the way from one to another. It claims to
> be able to steer its way through the flux. . . . This book has aimed at
> delimiting such pretensions. And so it can claim here only to end, not to
> conclude. We do not aim at a conclusion but an opening. We do not seek
> a closing but an opening up. [RH 293–94]

In reopening the book on RH, this metaphor of flux is insistent; it
would be the book's central metaphor, if it *were* a book, if it allowed
itself a center. But RH's claim not to be a book goes along with
its admission that nothing in its pages (and nothing signified *by* any
signifier) can contain the flux: "Such a hermeneutic comes to
pass only in the element of movement and *kinesis,* and it requires
ceaseless deconstructive vigilance to 'maintain' itself there . . ."
(RH 147).[3]

This metaphor of flux is not a single metaphor. I find in Caputo's
text at least two different metaphorics of the flux, and between them, a
wonderful and disturbing resonance.[4] One tone resonant here is the *difficulty* flux brings. RH introduces itself as "Restoring Life to Its Original Difficulty," recalling how we struggle to cope with the flux of a
life we never quite master. (Caputo cites Aristotle, Heidegger, and especially the Kierkegaard of *Fear and Trembling*.) There is a shaking in
the metaphorics of the difficulty of flux: we are shaken by it; we tremble. This trembling in Caputo's text is most pronounced in the face of
suffering. Trembling responds to the call of the other, and its theory
(after Levinas) is a phenomenology of the human face.

But laughter also shakes in Caputo's flux, its tones almost opposite
the trembling. If we suffer from the flux, our play is of the flux as well.
To affirm life (and not just its happier accidents) is to affirm it *in* its
ceaseless changes. We lose ourselves to our living, revel in its play:
life's flux finds its redemption as we laugh the laughter of Zarathustra's
ring dance. If the affirmation of flux in RH rings with Zarathustra's
laughter, its affirmation is also a Derridean celebration of textual play.
Text, too, is a kind of flux; the laws and lawyers of meaning will never
stop the signifiers shaking loose from Caputo's text.[5] What is a grave
matter for conservative hermeneutics—that the conclusive reading
never comes, that the book is always an open book—is a delight to

radical hermeneutics. This is laughter without phenomenology, only dissemination: a laughter laughed by the face of the text.

These are profound and powerful shakings: this trembling, this laughter. By a difficult logic indebted most to Derrida, radical hermeneutics practices the coincidence of these two shakings: the shudder felt of horror; the liberating *ébranler* laughing loose its chains. If radical hermeneutics accomplishes this connection (with or without its capitals), if it writes suffering and affirmation with a single tremor, this is a remarkable accomplishment: a wonderful, perhaps fearful, generation of new possibilities. This would be a deconstruction with (and not only against) a phenomenology. This would be a compassion (a suffering-with) at once laughing in life affirmed. It would be profound without seriousness, liberating without manifesto, true without ending its questions. If RH engenders all this, there are, already, many radical hermeneutics to come.

I will not argue that all of this is achieved in Caputo's unbook. I will suggest that its pages pose these questions, sometimes implicitly, turning loose these provocations to thought. Before coming to the trembling of radical hermeneutics, I will follow, at least roughly, the course of Caputo's text, first posing this series of questions: Why hermeneutics? Why so radical? How can it be both? I will then focus on two issues Marsh emphasizes in this critique of RH: the problem of rationality and the legitimation of action. It is in that connection that I will return us to the metaphorics of flux, and to the tension it solicits between the trembling and the laughter of radical hermeneutics.

## WHY HERMENEUTICS?

The hermeneutics of Caputo's title is most traceable to Heidegger, and in particular to the hermeneutic circle and existential analytic of *Being and Time*. Caputo has argued elsewhere—and well, I think—that Husserl and Kierkegaard are the two major figures feeding into Heidegger's existential analytic. Husserl's delineation of the horizon structure of meaning and of the corresponding acts of explication make his phenomenology especially suggestive for philosophical hermeneutics. Heidegger's hermeneutic circle is but a particular case of this—indebted to Husserl, but given an ontological focus (Dasein's understanding of Being) foreign to Husserl's more epistemic bent.

Yet it is Kierkegaard's existentialism that Caputo takes to be the controlling influence on Heidegger's early work. Kierkegaard's own delimitation of metaphysics anticipates Heidegger's destruction of the history of ontology, as well as his later "overcoming" of metaphysics.[6] But Heidegger takes the Kierkegaardian line and bends it to a more circular form. What for Kierkegaard is repetition forward ("to do again and again what one does now") Heidegger recasts as an ontology of retrieval. Here *kinesis* takes the circular form of "existing–falling–being-in-the-world." (Thus, a temporal circularity between the three moments of time; a circularity of thematic and prethematic in the understanding of Being; and a kind of circulation between Being and time—this last problem even encircling Heidegger's first and last publications.) It is against the weight of this (always-already) fall that hermeneutics must work its retrieval of the fallen, the sedimented, the lethic. Hermeneutics is not a violence *against* its medium, but *because* it is bent on retrieval.

Caputo stresses this, in one of the more telling instances of "both/and" to be found in the book: "There is no hermeneutic recovery without deconstruction and no deconstruction not aimed at recovery" (RH 65). This has a two-fold significance here. First, it emphasizes the element of strife persistent in Heidegger's thought (of *Aus-trag, Ent-eignis,* etc.), always complicating, deepening, interlacing this absence with the more present logos. Heidegger is on-the-way-to-Derrida.[7] But the second implication is that the deconstruction will not wrest free of hermeneutics, even if it says it does. All Derridean tracks mark out a way still, at least roughly, gone by Heidegger.

If Heidegger anticipated much of the differential logic we attribute to Derrida, he did not embrace it thoroughly enough to suit Caputo. Heidegger did move away from Husserl's epistemic concerns, and especially from his insistence on securing philosophy as a foundation. He also dropped the existential language and structures shortly after *Being and Time,* as his main concern had always been ontological. Later in his career he had broken with anything he would even call Hermeneutics. For Caputo, though (following Derrida), Heidegger never broke thoroughly enough with Husserl's reliance on direct intuition. Heidegger's meditative thinking refined that faith in intuition, ontologized it, but still sought the immediacy of presence in a nostalgia that would reach even farther than the pre-Socratics.

If Heideggerian thought has turned *too* far to the call of Being (past subjectivity, even past what is human in Dasein), one way to have a more critical hermeneutics would be to retrieve more of the existential, particularist stance so insistent in Kierkegaard. By making Kierkegaard a pivotal figure in his construal of hermeneutics, Caputo implicitly suggests such a possibility, without developing it in the first part of the book (and without taking Kierkegaard to be *sufficient* for these revisions). I propose you read the hermeneutics of Caputo's title as a confrontation between these two: the Heideggerian and the Kierkegaardian; the ontological and the existential; the epochal and the irreducibly particularist. The upshot is a hermeneutics already critical, not just set against a radical other, but divided in itself: tensed between almost opposite estimations of subjectivity; trembling between "God" and "the gods."

## WHY RADICAL?

So why must hermeneutics find itself radical if it is already at odds with itself? Why so radical? The most pointed radical to hermeneutics in Caputo's book is Derrida, a figure more upsetting to metaphysics than Kierkegaard (and more difficult to co-opt). If Kierkegaard inaugurated the delimitation of metaphysics ("the end of philosophy"), he surely didn't finish the job. That is hardly a criticism—more a mark of fidelity; it only alerts us to the inevitable limitations of the earlier work. Kierkegaard reversed the traditional line of metaphysics: from a recollection of pre-existing truth (whether Platonic or Hegelian), to a repetition forward that decides the constantly created self (and, in Christian existence, puts eternity ahead). But this reversed line of repetition falls short of the Heideggerian circle: Kierkegaard's is still conceived primarily in terms of individual temporality, resisting any conception of historicity as too Hegelian (RH 81–82).[8]

It is Derrida that Caputo pits against the seriousness of Heidegger's mythological pronouncements. For Derrida hermeneutics is not, as Heidegger had thought, the deconstruction of tradition; for Derrida, hermeneutics is of the tradition to *be* deconstructed.

Consider meaning, the most evident intent of hermeneutics. For Heidegger, meaning is not propositional content, but the structure that maintains understandability, the organizing component *in* what is understood, and upon which understandability depends. For Derrida, such structures are not themselves meaningful. Derrida's poststructuralism takes as its point of departure that the signified depends on the signifier (if we still want to use those terms), while signifiers depend upon their differential system. It is the field of differences between signifiers that is (if we still want to use the term) fundamental, not the positive, ghostlike entity the signified would be *an sich*. Thus, the signified itself, meaning itself, is an effect of systematic differentiation. Meaning depends upon something more basic, something not at all a thing and finally meaningless. Derrida links this motif of differing to another that is worked in detail in readings of Husserl (especially *Speech and Phenomena*): the deferral of presence, the impossibility of presence as such. In summary form, on Husserl's account the present is itself constituted by the traces of retention and protention; it is the cut of absence that allows the appearance of a present. The grafting of these two operations, differing and deferring, yields *différance*. *Différance* is generative of all differences (and of the difference between difference and identity), but this "generation" of difference is no more active than passive; it is undecided between the two.

Dissemination—seminal difference—exceeds the governance of meaning, but not from *outside* philosophy: philosophy, like Husserl's new point, is breached from within by its "other," built on what breaks it apart. This yields multiple critiques of logocentrism, of the dominance of logos in the multiple guises of reason (some of which are available in this volume). The logic of deconstruction no longer issues from logos in that sense.

This is the logic to which deconstruction (and radical hermeneutics) opposes itself: suppose a decided opposition, a hierarchy, if you will, in which one term is preferred and one excluded. A value claim is assumed as one term is valorized at the expense of the other, but there is also a more ontological assumption: that the terms *are* distinct, and that the opposition can be understood and mastered in those terms. Deconstruction sets upon both of these assumptions, making the little fish swallow the big one. We can no longer be sure what depends upon what in the food chains of philosophy. Philosophy has equipped itself for the indiscernability of identicals and the identity of indiscernibles, but Derrida offers instead an undecidability of opposites, an excluded middle turned inside out.

## Is Reason Caput?

It is easy to see why Derrida has been accused of irrationality, and Marsh is among these accusers. Because the radical hermeneutics willingly assumes Derridean directions, Marsh claims the most fundamental difference between himself and Caputo to be the following: "Is the tradition of modern, Western rationality simply to be overcome or is to be redeemed dialectically?" (PCM 261). We must look carefully at the alleged *ir*rationality that poses the rational as the problem here. (Could it be, Pythagoreans, that this irrationality belongs to the hypotenuse, and not to the geometer?) We must compare these two readings of Derrida's rendition of reason.

On Marsh's reading, Derrida claims that rationality (as western, modern, and evidential) is "simply to be overcome" or "simply to be jettisoned" (PCM xi, 255). Marsh locates the beginning of Derrida's error with Heidegger's project of overcoming metaphysics. Heidegger's critique of objectivity (preceded in some ways by Kierkegaard and Nietzsche, and followed in this by Derrida and Caputo) fails to distinguish the one bad sense of objectivity which *should* be critiqued—alienation—from the other seven senses Marsh enumerates, all of which are legitimate or even inescapable. Derrida compounds this error by his "undialectical rejection of presence and identity" (PCM 202), and by failure to recognize that *différance* must be *present* if it is to *make* a difference "and not leave us indifferent to the argument" (PCM 119). Further, Derrida's work admits to being parasitic on the metaphysical host. If that is a bankrupt tradition, why accept Derrida's check drawn on its account? But if Derrida has found bits of tradeable currency there, then the tradition wasn't bankrupt after all, was it? In sum, Derrida (with Heidegger and with a postmodernism that includes Caputo) takes a discourse outside philosophical reason and "bad" metaphysics to be the only alternatives; he completely overlooks the good metaphysics of new-and-improved critical modernism ("removes embarrassing performative inconsistencies").

Among anglo-analytic philosophers of language an example occurs repeatedly: Are Scot and the author of *Waverly* the same? Here: Is Derrida the same as the Marshian "Derrida" who thinks the tradition of rationality is simply to be overcome? This *is* a Derrida, and one familiar to too many, but this is not the author of *Grammatology*. Marsh's Derrida *needs* Caputo, and one of the greatest services of RH is that

many readers will find a saner Derrida than they might have expected
from accounts like Marsh's. (Unfortunately, Marsh's Caputo is not the
Caputo who can help Marsh's Derrida, as both figures seem to need
Marsh. I will leave other chapters to venture whether Marsh's Caputo
is the author of RH.)

Caputo reminds us (with David Wood and Christopher Norris,
among prominent others) that Derrida has not rejected rationality.
Caputo prefers to call his own stance a "postmodern rationality." The
most blatant error of Marsh's reading is that he could take either
Derrida or Caputo to hold that rationality is "*simply* to be overcome"
or "*simply* jettisoned." First, the overcoming of metaphysics was
never to have been a *simple* undertaking, and (for Derrida) the "end"
of metaphysics is continuous with its whole extent. It is not a limit line
to be stepped across; it is more a line that crosses *out,* but without obliterating what remains metaphysical. This is the complicated logic of
writing "under erasure," a trick of Heidegger's Derrida practiced in
his earlier texts. An X drawn through a word leaves the word legible—
legible, because we cannot do without it; crossed out, because, as it
stands, it will not do. This is a symptom of the "double gesture," an
undecidable relation between at least two hands: on one, Derrida (and,
more modestly, Caputo) wants at least at times to play beyond the
bounds of propriety, to enter into discourses that break the rules of discourse, to broach nonsense. (This is the "wild," "outside" Derrida,
so exemplary for certain English departments.) On the other, this discourse would also be "out of" the tradition, in that it is *from* the tradition. The two are inseparable in this operation, as every avant-garde
has insisted. To appropriate that tradition is a strategic necessity: there
is no other way to intervene, to "make a difference," as Marsh says.

But the necessity is not just strategic; it is as necessary as "logic"
gets. Caputo emphasizes this by recalling Derrida's first book, a dis-
sertation on Husserl's "Origin of Geometry." Derrida juxtaposes
Husserl's insistence on pure univocal sense with Joyce's attempts (in
*Finnegan's Wake* and elsewhere) to render language to its furthest plu-
rivocity. Derrida's point—and Caputo's—is that neither can succeed to
a pure form, but precisely because neither can entirely fail, either. It
belongs to the text of both, to *any* text, that some meaning perdures,
and that no identification of meaning could ever secure itself as *the*
meaning, could ever end the work of the text.[9]

In the conceptual fields worked by Derrida and Caputo, neither polarity can be what it is without its relation to the other. If there is no plus without its minus, it is just as true that there is no minus without a plus. Marsh sees this very clearly and, in that, he is absolutely correct. The problem is that he doesn't think Derrida and Caputo realize it too.[10] My diagnosis of Marsh's difficulty is this: While Derrida does accept the yang with the yin, while he never claims to accomplish pure deconstruction, Derrida does not admit to the logic of The Dialectic. Both Derrida and Caputo criticize the metaphysics of dialectic as yet another refinement in the historical privilege enjoyed by the concept at the expense of signs, by *arche* and *telos* at the expense of *kinesis*. Difference and otherness are included in the dialectic, but they are made to serve as moments in their own overcoming.

This, I think, is where we come to the crux of the issue between Marsh's modernism and the postmodernism of Caputo. Both depart from a logic of excluded middle; both take advantage of "both/and." But Marsh makes two interlocking mistakes that prevent him from appreciating his postmodernist adversaries. Because he takes Derrida and Caputo to "simply reject" metaphysics as a bankrupt tradition, Marsh reads them as *simply* taking the negative pole of absence over the positive pole of presence. Thus read, they fail to see the importance of "both/and"; thus read, they can offer no sound alternative to the dialectic, which is then the only game in town (other than an "uncritical" modernism).

Marsh would have us compare theoretical perspectives by considering which account of rationality is more rational, and which is more of a move forward in social theory (PCM 255, 261). Notice, though, that the *meta*theory here—with reason on its side—is set up for the choice of one and *not* both. If both radical hermeneutics and critical modernism embrace a "both/and" logic, for the latter there is only one kind of "both/and" that counts as rational and humane. The dialectic might be the true friend of difference (as De Nys cleverly argues), but only of differences *within* the dialectic, not of any difference *from* dialectic. Radical hermeneutics is (or should be) more pluralistic at even this metatheoretical level. Radical hermeneutics does not presume that there is one sort of theorizing that best advances the human condition in body, mind, and soul. Just as it presumes rationality without presuming the *adequacy* of what we take rationality to be, so, radical hermeneutics presumes a background of practices, strategies, and interventions without presuming their underlying theory to be adequate. As with deconstruction, we do not practice radical hermeneutics *instead* of critical theory, but in addition to the critical theories already being practiced. Action cannot be put on hold while we argue out our theories; our votes against the publicans will count with Marsh's.[11]

I want to conclude my rather summary critique of Marsh by granting *his* critique of Derrida the appearance of truth on an important point. After relating Derrida to the hermeneutics of suspicion, Marsh observes that Derrida fails to adequately relate suspicion to the hermeneutic moment of retrieval (PCM 202). There is truth in this. The critical edge of deconstruction is always against the logos, and one must read a bit closer to follow the less sensational passages admitting that logos, phenomenology, and dialectic aren't all bad. The reason is that these texts do more than transmit propositions; they intervene in hierarchy by trying to upset the privileged term. That strategy risks the appearance of contrary one-sidedness, and the truth of Marsh's observation is that this is exactly the perception of Derrida shared by most (especially those who read only accounts *of* Derrida).

But now a bit of irony. The more telling Marsh's criticism of Derrida is, the more important RH is. It is left to the less extravagant language of Caputo to rein the *reading* of Derrida back toward hermeneutics. In a double gain, hermeneutics becomes more radical, Derrida less irrational. By setting Derrida and Heidegger as epicenters to a more encompassing curve, Caputo contains the tension between suspicion and retrieval — as Marsh recommends — without effacing their difference — as we suspect Marsh of doing. Caputo's demythologized Heidegger is no longer attached to a primordial origin; that figure gives way to a more playful Heidegger, preoccupied with Greek only because he brings forth wonderful and undecidable possibilities from that language.[12] And Caputo's Derrida does not reject, but rewrites Heidegger's idea of authenticity. Like the stinging Socrates who returns us to a state of confused indecision, Caputo's Derrida retrieves for us the hermeneutic moment of speechlessness: as the shudder of *ébranler,* the solicitude that makes the whole tremble. Neither Heidegger's metaphorics or Derrida's free play can be free of the other; neither can simply "be" itself. Once more, "There is no hermeneutic recovery without deconstruction, and no deconstruction without hermeneutic recovery."

By carrying through on this formula, Caputo comes into his own in Part Three, beginning with a move (already underway) "Toward a

Postmetaphysical Rationality.'' Caputo's is a rationality that refuses to decide once and for all what *reasonableness* can consist in. (And perhaps the fear of this postmetaphysics is not so much that it abandons reason as that it opens that sanctuary to a more suspect congregation.) ''The problem with reason today is that it has become an instrument of discipline, not a mark of freedom, and that, when it is put to work, it is taken out of play'' (RH 211).

One of Caputo's examples is the shift of paradigms in science. In Kuhn's schema, the ''normal science'' that assumes its rules without challenge is an authoritarian establishment. (It is normal in Foucault's sense of ''normalizing.'') The moment of the paradigm shift is a violent one; the old paradigm is made to tremble as a whole. But a Derridean logic supports Feyerabend's ''dadaist'' view: that science is never free of that violence, never *wholly* normal (RH 222–33).

Even more than science, philosophy is the enclave of reason's hegemony. Caputo wants to wrest the *play* of reason from the *principle* of reason—Reason in its capital R—which makes everything accountable to itself, demands reason of all. This leaves no play *for* reason, for rea*sons* in their plural and more particular forms. Of course the principle of reason has no reason for itself; the ground it gives is just as much abyss.[13] Here the Heidegger of Caputo's earlier work makes the point by recovering the words of poetry: ''The rose is without why.'' This delimits the rational without just being *ir*rational, as the positivists would have it. But unlike Heidegger, radical hermeneutics will not give up reason to the Authorities: ''we should not give away the word 'reason' to those who have in mind only rule-governed processes and fixed decision procedures. . . . For I do not want to leave reason behind in the hands of *Technik,* like a retreating army abandoning its comrades to the enemy'' (RH 227).

The reason of such a philosophy is neither liberated nor captive, always at risk. It is a reason more like what Merleau-Ponty calls the hyperdialectic. Merleau-Ponty writes that ''the bad dialectic is that which does not wish to lose its soul in order to save it''; it is only a hyperdialectic that envisages ''without restrictions'' the plurality of relations and ambiguity.[14] All dialectics incorporate a plurality of relations; all hermeneutics, however conservative, admit ambiguity. But *without restrictions*: this is the clause rarely practiced. Every bad dialectic builds its restriction into the rules of the game. But for Merleau-Ponty, ambiguity cannot be treated as an add-on or as a subordinate clause to the main stuff of meaning. We live in that ambiguity.

Caputo's transitions from issues of reason to issues of life turn on the ambiguous, undecidable, logic-without-logos they share. The undecidability of sense and nonsense, truth and untruth, presence and absence is not only a matter of theory; its confusion of opposites extends to life as well. Caputo shows this connection especially well in the social capital of reason, the university, where reason is institutionalized, co-opted by the *Ge-stell*.

> The original enlightenment idea of reason—as a protest against entrenched authority—has so withered away that what nowadays calls itself reason is the latest and most dangerous authority of all. What we call reason today is a central power tightly circled by bands of military, technical and industrial authorities which together make up the administered society. This is why a philosophy . . . which speaks in the name of play, is widely perceived to be not only subversive—which it is; it means to be that—but also irrational, which it is not. [RH 234]

Radical hermeneutics thus practices a more specific double gesture (as Caputo quotes Derrida):

> . . . to ensure professional competence, and the most serious tradition of the university, even while going as far as possible, theoretically and practically, in the most directly underground thinking about the abyss beneath the university. . . . It is this double gesture that appears unsuitable and thus unbearable to certain university professionals in every country who join ranks to foreclose or to censor it by all available means. [RH 235]

"Supposing Truth to be a University"[15] . . . it is perhaps easier to appreciate the ambivalent relation of radical hermeneutics to "western Rationality." Both Anglo-American and continental philosophers have treated reason increasingly in terms of conventions and practices rather than atemporal truths; the step from convention to institution poses no difference in kind. So suppose reason to be the *particular* institution of the university. This reason, this university, is not something to be trusted *or* abandoned. It is hardly pure truth, but not unalloyed lies, either. It harbors us and subjects us to the most normalizing disciplines. We expose our students to subversive ideas, on which they are graded, the grades computed, and manpower sorted. This university, this reason, is a complicated site to inhabit; take it as an image of our Being-in-philosophy. This is why we practice such vigilant bricolage.

## THE ETHICAL, THE RADICAL, THE TREMBLING

*The Ethical.*

Having liberated hermeneutics from Heidegger's mythology, and reason from the tradition that has made even its enlightenment a danger, Caputo now comes to the liberation of action. It is not theory, not even ethics, that calls forth our action; we act because something has to be done.

Caputo tells a story of three ethics: of value theory (the ethics of modernity); of originary ethics (the primordial ethos of Heidegger, shared in part by McIntyre); and of disseminative ethics (urged by Caputo). Value theory is bad metaphysics: subjectivistic, calculative, enframed. A Heideggerian critique of value-based ethics could call for an ethics of *ethos,* of dwelling, of released letting-be. But this originary ethics (whether Heidegger's or McIntyre's) is modeled on a hierarchical, exclusionary *polis.* We cannot just revive the Greek polis by adding the few improvements of our later enlightenment; the polis is built on those hierarchies and exclusions. Even more telling, do you really want to take your politics from Heidegger? In that apolitical polis, the best we can hope for is the return of gods who have withdrawn. Only a God can save Heidegger's mortals; they cannot save each other and the single call toward which the best of them strain is of another frequency from the more human call for help.

Caputo rejects both this pessimism and its salvific language. And perhaps there is a connection between these two. Perhaps if we are willing to settle for less than salvation we can act where we see the need, even if we cannot make out the guiding voice of Being. Caputo's disseminative ethics is *also* an ethics of *Gelassenheit,* but he transforms Heidegger's releasement-to-things into releasement-toward-*people*. This third kind of ethics does not arise in spite of, but because of, the foundering of the first two: metaphysics and eschatology. It is precisely from the breakdown of all such standpoints and resting points that we begin to act, and this realization liberates action. No longer assuming an Archimedean point for its ethical leverage, action is no longer subordinated to the principle of reason. This is a morals without a metaphysics of morals.

The ethics of RH is disseminative in its counter-hierarchical force, in its suspicion of authority and exclusion, and in its affirmation of difference and plurality. These could even serve as formulae for the perceptions and inclinations we put into action—tendencies you can practice as extensively as you care to. These are also particularist ethics, more akin to Foucault than to Habermas (though Caputo's Foucault is the figure in these pages that *does* seem in need of a Marsh).[16] The ethics of radical hermeneutics is a lesson in humility, and in caution, since we cannot master the difficult flux of life. But this flux inspires our compassion, too, as we are "all siblings of the same flux" (RH 259). Caputo envisages a "community of mortals" in an image inclusive of the reader: "We huddle together for warmth in the night of this cold hermeneutics, shaken by the same trembling, by the same *ébranler*" (RH 259). This is one of the best offerings of radical hermeneutics. We will return to this image, to this metaphorics and ethics of the trembling.

## The Radical.

How radical is the radical of this hermeneutics? Surely not in conventional political terms: the motif of suspicion extends to every party, every metatheory of history, class, etc. Caputo's "radical" is the *root* of "radical," *radix*: root. This radical is not, for Caputo, a root that contributes foundation; it is a burrowing, gnarled, underground structure that is, however slowly, in movement, always implicated in its soil, as impacted as wisdom teeth. We should not expect the action of radical hermeneutics to conform to some theoretical stipulation, even to a rigorous anarchy. We should only expect this gnarled root to work its way into the classroom, the faculty senate, the APA; to touch local establishments of force with its underground movement. We can even hope that action at a distance can effect changes of this kind elsewhere.

But here is the first of my suspicions of RH: *Is* it underground? It is a liberation hermeneutics, but its liberation seems modeled on the liberation of Paris at the end of World War II, not Paris 1968—or 1968 elsewhere. While Caputo has good reason to be critical of political theory that supposes an ideal speech-situation,[17] the community of radical hermeneutics must also be one in which fair play is a (roughly) realizable end. The sphere of action most evident here is one of debate. Caputo lays his metaphors on the line in a key passage:

> I would say that the notion of free play is never more valuable than here, that what is required above all is the free play of ethicopolitical discourse, a kind of public debate in which we allow ethicopolitical reason to play itself out. Political and ethical rationality seems to me essentially a matter of free play. And, if it is objected that this is a metaphor, I would press the case of how one is to distinguish the difference between proper and metaphoric. We always have to do with metaphors. The crucial distinction is not between literal and metaphoric but between good metaphors and bad, and I am arguing that the flux and free play are good metaphors. [RH 261–62]

These *are* good metaphors, and we should hardly oppose the ideal of "fair play." But this metaphorics of fair play does not seem to me to be much underground, or to intertwine with the metaphorics of the root. My impression is that, for better or worse—and this may really *be* better: I frankly don't know—this is a "Very Liberal Hermeneutics."

(Ironically, it is at this point that I find Caputo closest to Marsh. For Caputo, the point is that "we keep the debate fair and free of manipulative interests"; just as Marsh distinguishes "appeal," which is rational and free, from "coercion," which is irrational and unfree.[18] They are equally suspicious of Foucault, too, who is characterized by Caputo as a metaphysical reductionist and dismissed by Marsh for "performative difficulties" stemming from his failure to distinguish coercion from appeal.)

It is in this light that I am surprised by Caputo's claim that Derrida has no "Rortian illusions about the charms of bourgeois liberalism" (RH 196). How different is the ethic of "fair play," or Caputo's claim that the *phronesis* we need today is "civility"? I would not agree with the affirmative part of Caputo's claim that Derrida "does not provide criteria but the conditions for a fair game"—which is fair in a way, since it is the most privileged who stand most to lose. My suspicion, though, is that Derrida's root metaphors drive farther underground than Caputo's, that there is less liberalism in Derrida's metaphors. I do not infer from this that Derrida's are better, or that the two are incompatible; I suggest only that there is a friction here, that this has implications for action, and that radical hermeneutics needs to continue its writing underground.

These metaphors are *supposed* to offer themselves for rereading; they themselves recommend this. The text is never secure, nor can the reader be. The whole is solicited, the whole trembles.

### The Trembling.

This is what troubles me the most in RH—perhaps the only difficulty that I feel in a palpable way. The problem is not the trembling— not at all. Rather, the voice of that text speaks of difficulty, of trembling, yet the voice of that text too rarely trembles. More often it is *about* trembling. After Derrida's exposure of phonocentrism we cannot speak with assurance of the "voice of the text," nor can we treat the text is if it *were* a voice—especially its "own." These deconstructive staples are by now familiar to almost all. But it would also be a mistake to think RH devoid of a voice. Marsh's reflection does well to commend the way Caputo's voice makes continental philosophy speak a "vigorous, eastern seaboard, Philadelphia prose."[19] The voice Marsh cites is a voice of confidence, if not authority, and it tells a good tale. All that would be fine, except that everything of importance is at stake in this trembling, more than anywhere else in this book.

My uneasiness is not just with the voice of RH, for I think it bespeaks an unresolved tension in theory as well. I want to suggest that the deconstructive element of radical hermeneutics shakes its phenomenology. And the metaphorics of trembling, while not the only site of this shaking, is where the issue becomes the most important: in the face of suffering.

It is not in the section on ethics, but in openness to the mystery that Caputo turns to the face as the origin of respect. If that respect is the very essence of the ethical, it issues *from* the abyss that each of us is. The human face is the face of the mystery. And it is also the face of suffering. If there can be a phenomenology of the face, it is because we are capable of trembling for the other. This is a human trembling, but a trembling not entirely belonging to the individual—almost a trembling between one and the other, like the fear and trembling before God (who, for Levinas, is almost metonymous with "the Other"). The "other" trembling of radical hermeneutics is the Derridean *ébranler* that shakes the whole—as metaphysics, "the tradition," "the book," or any other pretension to seamless wholeness. This trembling issues from textual points of undecidability. It is not a trembling felt by a subject. It can have no phenomenology.

Between these two tremblings, metaphorics of trembling, is there a kind of *meta*-trembling? a sympathetic shudder of contradictories? What tempts me to this thought is that the two tremblings seem both isomorphic and opposed. Their common structure is a Derridean excess of philosophy, of meaning, and of Marshian *ratios*. It is interesting and provocative to think a moral phenomenology ("The Face of Suffering") as embodying this deconstructure. But it is this coincidence that makes the *différance* of these tremblings reverberate here: What is most important is exposed—shaken from the shelter of inherited metaphysics. We do not know what this means, but something is shaking.

Radical hermeneutics registers that shaking. The danger is that what is human—what can be humanly felt, what could have a moral phenomenology—might be swept off in the play of a more Derridean trembling. In the final chapter of *Radical Hermeneutics,* for instance, there are five pages on the face of suffering, while I find that point dissipated by several other claims. Is "letting the play be" the best advice radical hermeneutics has to offer, as Caputo suggests (RH 264–65)? The last warning before "the Conclusion of the Book" is against the spirit of seriousness: "For all this talk about the abyss and dark nights is not supposed to be a midnight metaphysics . . . but a way of awakening to the play of the flux and hence in staying in play oneself" (RH 293). To oppose play in the name of suffering is the classic revolutionary excess, from guillotine to killing field. But it is left to the living to tremble and to play, somehow both. The contradictions of life, unresolved by dialectic, are no more resolved in this "free play" metaphorics.

The lack of resolution is perhaps a good thing, since it would be a distortion to claim life's problems solved by any book. But there is also this irony. RH does face up to the difficulty of the flux; but precisely because this hermeneutics does not shy away from the difficulty of life, because it *restores* that difficulty, our theory accounts for the dissonant tones of life. I think this is what nags at me: not that suffering is dismissed by this, as Caputo takes the tragic view of suffering to do, but that the extent of suffering could be accounted for at all. This hermeneutics has the satisfying ring of a well-rounded whole; its *theory* comes to a happy ending, as it includes everything a theory needs to include. Surely there are gaps, limitations, unresolved tensions; but without these "flaws" it could not *be* the theory it argues for. The faults of the text belong to its topography, consequences of its continental drift.

Caputo's text is not glib about this (as I fear I make it sound), but it is not a wounded text either. This is why I find between capital and uncapital practices of radical hermeneutics a question bigger than this text, a question I can barely put in the interrogative: between the face of suffering and the text of suffering — what?

As theory, RH is wonderful — even its perlocution. But this metaphorics of the trembling is so important, and so much a part of the book, that I want to feel it more in the reading, to carry that sense of trembling with me as a retention of reading, as the difficulty to be faced. Now I find I do feel this metaphorics of the trembling, but in the curious distance which locates me closer to it after all, as commentator on its absence. It comes to me as a suspicion yet to be confirmed.[20]


## WHAT IS TO BE DONE?

The most important issue looming here, between capitalized and uncapitalized radical hermeneutics, is not unique to these texts, nor is it new: What is theory to life? What is to be done? We can't turn to theory for reassurance here; there is no proof, no formula. We are without justification, just as Sartre observed, and perhaps the difficulty of the flux is *exactly* that of responsibility where there are no assurances.

In his reflection on RH, Marsh asks how Caputo, or any postmodern account, could justify preference for the marginalized, the poor, the dispossessed (*supra,* 19). These are surely the right choices to make, agrees Marsh, but how can RH justify them *as* choices?

The answer must depend on what justification you want. To *require* rational reasons is to accept that Rationality (with a capital R) is the best measure for such choice, and to grant its authority here. But it is just where we most feel the need for such an authority that we ought to be most suspicious of its claims. Consider: if the choice is clearly for or against life, for or against freedom, for or against human dignity — is there any way such a choice could be put on a more secure foundation? Surely we are most inclined to turn to "reason" to work out the muddier cases: *whose* life? *which* freedom? what *kind* of dignity? To think that our choices can be justified (in any strong sense) is to put theory before the flux of life. And too often that justification has been at the expense of the living. Suppose, though, a justification of another sort, of a need to do what can be done. This is the only justification Caputo aspires to, and this is where I find the most difficult politics of radical hermeneutics, where the trembling returns. We must respond to situations of urgency, we must act without assurance that we will succeed, or that our cause will succeed, or that some turn of history will prove us correct. We hope we are not ourselves spreading the plague. What is hard for the modernist[21] to give up is the idea of a transcending truth with which our transitory acts can be allied. We may no longer expect that truth of a god, of a transcendental ego, or even of history's inevitable course; but the modernist wants philosophy to be able *somehow* to validate the actions that seem necessary in a world in need of change. We admit the difficulty; we cannot see a solution in theory. Our best is compassion for our siblings of the flux, human, trembling.

Suffer the trembling.

The difficulty that faces Camus' rebel in this age of ideology is that violence seems both necessary and unjustified; we are not excused from one by virtue of the other, and we have no recourse to a logic of excluded middle. What is hard is the felt force of this deconstructive logic where human beings are at stake, where *campesinos* disappear in the night. Camus leaves us with a gun in our hands and a lump in our throats; I leave you only with a lump in my throat—or the thought of it. That is the difficulty: of *that*, I tremble . . .

NOTES

1. Marsh's title should read as *"Post-Husserlian Meditations,"* I think. Its focus and transcendental motif (the precedent from which the book takes its post) is much more in Husserl than in Descartes. In any case, I prefer the book with this title to the one with the alternative title.

2. This is dangerously close to a performative contradiction. But if the performance of the sentence has contradicted its content, what has been performed? Was anything read?

3. What leads up to the passage quoted here is also germane to the Caputo-Marsh controversy: "For if there can be a more radical hermeneutic, then that can never be turned into the latest philosophical standpoint, the newest position in the history of metaphysics."

4. To write "resonance" might seem "phonocentric," but I want to split the

"phono" from any evident centrism. This remains a *written* "resonance," and a resonance of writing. I will add "tone" and even "voice" to the play of this phonographics.

5. Including these.

6. See especially pp. 32–35 for Caputo's deconstructive Kierkegaard. That section ("Repetition and the End of Metaphysics") is an excellent instance of radical hermeneutics, and (in particular) of Caputo's contention that the ends of deconstruction and hermeneutics are really inseparable (a point to be discussed presently).

7. That Caputo has Heidegger anticipate Derrida is not only a claim of influence; it suggests too that it is Derrida's writing that establishes Heidegger's anticipation of it (as Borges writes of "Kafka and His Precursors").

8. There is, of course, much more to be done with the many voices of Kierkegaard's texts. A deconstructive hermeneutics will continue to expose the tensions between metaphysics and its overcoming in Kierkegaard. Again, that is not so much criticism or flattery as attention to the marvelous play those texts already achieve.

9. See p. 128 of RH for a fine discussion of this example and the larger point.

10. It is possible that I am only adding a misreading of Marsh to what I take to be his misreading of Derrida and Caputo, but radical hermeneutics can make better sense than critical modernism can of how all these texts allow such varied readings.

11. We face more difficult choices in Peru and South Africa.

12. "And Heidegger does that with the Greeks . . . because he is especially good at repeating Greek words in interesting and innovative ways, just as others are good at repeating the words of the scriptures or Plato or the *Tao*. The same thing could be done in other ways, with Meister Eckhardt's German, e.g., or with James Joyce" (RH 184). I find this one of the most suggestive moments in Caputo's book. What other languages, what other writings, what other media, lend themselves to this playfulness? There is no limit to the possibilities. RH opens an unlimited number of radical hermeneutics to be practiced and read and written. (Now that you've found another key, what are you going to play? . . . )

13. And again we encounter the undecidability, this time of foundation and the bottomless, and of the difference between them.

14. *The Visible and the Invisible,* ed. Claude Lefort, trans. Alphonso Lingis (Evanston: Northwestern University Press, 1968), p. 94. This motif of the "hyperdialectic" is interesting in the context of this debate because it offers a name and a "logic" which is neither dialectic nor deconstruction, while sketching a "both/and" that ought to be of interest to both Marsh and Caputo. I would argue that Merleau-Ponty's thought drew increasingly to directions not foreign to radical hermeneutics.

15. Quoted from Derrida's "The Principle of Reason: The University in the Eyes of its Pupils," trans. C. Porter and P. Lewis, *Diacritics* (Fall 1983), p. 16, quoted in RH, p. 235. Anyone concerned with understanding Derrida's view of reason should study this essay. This section of RH, "The Institutionalism of Reason," is another fine example of radical hermeneutics in practice.

16. I think radical hermeneutics has more to draw from Foucault than Caputo does in the book—but very carefully, and always along with Camus.

17. Doesn't it seem that critical modernists discuss political theory as if they are discussants in Plato's *Republic,* looking past the complications of the cave for a society ideal in theory?

18. Compare pp. 262–63 of RH with pp. 155–56 of PCM, from which I have cited their similar language, as well as their cautions about Foucault.

19. I refer to the third paragraph of Marsh's initial reflection on RH, reprinted in this volume.

20. I have only remarked a suspicion, a question, here. It seems to me to open on a number of wider issues, and that opening is only indicated here. See elsewhere for a more intensive pursuit of this in an essay that should be forthcoming as "The Trembling of *Radical Hermeneutics.*"

21. Marsh describes his position as a "critical modernism"; I am not familiar with anyone admitting to being an "uncritical modernist."

# On Being Inside/Outside Truth

## John D. Caputo

THE TIME HAS COME to be responsible. The police of truth (or of ''validity claims,'' which claim to be the same thing) are after us and it is high time to make the case that we are responsible citizens, not outlaws. Still the very idea of outlaw is not intrinsically bad, not bad by its very essence (if it has an essence). For suppose the laws are bad, then the ones outside the law would be outside what is bad, which is (presumably) good. Historically, some of the very best people have been judged and even punished as outlaws by the law, and were no doubt declared lacking in validity, judged invalid, by those who claim to be the guardians of the laws. But this outlaw matter is a dangerous digression (still, sometimes, dangers and digressions are more important than the safe straight-and-narrow) and it is just the sort of thing that gets me in trouble. It is not what I want to stress here. For in having stressed elsewhere (e.g., in *Radical Hermeneutics* ) the need for vigilance about (what calls itself) law and reason, for wariness about (what calls itself) truth and validity, I have left the distinct impression with the guardians of the law and truth that I am just an outlaw of a common garden variety, with no respect for law and order, truth and goodness, validity and legitimation.

So this is the time to come clean and to make the case that I am responsible too, that I want to respond to the sorts of things that responsible people respond to: to Being, the good, and the true. Perhaps I can even thereby respond to critical modernists like James Marsh who have unequivocally assured us that they are true guardians of the good, good servants of the truth, reliable keepers of the law, that they are true and sincere, that what they say is appropriate and comprehensible.[1] Critical modernists claim—validly, no doubt—to respect laws—above all, the laws of reason, which is for them the royal road to truth. Now as much as I distrust all royalty, perhaps the time has come to show that I too can put on kingly airs. Now I too must be equally reassuring, make a pledge to truth, pledge my allegiance to the flag of truth, and perhaps have my picture taken outside the factories where they make flags.

So let the word go forth here and now that I will not play around any more, not even a little bit. I have taken the pledge. I want to put everyone at ease, to calm racing hearts, take the red out of the faces of those who are angry with me or with what is called postmodernism. Let it be said here and now, in this venerable Jesuit university, this honorable house of Being, that I am for the truth. *Sapientia et doctrina:*[2] that will be the coat of arms on my flag. No one can doubt that this university, the university itself, we who work in the university, are for the truth. We respond to the call of the truth. If I can show the sense in which the "postmodernist" line that I pursue—by which I mean not much more than proceeding with the healthy distrust of the inflated claims of modernists from Descartes to Hegel (which would mean that postmodernism started in the nineteenth century at least)[3]—is "seriously" and "sincerely" committed to the truth, then what can be more responsible than that?

So I begin responsibly, with a point that has been obscured by all this talk about anti-foundationalism, relativism, and fictionalism, by borrowing a line from *Being and Time:* Dasein (that is, you and I, and in principle everyone else) is always and from the start *in the truth.*[4] Dasein is constantly bringing about the effect of truth, incessantly disclosing the world in this way or that, like it or not. This is not anything that Dasein can either choose to undertake or decide to drop. It is not something Dasein *does* at all, but something that Dasein *is.* Truth happens by the simple fact that Dasein exists, i.e., is there at all.

That means we presuppose truth from the start. Or rather, truth is a presupposition that in a sense has already been made for us, viz., by the very being which we ourselves are. Accordingly, the merely formal refutation of the skeptic, the charge of self-referential inconsistency—a charge that I am shocked and saddened to learn a famous guardian of the truth has made against me—is superfluous for Heidegger, who refuses to condescend to refutation: "And if a skeptic of the kind who denies the truth factically *is* [e.g., if he or she even shows up at a colloquium on modernism and postmodernism], he does not even *need* to be refuted." Dasein is already in the truth long before the talk of "validity claims" and of "performative contradictions" (which is strictly a second-order, "founded" way to talk about truth for Heidegger) can get off the ground. For Heidegger, truth already lays claim to us long before we lay claim to it. (Does that mean that Heidegger is even more aboriginally (*ursprünglicher*) sincere, comprehensible, appropriate, and "true" than Habermas? Another dangerous digression!) The only way to put an effective stop to this happening of truth, Heidegger adds, is by the desperation of suicide. Dasein may talk a skeptical line, but it cannot *be* a skeptic, cannot be "there" skeptically, cannot be the there of "Being" skeptically, not even if it wanted to.

To be sure, all this truth is not the achievement of singular, individual Dasein, but of a whole community, and not just of this community but of a whole string of communities which stretches from the Greeks to "us" (Germans and selected *Ausländers,* but not Russians or Americans; some of "us" seem to have more Dasein than others).[5] As soon as Dasein comes to be it finds itself on the receiving end of a rich, complicated, long-standing concatenation of beliefs and practices which it both takes in and takes over, which shapes its life, which provides the shape that truth will take for it. Some historical, factical, finite form of life is always already being forged; historical truth keeps on happening one way or another.

In short, to switch from a Heideggerian to a Derridean idiom, Dasein is always "inside" truth ("in the truth"); it can never be "outside" truth, try as it might and however mighty its skepticism might be.

But on the other hand—there is always another hand, many hands, usually more than two, more than just left and right— truth keeps happening, factically, historically, finitely, but we do not know why. Truth happens, Heidegger says, it just does. It is the inevitable exigency of our factical being there that it does, that it happens. So there is a kind of raw "facticity" in all this truth, an inscrutability, an abyss, that does not bear probing or yield further answers. Dasein is always *in* the truth, but it is *thrown there,* factically, and there is no grounding of that. Grounding (which would include setting forth the conditions under which "claims" would be "valid") is something we do in virtue of truth, so it is not anything to which truth "itself" submits. There is no *truth of truth* (which makes the "itself" in "truth itself" questionable). Truth (itself) is groundless. There is truth, Dasein, world, Being, history—Anglo-Americans, who have never been comfortable talking like this, would probably just say "a web of beliefs and practices"— and that is all. *Es gibt:* that's all.[6]

To put all this in the language of "responsibility," which is the point of the pledge I have taken here: we keep on responding to the claims which truth makes upon us, but when we ask about the source or the origin of that claim, about *what* is calling in the call which makes a claim upon us, we get no answer. We could, of course, try to go further and say that the claims of truth are "self-evident," that they shine with "a priori" clarity, that there is an in-built desire for truth, that the mind is, by its "essence," a "capacity" for truth, etc. But the long string of alternative explanations forthcoming from the history of "metaphysics" (the word I use when philosophy starts to make me uncomfortable) on this point, not to mention the merciless skepticism about such explanations voiced by people like Nietzsche, is rather more an indication that philosophers have begun to bump their heads against a wall than that they have been able to scale it. I do not see that we get any further than the *"Es gibt."*

So if Dasein is in the truth, it is no less in the *un*truth; or again, shifting from a Heideggerian to a Derridean idiom, we are not only inside the truth, but outside the truth as well. We cannot situate ourselves *wholly* within truth, within something which is true all the way through. Now that is reason enough to make one think twice about speaking "in the name of truth," since it is not clear what name that is or who has been appointed to speak for it. One of the real problems, inside philosophy and out, inside religion and out, inside politics and out, occurs when people feel called upon to speak in the name of truth or God or country. Thus, when it comes to the question of truth, the point of RH is not to "jettison" the whole idea, which is the way the critical modernists like to put it.[7] That is exactly the opposite of what we are doing, for the whole idea behind facticity is that we are thrown, hurled, in-"jected" into the truth and cannot even begin to throw (*jactare*, jettison) it out. Our point is rather to insist that there is much to be gained from recalling that, if we are always already inside truth, we are likewise always already outside, cast out of the house and home of Being, out-lawed from truth. For there is no truth of truth, no way that we can ground and found the truth in its truth, no way that we can establish our credentials to speak on behalf of the truth. We are thus both inside and outside the truth, neither quite inside nor outside. In a Derridean word (or two): (undecidably) inside/outside.

If I had thesis (or if a thesis had me, if it exerted its thetic-positing power over me and drove me to say this or that, which is what I think happens in critical modernism and which is what I distrust about theses) it would be that we are always inside/outside truth. But of course that would also mean that we are always inside/outside this or any other thesis (or antithesis or synthesis).

The (non)thesis, the claim/being-claimed, is that we are always inside/outside truth, that we do not get any further than the *Es gibt,* that truth is always inhabited by a kind of un-truth which prevents it from being truth all the way through and prevents us from reaching the truth of truth. This view has important implications for both the "historicality" and "transcendentality" of truth, implications which go to the heart of the disagreement between critical modernism and radical hermeneutics and which I wish to take up in turn. The historical point is a more Heideggerian issue; the transcendental point is more the Derridean issue.

First, the historical point: everything I have been saying up to now is a way of emphasizing the inescapable historicity of truth. The historicity of truth means that truth keeps taking historical shape, that we are constantly forging for ourselves one historical form of life or another. Truth in the Heideggerian sense that I have been pursuing here is the sphere of manifestness in which we think and act. Truth is not here taken as the correspondence between a statement—that Athena is the guardian of the city, that Christ will come again to judge the living and the dead—and the reality to which these statements correspond. Truth means rather that there is a "world" filled with Athena, the games, the agora, the temple, the statesmen and craftsmen, etc.; and a world filled with monasteries, clerics, towering Gothic cathedrals adorned with great works of art that tell the story of the life of Jesus, universities that treat theology as the paradigmatic and supreme *scientia,* etc. These are different "worlds," different constellations of truth, of manifestness. To be human (to be "there") is always to operate within one or another of such constellations, such "forms of life," and hence always to be in the truth. But it is also to recognize that there are many such historical constellations, that one form of life tends to give way to another, and that in general the one thing constant in this process is change.

The idea I am pushing here is that there are multiple human possibilities and hence multiple possibilities for truth. The Athenians who walked the agora and debated aloud the definition of justice, and the Florentian friars who walked the cloisters of a monastery adorned with the frescoes of Fra Angelico in silent prayer and meditation, are surely "different" from each other, but it would make no sense at all to try to rank-order them. Above all, it makes no sense—and here I use Heidegger against Heidegger—to treat the Latin Middle Ages as the "deformation" (*Verunstaltung*) of the Greeks.[8] Nor do I think one can get away with ascribing quite as much comprehensive unity to these constellations as does Heidegger. The best and worst thing you can say about these constellations is that they are not only in the truth but in the untruth as well, or that the way they are in the truth does not insulate them from, but rather exposes them to, being in the untruth—which goes for the Greeks as well.[9]

The forms of life of western men and women—and quite a few others, too—have been, on the whole, remarkably varied. The thrust of RH is to urge extreme caution in setting forth overarching standards by which to judge the past or to regulate the future. The idea behind RH is to maintain a sense of flexibility about human affairs—on the grounds that truth keeps happening in many ways—and to encourage a sense of forging something new, of staying on the lookout for little openings here and there which may catch on and have the effect of making some space where once there was none, which is the Kierkegaardian-Derridean sense of "repetition."

Now I come to the point about the transcendentality of truth. I begin by putting the matter in a way that will put Marsh and all other Lonerganians at ease. Truth *is* the transcendental condition of possibility of proceeding, of saying or doing anything, of even showing up at this colloquium. It is what we always presuppose, what is always already set out in advance—*eine Voraussetzung*—what belongs to the very fore-structure of human existence. That is true and I pledge to you that I believe it. Almost. It is almost transcendental, a certain kind of transcendental, a quasi-transcendental. By that I mean that truth goes hand in hand—with two hands, maybe more—with untruth. For it is just that in virtue of which we are able to have truth which casts us out into un-truth. So this transcendental is a queer one, a quasi-transcendental, one which makes it possible to have truth, but in one and the same stroke makes truth impossible, makes it impossible that truth can draw a circle around itself, enclose itself within the circularity of well-rounded *aletheia*. A transcendental condition of possibility and *impossibility*. This point about the (quasi-)transcendental is a more Derridean than a Heideggerian way of putting things and it needs some explaining.[10]

We are, in one and the same operation, always producing truth and always getting entangled in untruth. Let me illustrate this by returning to a famous example of Husserl's which Derrida discussed, in which Husserl tried (as an experiment, of course) to produce a string of signifiers which made no sense at all, not even a self-contradictory sense.[11] This proved to be harder to do than Husserl thought. Imagine a string of signifiers that would *not* make sense, that would not be true, could not even be *construed* to be true on some possible rendering, something which disqualified itself from ever being true in virtue of its very form. Husserl's famous example is "green is or," which Husserl tells us is truly an *Un-sinn,* not a mere *Wider-Sinn.* It is not contradictory (like "green is not green"), because what is contradictory is at least in good form, a form which admits of true substitutions (green is not red). But "green is or" is something which just fails to appear on the register of *Sinn* at all. It has bad form, is not well formed.

But no sooner has Husserl said that when industrious graduate students and young untenured assistant professors begin to buzz around it—they can fairly smell a term paper or a publication here—trying to find a sense for it. It would take no more than a simple recontextualization to make it true. For example, "green is or" could be construed as a response to the request: "List an English noun, copula, and disjunction, in that order." Or just: "Compose a string of three English words." You see how irrepressible the effect of truth is; it would be impossible to stop it up, close it off, suppress it, deny it. Truth is all around us; we are fairly inundated by it. (In particular, the powers that be, the guardians of truth, have ample supplies of it in well-stocked cellars of truth from which they can always select a vintage year.)

But you also see how it would be impossible to say anything that is always already true, only true, true through and through, true no matter how you construe it, so that it could not be thrown into confusion by recontextualization. Truth keeps coming unstuck, undone, like Husserl's claim that " 'Green is or' is an *Unsinn,* " or Husserl's claim about the pure presence of the ego to itself, or about first-hand givenness, or any of the rest of his phenomenological hardware. Now Derrida went on to offer a theory in virtue of which one could get this result with Husserl's example, and that is the quasi-theory of *différance.* The upshot of this notion, which is not quite a notion, is that meaning is an effect produced by the spacing between signifiers and that the "system" of such meanings is not a system, does not close over, but remains in a permanently open-ended condition analogous to the undecidability result which Gödel achieved in analyzing mathematical systems. Like Gödel, Derrida has a notion of formal undecidability which he extends to linguistic systems. That means that it is one and the same (non)thing, the chain of signifiers within which one operates, that makes it possible both to say something and impossible to nail it down definitively, decidedly. That is why we call it "quasi-transcendental."

Another way to put this Derridean point, which meshes it somewhat with the Heideggerian historical point, is that we cannot extricate ourselves from the rush of existence, from the flow of factical life, from the differential deployment of signifiers that make it both possible to get something said and impossible to get it said cleanly, which is, I believe, pretty much the point that Austin was making, but not Searle. We both do and undo things with words. We never get a chance to write from on high, we never win the transcendental high ground. We write from below, slowly and painfully forging unities of meanings from the flow of signifiers (or of internal time consciousness, or of perceptual multiplicity, or of the Heraclitean stream), unities about which we keep our fingers crossed that they will get us through the day. We are always inside and outside truth, unable to stop the rush of truth, yet unable, too, to hold truth in place and stop its rushing off.

Inside/outside.

This fix that we are in—that there is no quick or final fix—this quasi-transcendental, historical fix, is what I would call the hermeneutical situation. The hermeneutical situation is the sphere of factical givenness, of our concrete comings and goings, of our commerce and communication with others, of our practices and beliefs. The hermeneutical situation is always already in place, and no one yet, from Diogenes to Derrida, has succeeded in leaving it behind save by taking the extreme measure of dying in order to prove their point. In pursuing a radical hermeneutics, we are not out to deny truth but to take some of the steam out of the rhetoric about life, world, the things themselves, living presence, being, pure truth, and all of the other lures and comforts of philosophy (maybe even out of *sapientia et doctrina*). We want to show how much acutely critical methods—like phenomenology and Marxism—leave uncriticized and unreduced. We show the extent to which what we like (what we "desire") to think of as being, truth, life, and presence are *possible* only under conditions which philosophy tends to *exclude* under the names of convention, death, and absence. We do not deny the world, but insist on its mediated, constituted character. Every time we hear someone sing the praises of living dialogue we like to remind them about writing and meditation. We do not deny tradition, communication, intentionality, truth, being (or whatever else you need), but we just want to show their complexity, density, instability. We just keep breaking the bad news to metaphysics, for which a lot of people want to kill the messenger.

Radical hermeneutics operates within a truth which is always already in place, within the world of intentions, desires, motives, subjectivities, authors, histories, institutions, and everything else which populates the historical world. Far from withdrawing into a worldless playing with signifiers, we move about, always and from the start within the concrete world of the historical, social, political, and institutional embodiment—let us say the worldly contextualization—of signifiers. Radical hermeneutics does not take philosophy and literature to be pure or worldless writing, cut off from the concrete institutions and systems of power in which they operate, as in some forms of anemic, apolitical aestheticism. On the contrary, everything we say strains against allowing this pure cut, this detachability and unlacing of the work—of art or of philosophy—from its enframing social and political context.[12] Texts are always already enframed, by other texts, of course, but also by political frameworks, by hierarchical systems which want to decide in advance who has the right to determine their truth, whose voice has a right to be heard. Radical hermeneutics is not bent on "jettisoning" the ideas of reason or science but on putting into question certain assumptions, e.g., that the privilege of the logos belongs exclusively to fathers and sons and brothers, or that the destiny of scientific rationality has always been the exclusive vocation of the West as opposed to the "primitivism" of the East or the African.

That is why Derrida is driven to impatience by suggestions that deconstruction denies reference, or intentionality, or subjectivity, or truth, or that deconstruction locks us up in a kind of linguistic idealism— suggestions for which he can offer, perhaps in a moment of frustration, no other explanation than "stupidity."[13] The denial of the transcendental signified is not the denial of reference but of reference-without--difference. It is a denial of the claim that we ever make contact with the uninterpreted facts of the matter, with pure givens, with naked data.

Radical hermeneutics moves about in the world of truth: of sense and reference, of historical agents, of social structures, and of political institutions. Its work is not to scatter truth to the four winds but to let the various hermeneutical agencies know how much trouble they have bought for themselves by trying to sell us one interpretation or the other and to remind them how many other possibilities there are. The truth is always already in place. Mundane intentions and transactions are continually transpiring. Dasein is always in the truth, like it or not, whatever its *vouloir-dire*. The radical in radical hermeneutics does not mean well-grounded and foundational but the racinating, the knotted system of roots that no one can disentangle. Hence, the task of a radical hermeneutics is to show that our comings and goings, our beliefs and our practices, our multiple hermeneutic transactions have roots which extend far below the surface, into the depths of textuality, of the unconscious, of history, and of who knows what else, and that we have only limited hope of disentangling them.

What then? What can we know? What are we to do? What can we hope for? Where do we start? We begin where we are, in the truth, not a little sure about some things, uncomfortably unsure about others, and we push ahead, looking for an opening here and there. This is not the denial of truth, but a more merciless account of what truth is like. The world is a concatenated web, a textual system of its own, and it tends to close down the possibilities and to discourage initiative. We tend to be carried along by its lines of force, repeating it lifelessly in dull, uninspired reproductions, lulled into taking the easy way out. For us, the "received" truths are like the charts that oceanographers draw which show how objects dropped on the surface of the sea tend to drift in patterns set by prevailing currents. They reflect the dominant tendencies. But RH is looking for a counter current which moves against the stream, a break, a tear, a Kierkegaardian *Augenblick,* a little innovation here or there which can appear in the blink of an eye.

One sees now the wrongheadedness—dare I say the untruth?—of Marsh's critique of RH which appeared in the distinguished journal published by this venerable Jesuit university, published in the name of *sapientia et doctrina*.[14] It begins with praise, high praise, and I am humbled by it, for it captures much of the spirit of the text. Almost. For we postmodernists have learned to sense an ambush. In my view, Marsh has missed the inside/outside, the double gesture, the slash between truth and untruth upon which RH balances itself. He wants to keep the inside for himself and push RH to the outside. He thinks that RH argues for "pure flux," that it stands "outside the tradition," that it takes truth claims to be "wholly arbitrary," that it has "no criteria" for its preferences. But of course that goes clean against the grain of RH, which is to take such clean breaks as the essence of metaphysics.

The thrust of RH is that one must begin where one is, in the truth, in the factical situation into which one has been put, with one's inherited beliefs and practices, traditions and values, with all the multiple, irrepressible truths that have been handed down to us (Gadamer) and sometimes forced down our throats (Derrida). Nobody succeeds in getting a clean start in the rush of existence, in leaving their factical life behind.

If RH is a bit of postmodernism, a little postmodern fragment, it is certainly post*modern,* i.e., has passed through, or is still passing through, has not yet left behind, modernity; it never manages to shake modernity off or to shake loose from it. We take the side of Galileo against Bellarmine (even so, we still believe that the Jesuits are in the truth, for Rorty has shown that Bellarmine had the better philosophy of science), of Locke and Rousseau against the royalists and divine rightists, of critique against superstition, etc. We bend our knee, or at least tip our hat, before most of the gods in the modernist pantheon; indeed, we even use a computer. We are responsible citizens and we respond to the claims which modernity makes on us, to democracy, equality, truth, emancipation, suffrage. We have pledged to be responsible.

Whatever bit of trouble RH manages to stir up, it does so only in virtue of borrowing the resources of the very thing it criticizes. We want to out-Locke Locke, out-Marx Marx, maybe even, were it possible, out-smart Marsh. Where else would we get our resources, our ability to make trouble from the factical world into which we have been thrust, thrown, injected? (Unlike Marsh, we do not claim to have dropped from the sky, or to be the secret longing of the West.[15]) This may seem ungrateful on our part, but it is true, and for now, at least, I am pledged to tell the truth.

But RH also wants to exercise responsibility *for* what claims our response.[16] We want to know what is calling to us in what all too quickly *calls itself* reason and truth. We want to know whether anything is being silenced by all this sounding brass, whether anything is being deprived of its voice by what calls itself reason, democracy, truth, the university, *sapientia et doctrina.* Like Kierkegaard, we always find ourselves wondering whether or not those who now praise the prophets' memory most loudly are not the very ones whose fathers killed the prophets in the first place.[17] We are interested in what is being excluded under the name of untruth by everything which calls itself the truth. We want to call into question whatever calls upon us to respond and demands our responsibility. Where, for example, is one standing when one hands down the conditions of truth? Moses claimed only to have had the commandments handed down to him by God. Where is Habermas standing when he enunciates the four conditions for validity claims, when he lays claim to the conditions under which it is possible to lay claim to anything at all? Why not three conditions, or five? Suppose we have left one out or added one too many?

For critical modernists like Marsh this business of borrowing from a tradition which one also makes questionable, of learning to live with truths whose coefficient of untruth one has also recognized, of aiming at getting through the day rather than at ahistorical transcendentality, all of this is a mark of a "performative contradiction." That means, according to Marsh, that it denies truth in the name of truth by claiming that it is true that there is no truth. But that is a singularly vacuous kind of argument, as Gadamer has already shown,[18] and a singularly dense way to interpret the rather Derridean version of postmodernism I defend. A performative contradiction consists in acting upon the basis of what one has *denied,* deploying something of which one has *forbidden* the use, depending on something which one has already *destroyed, sawing* off the limb upon which one has perched oneself. But the Derridean deconstructive strategy to which I have recourse consists rather in proceeding on the basis of what we ourselves have made *questionable,* using something about which we ourselves have urged *vigilance,* depending on something about which we can offer *no assurances,* noticing that the limb upon which we are perched is *breached* in a critical place.

You see the difference between conceding the *différance* which inhabits everything and a performative contradiction which would act against its own flat-out assertions or denials. RH does not act against its beliefs or disbeliefs but rather describes the condition of action as one of forging ahead in the midst of truths which are inhabited by a certain contingency and historicality, truths which harbor within themselves their own untruth, sayings which contain within themselves the seeds of their own unsaying or undoing. Marsh has missed the deeply *experimentalist* sense of truth in RH, its sense of proceeding ahead— repeating forwards—because that is the direction in which life is headed, but with a salutary sense of trepidation, revisability, contingency, undecidability. Undecidability is not indecision, but the capacity for decision in the face of the undecidability which inhabits our lives. Undecidability does not undo decision; it is a condition of deciding. RH makes no sweeping denials of the true or good, which it then proceeds to ignore in practice. It simply blows the whistle on the excessively apodictic frame of mind endemic to metaphysics and urges in its place a sense of raising truth from below, of forging certain contingent unities of meaning which may become unstuck at any moment, or which may take on an unexpected sense at a later date which will lead us to revise them radically. RH does not fall into contradiction with itself simply because its *dictio* never gets so far as the apodictic denials that Marsh attributes to it. It does its level best to avoid saying anything apodictic, sweeping; it leaves that to the guardians of truth and the law and the promulgators of the conditions of possibility of all possible validity claims.

RH regards the tradition as neither good nor evil, as both good and evil; it regards it as a maze-like complex which is at once a major resource and a major obstacle to progress. It falls back upon the resources of the tradition time and time again, even if it suspects that "the" tradition is a bit of fiction and a bit of violence, that it is a much more complicated, involuted, repressed, and multi-form phenomenon than people like Gadamer make it out to be, that in fact there are many traditions competing and struggling within what Gadamer and Heidegger all too placidly call "the" tradition. RH is interested in all of the materials from the past that the mainstream tradition has erased, in part just because they have been erased (it wonders what everyone is afraid of.) I admire, for example, the way feminist scholars approach the New Testament, by wondering what happened to all the women who must have played a part in those times and whether the women whose roles have been recorded have been played down.[19]

RH is not above dealing with the tradition opportunistically, taking what it can use, while declining to offer a general theory that the tradition is either deeply true on the one hand or deeply fraudulent on the other hand. That even goes for having a general theory of the history of metaphysics. I tend to use the word "metaphysics" in RH for everything I distrust about philosophy, for the tendency of philosophy to become apodictic, ahistorical, sweeping, universal. But if metaphysics *is* philosophy, as Heidegger says, then my view is that we are always inside/outside metaphysics, never above the fray, never able to overcome (*über-winden*) it but at best always struggling not to be overcome by it, which seems to me what Heidegger meant when he suggested occasionally that what we need vis-à-vis metaphysics is not *überwin-den* but *verwinden,* which is a way of saying "inside/outside" meta-physics, a Heideggerian nuance never noticed by Marsh.[20]

Let me conclude this confrontation of radical hermeneutics and crit-ical modernism with a single issue that brings a lot of this to a head. RH takes the side of the marginalized and excluded. But why prefer the marginalized and the dispossessed, the guardian of truth wants to know, not because he thinks this judgment is not "true," but because he thinks it has not been "legitimated." How can one prefer the op-pressed to the oppressor without a criterion of truth? Can this choice be justified, legitimated, the philosopher of validity-claims demands to know? Yes and No: I am on the slash, inside/outside truth and validity and legitimacy.

Let us take the down side first, the "no," by beginning with the grimmest, coldest objection to justifying ethics or anything else that I know of:

> In some remote corner of the universe, poured out and glittering in in-numerable solar systems, there once was a star on which clever animals invented ["ethics."] That was the haughtiest and most mendacious minute of world history—yet only a minute. After nature had drawn a few breaths the star grew cold and the clever animals had to die.[21]

(Those who know this text know that I changed one word, that Nietzsche spoke of "knowledge," not "ethics." Still, the point is the same.) The cosmos does not know we are here. That merciless fact Nietzsche calls the great cosmic stupidity. I do not know of any re-sponse to that objection. I have certainly never heard any from Husserl or Habermas, Marx or Marsh. "Racism is unjust," the critical mod-ernist shouts from the surface of the little star, his hand cupped to his mouth. The cosmos yawns and draws another breath.

Now this is not to say that postmodernists, who like Nietzsche quite a lot, have undergone a deep moral rot, that they have ice water for blood, that they (we) are depraved and monstrous. It is just a way of saying that all our little truths are inhabited by untruth, that they are not true all the way through, that they lack the apodicticity which transcen-dental philosophy desires, and hence that we should be wary of truths which pretend to something which they cannot deliver.

But this is not the end of the story. For even if our ethical claims do not achieve absolute validity, that does not mean that they are up for grabs, that one can claim just about anything, that one claim is as good as another. Short of finding cosmic support for our beliefs, there are still choices to be made and reasons for making them, some of which are better than others. I do not think that one choice is as good as another. But I very much doubt that Marsh has any better reasons for condemning racism or preferring the marginalized than I do, or that he has a hotline to some ethico-metaphysical value center that supplies him with knock-down arguments as the occasion arises. I think the difference between him and me on this point is that he tends to jack his justifications up a notch or two and then to pat himself on the back for having legitimized them, whereas I distrust all heights and am content to remain on the surface of the little star, which is what I mean by the hermeneutic situation.

To begin with, the two of us are very much embedded in a Judeo-Christian facticity and we are both taken (impressed, persuaded) by the views voiced by liberation theologians which show the systematic preference that Jesus showed for the poor, the lepers, the lame, the prostitutes, the Samaritans, the tax collectors, and the prodigal son—in short, the marginalized. (The sort of people Jesus favored and to whom he directed his attentions are a lot more like the people about whom postmodernists write than the mainstream Christians of today who, as Kierkegaard said, have made a profitable business out of the Crucifixion.) Furthermore, we are also both impressed by western ideas about democracy and justice, although I do not think the West has a monopoly on such ideas, given what we have to learn from Gandhi. We find those ideas more reasonable, fairer, better, more persuasive.

So there are certain factical reasons for our agreements in ethics and politics. But this needs to be pressed harder. Why do we both tend to draw on the same side of our inherited tradition when there is ample supply of conservative, rightist politics in our common political and theological traditions? I would say because something *calls* to both of us from the "marginalized" or the "other," something very powerful, and we *choose* to *respond,* that is, to be *responsible.* So I come back to the pledge to be responsible. Responsibility, responding to the claims that are made upon us, goes to the heart of what I think ethics is. Now since I conceive of my supposedly/admittedly postmodernist views in terms of responsibility, I would say that RH pursues an essentially ethical line (were it not for the fact that I distrust all talk of essences). This response is not arbitrary: it answers to something which addresses it from without, which overtakes it, seizes it, lays claim to it. So I am less inclined to erect "racism is unjust" into an assertation and look for the basis of the "validity" of this "claim" than I am to speak of my "being claimed" by something which lays claim to me. I think there is something "there" which claims me, although I do not think it is an unmediated, naked datum, and I do not try to vest it with the authority of a categorical imperative. I would rather call it a powerful appeal, an appeal for help, friendship, respect, love, or whatever the other needs. I think this appeal is the sharpest and the most compelling when it voices the appeal of those who suffer.

It is just because this appeal is not "categorical"—unequivocal, un-ambiguous, an uninterpreted fact of the matter—that I speak of "choosing" to respond. There is always an element of choice. It is al-ways possible to walk away from it, which is something that is always being done, by us as well as by others. I myself am at a loss to make this choice more compelling, to give better "reasons" for it, than by undertaking a careful hermeneutics of the other, particularly of suffer-ing. There is an important development of just such a hermeneutics in RH (pp. 273ff) which occupies a crucial place in its argument and I am surprised that Marsh does not spot this or notice it doing the work of what he would call a "criterion." We both think that the arguments against apartheid are better than the ones for it. I think that means that whatever reasons the white minority has for perpetuating the current system are not worth the suffering they are inflicting on black people in the form of inferior housing, hospitals, and jobs and all the attendant family instability and personal misery such things bring with them. But neither of us has any cosmic or transcendental support for our beliefs, for not inflicting suffering in the first place, although I believe I am in the stronger position for owning up to this limitation, for not putting on universal, a priori airs—which is a philosophical gesture we all recog-nize (from Socrates).

PCM comes close to recognizing the point I am making here when it says that critical theory is a kind of phenomenology, viz., a phenome-nology of the alienated world to which capitalism gives rise (see pp. 212ff). That, I think, is a fine and also a telling point about Marxism. What is truly persuasive about Marxism is that it is able to describe in a convincing way what harm people do to one another when they exploit the labor of others and what harm they do to themselves when money becomes a fetish. But it is also a telling point against Marxism inasmuch as it points to the danger of jacking this claim up any higher and draping it in the terms of a theory which lays claim to the meaning of history, or which sees itself as history's vanguard, which thinks that it knows something about historical destiny or even that there is such a thing as destiny instead of just the *es gibt*. That sort of thing breeds violence. The one thing Heidegger said he liked about Marxism—and this, we can safely say, is the only thing—was that it had a theory of history and hence of historical destiny. But that was the truly dangerous thing in Marxism and in Heidegger in the 1930s as well.

In RH the idea is to be content with a good hermeneutics, a vivid account of the injury we do one another, and to drop the overarching theories of history, the metanarratives about alienation, and the metaphysics of validity claims. Marsh and I share a fair number of ethical and political judgments; but his judgments have undergone a gross and unwholesome swelling. He has nothing better to back up his views than I do, viz., the attempt to make those who oppress and exploit look as bad as possible by doing a phenomenology of an alienated and oppressed existence. But he tries to produce something more, and the result is inflation, or even a bit of ludicrousness. Thus we are told that what is wrong with kidnapping is that it violates the second and fourth requirements for validity claims (truth and appropriateness), which arises from the fact that kidnappers have no confidence in the merits of their argument (for ransom money) and so kidnapping is definitely not an instance of an ideal speech situation.[22] That, of course, is extremely illuminating and we can all be grateful to Professor Marsh (and ultimately to Professor Habermas, who inspired this incisive observation) for having pointed this out. It will no doubt help to stem the rising tide of kidnapping in the United States in the future.

The objection of a "performative contradiction," which Marsh makes against RH (or which Habermas makes against Derrida or postmodernism generally), is utterly misbegotten. It all goes back to the question of how much inflation one's notion of truth undergoes. We all begin where we are, on the little star, with our inherited traditions, little truths and untruths, with the factical life into which we have been thrust, "in the truth" which can not be insulated from the untruth, inside/outside truth. We do what we can, forging such truths as our mortal conditions permit, courageous enough to press ahead, but wary of our own limits. The idea behind RH is not to "jettison" truth, to throw it out, throw it over, which would be to think that one can get outside it or overcome it (in some final and thorough-going way). Rather, the idea is to repeat forwards, to forge the truths we need, while making little alterations along the way. We move about the hermeneutic situation with a kind of undecidability, inside and outside truth and goodness, inside and outside the law. We roam the streets on the lookout for something new, even as we suspect that we are being followed by the police of truth.

NOTES

1. PCM, pp. 148ff.

2. The motto of Fordham University.

3. I prefer to describe my own view as "radical hermeneutics," not as "postmodernism." But Marsh describes RH as a work of postmodernism, presumably because of its debt to Derrida (who also does not use the expression). For the sake of staking out the broad lines of disagreement and getting a discussion going I am willing to use the word.

4. For the discussion which follows see Martin Heidegger, *Being and Time,* trans. J. Macquarrie and E. Robinson (New York: Harper & Row, 1962), p. 44; for the texts I am citing, see pp. 263, 270–72.

5. Heidegger had a life-long antagonism toward America and Russia; it is manifest not merely from the famous pincers passage in *An Introduction to Metaphysics,* trans. Ralph Mannheim (New Haven: Yale University Press, 1959), pp. 37–38, 46; he has not budged a bit as late as the 1966 *Der Spiegel* interview: "Only a God Can Save Us," trans. M. Alter and J. Caputo, *Philosophy Today* (Winter 1976), pp. 276, 280–81.

6. The *es gibt* language is to be found in *Being and Time,* p. 269, and it recurs in an important place in "Time and Being" in *On Being and Time,* trans. Joan Stambaugh (New York: Harper & Row, 1965.) For the interpretation of "Time and Being" which I am using here see RH, pp. 171–86.

7. For samples of Marsh's unnuanced account of postmodernism, see PCM, p. xi: "simply to be jettisoned"; p. 255: "jettisoning . . . rationality"; p. 254: "simply reject;" as well as his reflection on RH reproduced elsewhere in this volume: p. 462: "opting for pure flux"; "all truth claims are imposed arbitrarily"; p. 464: "apparently arbitrary manner." Given what Derrida has to say about undecidability, one might venture the observation that the main point of deconstruction is to make questionable the whole idea that a thing can ever be treated as "simply" this or that.

8. *An Introduction to Metaphysics,* p. 13.

9. For a critique of Heidegger on this point, see my "Demythologizing Heidegger: *Aletheia* and the History of Being," *The Review of Metaphysics,* 41 (1988), 519–46.

10. For an outstanding account of the "quasi-transcendental" in Derrida see

Rodolphe Gasché, *The Tain of the Mirror.* (Cambridge: Harvard University Press, 1986).

11. See Husserl, *Logical Investigations,* trans. J. N. Findlay, 2 vols. (New York: Humanities Press, 1970), *First Investigation,* p. 15. See Derrida, *Speech and Phenomena,* trans. David Allison (Evanston: Northwestern University Press, 1972), pp. 88–101. See also RH, Ch. 5.

12. See Jacques Derrida, *The Truth in Painting,* trans. G. Bennington and I. McLeod (Chicago: University of Chicago Press, 1987), pp. 83ff.

13. See "Dialogue with Derrida," in *Dialogues with Contemporary Continental Thinkers,* ed. Richard Kearney (Manchester: Manchester University Press, 1984), pp. 123–24. This interview is a particularly salutary rebuttal of the sort of portrait of Derrida forthcoming from Marsh and Habermas.

14. I refer to Marsh's reflection on RH reproduced elsewhere in this volume.

15. PCM, p. 252. I have poked some Derridean fun at this passage at the end of my initial reflection on Marsh elsewhere in this volume.

16. I have discussed this side of deconstruction with some care in "Beyond Aestheticism: Derrida's Responsible Anarchy," *Research in Phenomenology,* 18 (1988), 59–74.

17. See "What Christ's Judgment Is About Official Christianity" in *An Attack on Christendom,* trans. W. Lowrie (Princeton: Princeton University Press, 1968), pp. 115ff.

18. I discuss this in my reflection on PCM reproduced elsewhere in this volume.

19. See, e.g., the works of Elizabeth Schüsler Fiorenza, especially *In Memory of Her* (New York: Crossroads, 1986).

20. See Heidegger's Letter to Ernst Jünger *"Über die Linie"* in *The Question of Being,* trans. Jean Wilde and William Kluback (New Haven: College and University Press, Twayne Publishers, 1956).

21. Nietzsche, "On Truth and Lying in the Extra-Moral Sense," in *The Portable Nietzsche,* trans. Walter Kaufmann (New York: Viking Press, 1954), p. 42.

22. PCM, p. 151.

# Understanding and Difference: Reflections on Dialectical Phenomenology

## Martin J. De Nys

IN THE *DE LIBERO ARBITRIO*, Augustine and Evodius discuss the excellence that belongs to knowing and the end to which understanding properly aims.

> Augustine: Now let us see how man himself may be most ordered from within. . . . Tell me, are you very sure that you are alive?
>
> Evodius: What could be more certain than this?
>
> A.: Can you make the distinction that it is one thing to live and the other to know that one lives? . . .
>
> E.: I am no longer in doubt. Go on the next point: I have now learned that it is one thing to be alive and quite another to know that one is alive.
>
> A.: Which of these things do you think is more excellent?
>
> E.: Why clearly the knowledge of life [*scientia vitae*].
>
> A.: Do you think that knowledge of life is better than life itself? Or perhaps you understand that a certain higher and truer life consists in the knowledge of life, which no one can have except those who have understanding. For what is understanding but living more clearly and perfectly by the very light of the mind. Therefore, unless I am deceived, you have not set something else above life, but rather have set a better life above a mere life.[1]

That classical and modern philosophical claims concerning reason are suffering a fundamental critique on the current scene is well known. What is not always sufficiently grasped is that the philosophical tradition, classical and modern, has regularly subjected its conception of claims concerning reason to painstaking, radical scrutiny. The turns in the history of philosophy from Plato to Aristotle, from medieval neo-Platonism to Aquinas, from late scholasticism to Descartes, from modern rationalism and empiricism to Kant, from Hegel to Marx, all attest to the power with which the western philosophical tradition constantly reassesses and redevelops its own conception of rationality.

The work that James Marsh does in *Post-Cartesian Meditations* stands in the tradition of philosophy's self-interrogation concerning reason. His philosophical questioning begins from the wonder that humans experience at the world and from the alienation that humans experience from themselves and the world. It also begins from a critical consideration of the concern of modern philosophy and phenomenology for philosophical beginnings. By way of an assessment of Descartes and Husserl, Marsh proposes a dialectical phenomenology. This phenomenology "is dialectical insofar as it is historically rooted and insofar as it overcomes 'either-or' opposition and moves towards 'both-and' mediation."[2] It is descriptive in three ways. It describes "phenomena of experience with as few presuppositions as possible."[3] It understands and affirms "essential structures on each level of human experience, as well as essential relationships between and among levels."[4] And it moves "into the egological-ontological reduction in which the self in the life world is the source of meaning in that world, in the sense that for each meaning or level of meaning there is a corresponding act of discovery, creation choice, and so on."[5] As conceived by Marsh, phenomenology is "the universal reflective, conceptual thematization of human subjectivity in relation to being. Being is the life world as ultimate context, as unity of subject and object."[6] Dialectical phenomenology follows a transcendental method which, "in the full sense is an explicit experience, understanding, judging, and choosing of myself as an experiencing, understanding, judging, deciding subject in the world, relating through those activities to various noematic objects."[7] Dialectical phenomenology aims at a comprehensive recovery of the life world, the circumambient contexts of meanings and involvements that situate the self. It contrasts the life world with the world as given in the objectifications of science. It understands the life world as the whole which grounds scientific knowing and includes scientific objectifications within itself.[8] It identifies the life world as the proper focus of philosophical knowing, and this identification is the basis for a critically enhanced understanding of reason. Simultaneously, dialectical phenomenology aims at a recovery of the self,[9] at a full and concrete understanding of those acts and involvements through which the self brings about the multifaceted domain of meanings that situates it and allows the sort of self-unification proper to it. This recovery of the self goes hand in hand with the recovery of the life world, and reinforces the critically enhanced understanding of reason that dialectical phenomenology unfolds.

Dialectical phenomenology, then, is not only a body of positions but also a program. This essay will be an effort to participate in the program that dialectical phenomenology outlines. I want to probe the resources for philosophizing on which dialectical phenomenology draws, to discuss how one of those resources offers dialectical phenomenology a strategy that grounds its achievements, to examine some of the claims that Marsh makes as he develops this program for philosophizing, and to focus briefly on the goals that dialectical phenomenology defines as properly philosophical.[10] Throughout, my intention will be to discuss in various ways the account of reason that defines the "critical modernism" that Marsh espouses.

I

Mention was made above of some features which render dialectical phenomenology phenomenological. While not minimizing the importance of any of these, one may suggest that this program for philosophizing is phenomenological in even a deeper way, finding a resource in a very basic achievement of Husserlian phenomenology that grounds the aforementioned senses of descriptiveness. Dialectical phenomenology consistently operates in light of the possibilities opened by way of the phenomenological reduction and the doctrine of intentionality.

In *Ideen I,* Husserl develops at least two arguments, quite interdependent but also different, concerning the reduction. I call these the argument from apodicticity and the argument from radicality.[11] On the one hand, things given only in profiles and therefore presumptively in the natural attitude are given in an absolute way when considered as phenomena for intentional consciousness. This makes possible the apodicticity that strict knowing requires.[12] On the other hand, the world, understood as a domain of sense or meanings and imaginatively annihilated in its natural facticity, continues to present itself as a correlate of consciousness. This shows that "the whole *spatio-temporal world,* which includes human being and the human Ego as subordinate realities, is *according to its sense a merely intentional being.* . . . It is a being posited by consciousness in its experiences which, of essential necessity, can be determined and intuited only as something identical belonging to motivated multiplicities of appearances. . . . "[13]

The phenomenological reduction, as Husserl discusses it, achieves a standpoint in which things can be considered in an apodictic way and in a more radical way than available to the natural attitude. The latter is the case because, given the reduction, one can consider things not as assumed facticities, but with regard to the manner in which they appear or present themselves to consciousness, in correlation to those perceptual and categorical acts and achievements through which the conscious subject allows things to appear. Phenomenological description proceeds in light of the radicality that the reduction makes possible. In pursuing it,

> I describe an object not in light of the special features that it has, but in terms of the ways in which it can be experienced. I describe the modes of experience and the modes of presentation, not the contents of what is presented. I can describe noematically, in which case I describe the presentational forms of the object experienced, or I can describe noetically, in which case I describe what I and anyone else must do in order to let the object appear.[14]

But in either case, a phenomenological consideration of things achieves a unique radicality, just because it understands things not with regard to their particular characteristics but in relation to their "presentational forms" or modes of appearing.

Husserl continues to underscore this radicality in the *Crisis,* where, of course, explicit consideration is given to the life world. A properly phenomenological consideration of the life world is definable by way of two contrasts. First, one understands the life world by way of contrast with the world as it is represented in "the cognitions of the objective sciences . . . ,"[15] in formal and quantified hypotheses, laws, and theories. Second, a phenomenological approach to the life world sets itself off from the attitude toward the world that operates in "natural and normal world life . . . ," the attitude at work in "straightforwardly living towards whatever objects are given, thus toward the world horizon. . . . ''[16] The abstention or bracketing of that attitude permits an inquiry directed toward ''asking after the how of the world's pregiveness.''[17] The phenomenological attitude permits the appreciation of the world as a ''world horizon''[18] that contextualizes the appearance of all that appears in it, and an appreciation of all that appears in it—material objects, living beings, humans, works of art, cultural and political institutions, bodies of knowledge—again with respect to what Sokolowski calls their ''presentational forms,'' the manners in which they show up, make appearances in the contextualizing world of life. Here again, but now in a full and concrete way, phenomenological inquiry attains an otherwise unavailable radicality insofar as it can, and does, consider things not with reference to their givenfeatures but in relation to their modes of worldly giveness or manifestation.[19]

Phenomenology, taken in Husserlian terms, is an attempt to rescue appearances from the philosophical attempt to think through and beyond them to a reality which subtends and opposes itself to what appears. At the same time the way into the phenomenological standpoint from the life world gives the subject matter of phenomenology a peculiar density, and introduces a unique set of problems into inquiry. The life world bears within itself the funding and effects of its own historicity. The historicity of the life world, in turn, is born by traditions that are conveyed by discourses which become fixed in texts. Things appear and selves are in the life world through the mediation of traditions. The project of understanding the life world calls forth the task of interpreting the discourses and texts that convey the historical traditions that allow things in the world to appear as they do and selves in the world to be as they are in their historicity. But recognizing the necessity of this hermeneutical task involves ''not transcending phenomenology into thought, but transcending transcendental, Cartesian phenomenology into existential, hermeneutical phenomenology.''[20] Moreover, traditions can become distorted on account of the social structures which come about through them and which house them. Considering tradition calls for critical reflection on such social structures. But ''tradition nourishes critique and critique redeems tradition.[21] Hermeneutical reflection and critique are not just others to each other. Hermeneutics needs critique if authentic and distorted forms of a tradition are to be distinguished and assessed. Critique needs hermeneutics in order to find normative bases for its own procedures and criteria for assessing its proposals and projections.

These remarks are only suggestive as to how phenomenological thinking opens out to hermeneutical and critical tasks. Rigorous analyses of this issue are needed.[22] The point of my comments is not even to begin those analyses, but to indicate that as dialectical phenomenology moves from description to hermeneutics to critique on a procedural level, it does not cease to be phenomenological. On the contrary, the hermeneutical and critical gestures that are made in the process of understanding the life world belong, as Marsh's comment on this indicates, to a hermeneutical and critical phenomenology. Descriptive immediacy gives itself over to the mediations of hermeneutics and critique for the sake of enabling comprehension of things and selves in the life world. But this does not bypass what Ricoeur, in a slightly different context, calls the "immense and unsurpassable discovery of intentionality."[23] Description, hermeneutics, and critique play off and into each other so as to allow, in differentiated ways and together concretely, things and selves in the life world to be considered as they appear and with reference to their modes of appearing. Dialectical phenomenology operates out of and preserves the radical standpoint that phenomenology defines, even if it recognizes radicality in a way that qualifies phenomenological claims to apodicticity. Recognizing that judgments are secured by the evidences that phenomenology attains, dialectical phenomenology admits to claims of apodicticity. Recognizing that evidences are attained within a process of hermeneutical and critical reflections ever in need of extension, testing, and specifications, dialectical phenomenology acknowledges that even judgments for which apodicticity is claimed are in need of subsequent verifications and modifications. Claims to apodicticity are qualified and wedded to fallibilism.[24] The linking of apodicticity with fallibilism does not deny the former. It redefines it in light of the procedures followed for the sake of achieving and maintaining the radical standpoint and ends proper to phenomenology.

Dialectical phenomenology, then, endeavors to be phenomenological through and through. It also endeavors to be dialectical through and through. It draws upon and assumes into itself those resources from phenomenology that allow for radicality in thinking. It draws upon and assumes into itself those resources from dialectical philosophy that allow for concreteness and comprehensiveness in thinking.

I have already mentioned what Marsh says by way of introducing the dialectical dimension of his philosophical program. Reflections on the life of the world call for considerations of its historicity and for surpassing oppositions with mediations. Moreover, as PCM develops, its analyses commonly move through dialectical considerations of abstract oppositions to concrete, descriptive, hermeneutical and critical understandings. I want to suggest that the interrelated aspects of the dialectical dimension of this philosophical program find their principle in a fundamental understanding that belongs to dialectical philosophy and that is achieved with fullest consciousness and clarity with Hegel, namely, the dialectical understanding concerning identity.

Hegel explicitly considers identity as a category in the second chapter of the first section of the second book of the *Science of Logic*. By then, thought has gone through incredible labors so as to arrive at a standpoint that permits express consideration of the category of identity. Subsequently, thought must go through even more extensive labors to fully articulate the content and import of those considerations. The following remarks do not intend to indicate the nature of those labors, but to give some indication of the sense, complexity, and fundamentality of the category of identity for dialectical phenomenology.

Throughout the first major division of the *Science of Logic*, "The Doctrine of Being," categories immediately pass over into other categories and immediately surpass others, so that the reference of logical categories to others is only implicit in them. But that reference begins to appear as the logic of Being culminates. Its explicit appearance marks the passage from the logic of Being to the logic of Essence. Essential categories are, in fact, pairs of categories that mutually refer to each other. Given the logic of essence, the "dialectical process is no longer the mere success of *Übergehen*," but rather "the dual movement of *Reflexion*,"[25] a movement in which categories refer to each other, and return to themselves and determine their senses through these references. This notwithstanding, a category belonging to the logic of essence "can be distinguished as a self-contained category because thought has dissolved the immediacy of simple being, and then has taken this act of dissolution for its content."[26]

These comments set the stage on which Hegel presents a consideration of identity. Because essence, throughout the categories of essence, refers to or reflects itself in its other and thereby straightforwardly comes to self-determination, "Essence is therefore simple identity-with-self.''[27] It is simple, self-contained. It is an identity-with-self, in that its other is not another, but essence's own self-reflection. Nonetheless, it is an identity *with* self, in that essence returns, through its self-reflection of reflection in its "other," to its self-determined sense. The identity that essence is, what identity itself is, presents itself not as isolated, unrelated datum but as relation-to-self, as self-relation.

To conceive of identity as self-relation is to conceive the same in relatively concrete and synthetic terms, rather than in an abstract and analytic way.[28] But self-relation implies that that whose "otherness" the identical surpasses is nonetheless that through which self-recovery is necessarily attained, and is, in this sense, not surpassed. Inasmuch as identity defines itself as self-relation, it defines difference as an essential determination of itself. Difference seems to be subsumed in identity, but on the other hand, identity is attained only through this subsumption. "Difference is therefore itself and identity. Both together constitute difference; it is the whole, and its moment."[29] It is a moment of the self-related whole. But it is also the whole as such, the indispensable and enduring moment of self-relation.

Identity, then, defines difference as an aspect of itself and defines itself in terms of difference. These two sides of itself appear at first just to fall apart, to be merely other from each other, diverse from each other.[30] But because each is determinate only by way of contrast with the other that its determinateness excludes, they are opposed.[31] And because this opposition falls within the self-related whole that identity is, it defines identity in terms of self-opposition, contradiction.[32] But at just this point, inner self-opposition or contradiction reveals itself as the genuine ground of self-recovery. Self-recovery or self-relation achieved through inner differentiation, which at first seems to oppose it, is in fact the only kind of concrete identity that there is. Self-relation occurs only through inner differentiation. Identity defines itself concretely when it allows its other, difference, fully to be itself, to contradict it, and then reconciles this contradiction not by annulling the other but by defining itself in terms of its other, fully realized. Identities come about as differences play off and into each other so as to bring about the very determinateness of self-relation or identity.

Heidegger says that

. . . throughout the history of Western thought, identity appears as unity. But that unity is by no means a stale emptiness of that which, in itself without relation, persists in monotony. However, to get to the point where the relationship of the same with itself—which prevails in that identity which was implicitly present very early—emerges as this mediation in a decisive and characteristic way, and where an abode is found for this radiant emergence of mediation within identity, Western thought required more than two thousand years.[33]

Hegel struggled toward a concrete conception of identity in his early theological and philosophical writings, and expressed that conception in the earliest of his mature works.[34] But it is in the categorical articulation of the *Logic* that the conception attains its fully conscious and normative development. And one can note, again with Heidegger, that "since the era of speculative Idealism, it is no longer possible for thinking to represent the unity of identity as mere sameness, and to disregard the mediation that prevails in unity. When this is done, identity is represented only in an abstract manner."[35]

Dialectical phenomenology acknowledges the normative role of a concrete conception of identity. Its task is the rational and radical recovery of the life world and the self. It endeavors to construe the identities of things as they appear in the life world. Because it operates with a concrete conception of identity, it can construe discrete phenomena in terms of the multifaceted, inner differences which play off each other and are resumed in their self-related identities, and can understand differing phenomena in the life world in terms of the way they interact toward the formation of larger, differentiated unities. In this way understanding is concrete and comprehensive. Moreover, because dialectical phenomenology takes up the conception of identity that finds categorical expression in Hegel, it possesses a warranted basis for its attempts to overcome "either-or" oppositions and move toward "both-and" mediations. And the conception of identity that dialectical phenomenology takes up gives normative direction to its considerations of the life world in terms of its historicity. The life world in its contemporaneity has its identity in virtue of the findings of its past which it bears in itself and in its relations to the future which it reflects in its possibilities. The differences constitutive of historical time are preserved and resumed in the concrete identity of the life world. This identity motivates the thought that considers the life world to achieve an historical rooting.

Dialectical phenomenology, then, draws upon and integrates fundamental possibilities for thinking that belong to phenomenology and dialectical philosophy, to Husserl and Hegel, taking these up as resources for its own developments. It critically retrieves the notions of intentionality and identity so as to propose for itself the aims of radicality, concreteness, and comprehensiveness in thinking. This is no eclectic borrowing from disparate philosophical sources, but a critically disciplined reflection that tries to bring phenomenology and dialectical philosophy together in order to realize fully and properly the possibilities that belong to each.

## II

It will be no surprise, given the previous comments, to note that, according to Marsh, "Dialectical phenomenology emerges as the true friend of difference."[36] Marsh makes this comment specifically with reference to the distinction he draws among "five essential kinds of power: appeal, influence, manipulation, coercive non-violence, . . . and straightforward violence."[37] He contrasts these distinctions with the account of power offered by Foucault, which is claimed to be " 'dedifferentiated' . . . an obliteration of difference contrasting ironically with the postmodernist's proclamation of *différance.*"[38] In fact, dialectical phenomenology befriends difference in a way whose importance exceeds the boundaries of the conversation March carries on with Foucault. It recognizes difference in a series of interrelated ways that lead to some of its more significant achievements.

One can approach a first consideration of the way dialectical phenomenology befriends difference by way of the issue of objectivity. A central tenet of dialectical phenomenology grows out of the distinction among various senses of objectivity that Marsh draws. He distinguishes among understandings of objectivity associated with perception, the universal, thematizing, judgment, alienation, normativity, experiment, and expression.[39] This enables one to identify "the thematization that is proper to philosophy," and to contrast it with "perceptual, scientific, alienating, or experiential objectification."[40] Thematization is a kind of objectifying that moves between the extremes of pure observation and complete belonging.[41] It permeates all other senses of objectivity and is a unique way of objectifying it.[42] It encompasses thinking that "is conceptual because it is universal and expressive, a working-out into language of notions initially vague and incomplete. What the thinker experiences is a movement from an initially indeterminate, vague, incomplete notion to one that is determinate, explicit, and complete."[43] Views that assert the inadequacies of objectifying thinking concerning self, others, or the world misfire because they confuse the sense of objectivity that thematizing realizes with distinct senses of objectivity proper to perception, science, or alienation.

Thematization, it seems, is nothing less than "to let that which shows itself be seen in the very way in which it shows itself."[44] These words from Heidegger seem faithfully to express the intention of thematic objectifying in dialectical phenomenology. But that intention is realized just insofar as reflection in this approach to philosophy acknowledges and befriends difference. It is a procedural and substantive acknowledgement of differences that allows one objectively to thematize the life world as a domain of universal eidetic structures, funded by historical, linguistic, textual traditions, dominated and regulated by a concrete form of life whose contradictions can attack and distort the possibilities that human existence can achieve and that tradition opens. Only a reflection that attends to the life world with reference to differentiated dimensions that belong to it can approach comprehending the life-world, can succeed at philosophical comprehension. Moreover, each of these differentiated dimensions is itself a domain of differences which need to be understood simultaneously as differences and as interrelated in order successfully to be thematized and objectively known. Perception, expression, and reflection, motivation and decision, self and other, need to be understood as interrelated differences. Self and tradition, interpreter and text, need to be understood in terms of the way in which each plays off the other so as to be related to the other and to be itself. Use value and exchange value, social labor and privately owned forces of production need to be understood in terms of the way in which each simultaneously requires and is opposed to the other.

Now at one point Marsh states that "A . . . consequence of my analysis is that a conceptual knowledge of being or the life-world can reveal and enlighten. Conceptual, representational thinking is not, as Heidegger claims, necessarily a thinking that distorts and covers up being."[45] I think that a refinement is possible with regard to this statement, and I hope that the comments that suggest it are not merely a quibble over a word. Representational thinking, as we all know, has come in for a great deal of grief from those whose thinking is inspired by the later Heidegger and by postmodernism. As John Caputo has recently reminded us with reference to the later Heidegger, representational thinking is "thinking which is willing *Vorstellen,* which means the way the subject 'sets' (*stellt*) things forth (*vor*) for itself. . . . Heidegger criticizes not only the *stellen,* the willfulness of setting things out in a way that suits us, but also the *vor,* the setting *forth,* putting these things forward in an order of our own devising, a construction of our own making, made in our own image, made to suit us."[46] Given representational thinking, things are "stood up like objects against a horizonal screen or backdrop so they can stand before us (*Gegenstehen*) . . . in a projective framework of our own devising."[47] Representational thinking, on this construal, lays things out before us in terms of its all-encompassing constructions or assumptions. It flattens and levels multiplicity and difference. It projects, as the above comments state, a horizon against which things stand out, thus claiming knowledge while at the same time blocking the possibility of things showing themselves from themselves.

I would not deny that philosophy, in the course of its history, has succumbed to the inadequacies of representational thinking, as just construed. I believe that the critique of representational thinking is valid and well focused. But I would argue that through historical critiques of reason philosophy has just as often resisted falling into the grasp of representational thinking—sometimes, ironically, while making the very moves that also led it into that grasp. And I would argue that it is the very danger of representational thinking that dialectical phenomenology is designed to—and does successfully—avoid, by befriending difference in the way that it does. When dialectical phenomenology, for example, distinguishes among different modalities of power, and then exhibits the ways in which these modalities differ as eidetic variants and as modes of power embedded in a concrete form of life such as capitalism, it is trying to allow the differences that belong to the phenomenon of power to show themselves, once in universal, descriptive terms, and then again in terms of the way they are critically discovered to occur in a form of life, so that the phenomenon may show itself in its differentiated integrity. To do this is also to acknowledge the ambiguity of power, by recognizing that its different modalities slide over into each other, as each points to the others, bears traces of the others, and is therefore not just simply and neatly itself.

Taking another example, to say and to display evidence for saying that "I constitute my having been constituted by the other"[48] is to indicate that self-relatedness is achieved in an already accomplished transcendence of the self, and that intersubjectivity is intelligible as the relation which integrates these differences by preserving them. A claim such as this tries to allow selfhood, otherness, self-transcendence, and intersubjectivity to show themselves as they are by showing them as differences which distinguish themselves from each other at the very moment at which they allow each other to be. Marsh wants to argue that conceptual thematization differs from other forms of objectification that would improperly comprehend the life world. I want to argue that conceptual thinking, as understood in dialectical phenomenology, should also be distinguished from representational thinking, as Heidegger and Caputo understand it. Because of the way conceptual thematization in dialectical phenomenology considers differences, it does not re-present things in a way required by the dictates of a putatively occluding thought. It rather allows things to manifest themselves as they are in light of differentiated thinking.

Further, a claim in dialectical phenomenology is evidential just insofar as it traces the way in which differences distinguish themselves from each other, insist that they be recognized as differentiated, and also establish identities by way of their self-relatedness to what is other than themselves. Evidential knowing in phenomenology follows from a true friendship for difference. Apodicticity "is based on insight into necessary connections among moments which become articulated in reflective thinking," and this insight, in turn, follows from and preserves an appreciation of those moments as different.[49] In these ways, a dialectical acknowledgement of difference is an integral aspect of the thematizing achievements of phenomenology that lead to objectivity.

There is a second way in which dialectical phenomenology befriends difference, hinted at in the foregoing remarks. Dialectical phenomenology aims at the reflective recovery of the self in its worldly projects, or at the reflection on " 'the world in its human involvement.' "[50] The humanly involved world is, again, a dense domain of universal structures and inherited historical and linguistic traditions, enframed within a concrete form of life. Even when considering a basic and all-pervasive level of experience such as perception, it is necessary to recall that "we contribute a practical interest and linguistic form to our perception,"[51] and that our funded interests and our language are affected by the form of life to which we belong. That is to say, any phenomenological thematization occurs in relation to numerous determinants which have not been thematized. Dialectical phenomenology attempts to uncover and comprehend the presupposed determinants of lived experience. In the by-now classic words of Merleau-Ponty, it "slackens the intentional threads which attach us to the world and brings them to our notice. . . . "[52] At the same time, because it acknowledges historicity and contextuality, this phenomenology reveals the "world as strange and paradoxical," resisting the idea of a "thought which embraces all our thought."[53] It envisions philosophy as an endless reflective process which swings between varying degrees of equally necessary universality and concreteness.

All this is to say that dialectical phenomenology acknowledges and proceeds from a recognition of the difference between reflective knowing and the matter of its concern, its "object," if you will. One must be very careful in using, interrelating, and distinguishing terms here. It is not true to say, using language Hegel suggests, that reflective knowing is an instrument or medium capable only of knowing an object as it affects or is affected by it. Nor is it true to say that thinking proceeds from and is enabled by an abyssal granting that forever escapes its grasp, which thought can acknowledge only as an illumining self-concealing. It is appropriate, on the terms of this phenomenology, to say that the matter of concern to knowing offers itself to knowing and exceeds knowing in that very offering.

Reflective thematization allows universal and concretely historical necessities to occur for it—the necessarily perspectival nature of perception, the necessarily intersubjective nature of selfhood, the necessity of surplus repression in capitalism—while at the same time recognizing that such necessities are lodged in matrices that exceed its conceptual grasp. An identity-in-difference of knowing and its object is defined in a way which respects difference and identity equally. Now, granted, dialectical phenomenology does not hold that that which appears to knowing differs from and defers itself in its many possible appearances, such that claims to apodicticity must be abandoned. This may seem an insufficient way of befriending difference. But what are friends for? Sometimes a friend needs to tell me that I am important, but not more important than someone else. Perhaps philosophy best befriends difference by telling difference that it is as important, but not more important, than the identity of the object with, and in, knowing. This is to remind difference that, on account of it, philosophy is a project of infinite tasks, but not a self-subverting process.

At one point Marsh discusses the relationship of knowledge to this object with reference to the question of being. As already noted, he identifies being with the life world, "the ultimate context of subject and object."[54] He notes that being is not an object as is the thing perceived, known scientifically, dominated, or reified. But as "the implicit context or ground within which things appear,"[55] being is susceptible to objective thematization and conceptual appreciation. This does not argue for "a total comprehension of being. Such a claim would be alienating in the broader sense of that word—an inappropriate objectification."[56] But it is a claim that may reopen the possibility of metaphysics.

I think that one does not approach the question of being in a fully adequate way in identifying being with the life-world. Being is both distinct from beings and is the being of that which is. It is that which enables beings to appear in and through the differences that belong to their appearing. It is toward that which thinking transcends in its most radical efforts at comprehension. One approaches the question of being by considering that which is both distinct from beings and permits them to appear in the life-world. The being of things, one might suggest, has to do with the way beings distinguish themselves from other beings and present themselves in the manifold and different appearances they make in the life-world, a presence that is necessarily correlated with and therefore does not annul absence. In these terms the question of being is not best approached by identifying being with the life-world. But the suggestion that being is susceptible to a specific objectifying thematization which allows being to enter into and exceed conceptual knowing, the suggestion concerning the intelligibility of being that reopens metaphysics as a possibility, is an intriguing and important consequence of dialectical phenomenology.

Dialectical phenomenology befriends difference in still a third way. As it moves from description to retrieval to critique, this reflective and transcendental praxis points beyond itself to its other, to material praxis, to political and social action. Experience occurs and traditions are received within a form of life, a concrete totality of internal political, cultural, social, and economic relations.[57] Reflection is responsible to its own demands when it moves from the description of the eidetic intelligibilities and the recovery of the intelligibility of traditions to the consideration of the rationality of the form of life that situates us, conditions our experience, and assigns roles and possibilities to the traditions we receive. This consideration becomes critical as one discovers the form of life currently dominating much of the globe, capitalism, to be a domain of contradictions, of irrationality. In economic terms, the personal independence of working people is matched by objective dependence on forces of production, including their own labor power, over which they exercise little meaningful control. In social terms, capitalism establishes a community of increasingly atomized individuals. In cultural terms, capitalism leads to the commodification and privatization of aesthetic, moral, and religious values, to the positivistic and scientistic definitions of knowledge. In political terms, capitalism burdens the state with the necessities of giving free play to privately owned forces of production and of restricting that free play in an effort to combat economic and other damages.

These remarks only suggest the detailed critical analyses which dialectical phenomenology, obviously drawing on the resources of Marxism, offer concerning capitalistic society. It is not my intention to develop those critical analyses. The issue of importance here is that dialectical phenomenology, through the critical analyses that it performs in a reflective, theoretical way, claims to show that theoretical reflection is both necessary and insufficient. It is necessary because it is the indispensable way to self-clarification. It is insufficient because the clarification it achieves leads to the identification of contradictions in the currently dominant form of life which are surpassed not through reflection alone but through material praxis, action undertaken for the sake of economic, social, cultural, and political change.

I think Marsh would agree with Habermas that critical theory does not immediately and of itself dictate the necessities of action.[58] This is the case for at least two reasons. First, critical theory must allow its claims to be confronted by opposing analyses of capitalist society. Its claims remain credible only insofar as it succeeds in defending them against such counter claims. It recommends action only through the mediation of such successes. Second, judgments concerning actions must define ends to be achieved and means of achievement not only with reference to the conceptuality of critical analysis, but also with reference to the particular circumstances that locate the agent. But critical theory does illumine action, does illumine the thinking and judging that belong to material praxis. It does this just by being theory, by uncovering structures, relations, and effects that operate otherwise unconsciously in capitalism as a form of life. As dialectical phenomenology progresses to the moment of critical theory, it relates to and surpasses itself in its other, material praxis, while respecting the integrity of the other. Material praxis, from its side, is able to recognize its otherness from and dependence on the clarifications and conceptually self-correcting understandings that critical theory provides.

## III

I have suggested three ways in which dialectical phenomenology acknowledges and respects, or befriends, difference. It thematizes phenomena in terms of the differences that play off each other to form identities. This enables phenomena to show themselves, and it enables knowing to be objective and evidential, insofar as it traces the necessities with which things have identities because of the differences that belong to them and because of the way they distinguish themselves from other things. Dialectical phenomenology also befriends difference by understanding as it does the relation of thinking to the object and to being. This is an important aspect to the critical dimension of critical modernism. The modern notion of reason is defensible insofar as methodic, rational activities allow the subject to appear in knowing and to be known truly. The modern notion of reason is corrected and surpassed in that the object is identified as appearing in and simultaneously exceeding rational knowing, thereby making claims to apodicticity fallibilistic rather than pure, and reason a process that leads to evidential comprehension but not totalization. Finally, reflection in a dialectical phenomenology surpasses itself in material praxis while showing, in its way, the need that praxis has for reflective theory.

These ways of considering difference, I have claimed, find their ground in an appropriation of the conception of identity to which Hegel gives normative, categorical articulation. But the efforts at concrete and comprehensive understanding that are guided by the Hegelian notion of identity are always joined with the project of radical understanding that Husserl defines. This is the case with regard to attempts at understanding the world that situates the self and the self as such.

Marsh finds in the practice of phenomenology, as Husserl discusses it, the process of seeking adequate descriptions of experience that are consistently framed in evidential judgments in a process chosen with deliberate consideration, a conception of the self that yields "four transcendental precepts . . . , 'Be attentive,' . . . 'Be intelligent,' . . . 'Be reasonable,' . . . 'Be responsible.' "[59] The self is one who experiences, understands, judges, and chooses in the world. Faithfulness to the transcendental precepts, whose discussion clearly betrays the influence of Lonergan on Marsh's thinking, defines the possibility of authentic selfhood. Because the self is embodied, historical, and social, its possibilities are limited. Because the self is reflective and free, its possibilities transcend those realized in any current state of affairs. Authenticity is realized in those attentive and intelligent judgments and choices made in the tension between limitation and transcendence.

I have mentioned the way in which dialectical phenomenology is a form of transcendental philosophy, and referred to the claim that it is on its own terms a kind of praxis. It is now possible and appropriate to discuss that claim somewhat more fully, albeit briefly. Dialectical phenomenology leads to the view that, "insofar as the choice of myself as perceiving, reflecting and choosing subject is essential to transcendental method, transcendental method is a kind of praxis, the most fundamental kind of self-recovery that grounds and founds all other forms of praxis."[60] Praxis is undertaken by the self in the world for the sake of recovering the possibilities for unity and freedom proper to it. The practice of transcendental philosophy discloses the self as, and calls upon the self to choose itself as, one who authentically experiences, understands, judges, and chooses in the world. Attentive experience, intelligent understanding, reasonable judgment, and responsible choice are a principle ingredient in all forms of praxis. But it is also a form of praxis on its own terms, undertaken for its own sake. It is a fundamental retrieval of the self with regard to the possibilities constitutive of it and the authenticity open to it. And it can be this, in light of dialectical phenomenology, insofar as rational thinking possesses the capacity for a conceptual and evidential comprehension of what is basically constitutive of and open to selfhood. This comprehension does not put an end to efforts at self-understanding. It defines the fundamental standpoint from which all such efforts proceed and gives them orientation. Nor does this comprehension replace ambiguity with abstract clarity, fallibilism with abstract apodicticity, or differentiated understanding with abstract conceptual totalities. It does claim to illumine fields of experience which nonetheless continue to exhibit ambiguities, to secure evident judgments which continue to stand in need of future verifications, and to bring about comprehensive understandings whose concreteness acknowledges the inescapability of difference. It does claim for conceptual, evidential reason the ability to achieve radical and comprehensive understandings concerning the world and the self, understandings whose warrants can continue to be shown in a process that is public and philosophical. Finally, then, the radical and differentiated reflective activities that dialectical phenomenology involves, and the achievements to which they lead, enable it to occur as the fundamental transcendental praxis it claims to be, and thus an effort at that ''living more clearly'' with which Augustine identifies understanding. The methodic exercise of evidential reason leads to a conceptual recovery of the life-world and of the self who is involved in the life-world. It leads to comprehension of the necessities that situate and sustain us, the possibilities open to us, the challenges and demands that face us. These achievements help to indicate that the proper response to inadequate or impoverished notions of reason is a rationality more comprehensive and adequate to reason's tasks. They also suggest that the proper attitude to attacks on rationality involves an attempt to determine the degree to which those attacks are predicated on inadequate definitions that reason has offered of itself. This response and this attitude occur of necessity not once but repeatedly in the history of philosophy. They assume their best forms when they allow demonstrative rigor to lead to understanding as Augustine conceived it.

NOTES

1. St. Augustine, *On Free Choice of the Will,* trans. Anna Benjamin and L. H. Hackstaff (Indianapolis: Bobbs-Merrill, 1964), pp. 15, 17.

2. PCM, p. 38.

3. *Ibid.*

4. *Ibid.*

5. *Ibid.*, p. 39.

6. *Ibid.*, p. 87.

7. *Ibid.*, p. 111.

8. See *ibid.*, pp. 21–22.

9. See *ibid.*, p. 106.

10. *Ibid.*, p. 255.

11. See Robert Sokolowski, *The Foundation of Husserl's Concept of Constitution* (The Hague: Martinus Nijhoff, 1964), pp. 123–33. Sokolowski calls these arguments the "Cartesian way" and the "ontological way" to the reduction.

12. Edmund Husserl, *Ideas pertaining to a Pure Phenomenology and to Phenomenological Philosophy: First Book,* trans. F. Kersten (The Hague: Martinus Nijhoff, 1983), p. 102.

13. *Ibid.,* p. 112.

14. Robert Sokolowski, "The Theory of Phenomenological Description," *Man and World,* 16 (1983), p. 223.

15. Edmund Husserl, *The Crisis of European Sciences and Transcendental Phenomenology,* trans. and intro. David Carr (Evanston: Northwestern University Press, 1970), p. 135.

16. *Ibid.,* pp. 146, 144.

17. *Ibid.,* p. 154.

18. *Ibid.,* p. 143.

19. See *ibid.,* p. 189.

20. PCM, p. 165.

21. *Ibid.*

22. Marsh develops this issue, *ibid.,* pp. 160–82. Valuable contributions to a discussion of the relation of critique to hermeneutics and of hermeneutics to phenomenology appear in two essays by Ricoeur, "Hermeneutics and the Critique of Ideology," and "Phenomenology and Hermeneutics." See Paul Ricoeur, *Hermeneutics and the Human Sciences,* edited and trans. John B. Thompson (Cambridge: Cambridge University Press, 1981), pp. 63–128.

23. Ricoeur, *Hermeneutics and the Human Sciences,* p. 105.

24. See PCM, pp. 254, 256.

25. Malcolm Clark, *Logic and System* (The Hague: Martinus Nijhoff, 1971), pp. 90–91.

26. John Burbidge, *On Hegel's Logic: Fragments of a Commentary* (Atlantic Highlands: Humanities Press, 1982), p. 64.

27. *Hegel's Science of Logic,* trans. A. V. Miller (London and New York: Geo. Allen and Unwin, Ltd., and Humanities Press, 1969), p. 411.

28. *Ibid.,* pp. 411, 416.

29. *Ibid.,* p. 416.

30. *Ibid.,* pp. 418–24.

31. *Ibid.,* pp. 424–27.

32. *Ibid.,* p. 431.

33. Martin Heidegger, "The Principle of Identity," in *Identity and Difference,* trans. Joan Stambaugh (New York: Harper & Row, 1969), p. 25.

34. See *Hegel's Phenomenology of Spirit,* trans. A. V. Miller (Oxford: Clarendon Press, 1977), p. 100.

35. Heidegger, *loc. cit.* I am aware that I am abstracting these comments of Heidegger from the context in which he sets them, and therefore from the role they play in the development of his own thoughts.

36. PCM, p. 156.

37. *Ibid.*

38. *Ibid.*

39. *Ibid.*, pp. 81–85.

40. *Ibid.*, p. 87.

41. *Ibid.*, p. 83.

42. *Ibid.*, p. 86.

43. *Ibid.*, p. 87.

44. Heidegger, *Being and Time*, p. 58.

45. PCM, p. 87.

46. RH, p. 99.

47. *Ibid.*, p. 101.

48. PCM, p. 131.

49. Robert Sokolowski, *Husserlian Meditations* (Evanston: Northwestern University Press, 1974), p. 15. Sokolowski is using "moments" in its technical, Husserlian sense, as am I.

50. *Ibid.*, p. 174. Sokolowski is citing Francis Slade, "Socrates: The Nature of Philosophical Inquiry," unpublished note.

51. Graeme Nicholson, *Seeing and Reading* (Atlantic Highlands, N.J.: Humanities Press, 1983), p. 2.

52. M. Merleau-Ponty, *Phenomenology of Perception*, trans. Colin Smith (London: Routledge and Kegan Paul, 1962), p. xii.

53. *Ibid.*, pp. xii, xiv.

54. PCM, p. 87.

55. *Ibid.*

56. *Ibid.*, pp. 87–88.

57. *Ibid.*, p. 216.

58. Jürgen Habermas, *Theory and Practice*, trans. John Viertel (Boston: Beacon Press, 1973), pp. 19–21.

59. PCM, p. 112.

60. *Ibid.*

# Ambiguity, Language, and Communicative Praxis: A Critical Modernist Articulation

## James L. Marsh

EVEN THOUGH IT IS AN HONOR, I wish politely to reject Jack Caputo's description of me as a "guardian of truth." The truth does not need guardians or police; indeed, that conception of truth is one that *Post-Cartesian Meditations* spends a good deal of time arguing against. To talk in this way is to assume a Cartesian, monological sense of truth that the intersubjective truth argued for in PCM invalidates. The truth can use servants; that is the most I would claim for myself: one who in the process of a communicative dialogue may have a few things to say that illumine our human situation. But whether the truth has guardians or servants, it has a way of "willing out," even about claims such as Jack Caputo's to be "in the truth," using the language of Heidegger I, when Caputo claims to have transcended even Heidegger II. We do not need guardians to determine the validity of claims like that, only to keep our wits about us in the course of philosophical dialogue and in that sense to serve the truth.[1]

I wish to thank Bob Johann and the Fordham University Philosophy Department for hosting this event, the panelists, all of you, for coming, and especially Brian Leftow for his hard work on the practical details of arranging the Symposium. It is a form of serendipity. Along the trajectory of what we might call the Fordham-Villanova, New York-Philadelphia axis, with a detour to George Mason University, we have an encounter between representatives of the two main wings of contemporary continental philosophy: critical modernism and postmodernism, dialectical phenomenology and radical hermeneutics.

Jack Caputo explores continental philosophy along a line extending from Kierkegaard and Husserl through Gadamer and Heidegger to Nietzsche and Derrida. I explore a strand of the tradition that begins with Descartes and Husserl, moves through Merleau-Ponty and Ricoeur, and concludes with Marx and Habermas. We have here two different readings of the modern philosophical tradition, interpretation, rationality, critique, selfhood, politics.

With all of the differences between us there is much common ground that merits discussion as well. Both Jack and I are engaged in a radical leftist project of critique and overcoming the wasteland of contemporary industrial society. Both of us are committed to mediation and interpretation in theory, the avoidance of any naïve immediacy, an account of the political uses and abuses of reason, a critique of sexist, racist, and classist forms of marginalization and exploitation, and a God and Christ who is identified with the poor and oppressed—a philosophical version of the preferential option for the poor. Caputo's is an anarchist, postmodernist, post-Marxist Christian leftism; mine is a communitarian, critical modernist, Christian Marxism leftism. To those of you in the audience suspicious of radical leftism in any of its guises and disguises, this may seem like picking your poison. You may wish, in the discussion, to show us the error of our ways.

Jack and I have a personal and intellectual relationship going back many years, in which it has been my privilege to be challenged, to learn, and to grow through many intense, spirited discussions and exchanges with him. The critical modernist/postmodernist debate between us has already gone through many stages in the form of conversations, letters, conferences, my reviews of his three books, and his review in IPQ of my book. I am already on record about how good I think his recent book is: challenging, courageous, insightful, well-written, provocative. Caputo is a *thinker* in the best sense of that word, inviting us—poking and prodding us—to move out of our pre-modern or modern dogmatic slumbers.[2]

However, there are differences. And to catch some of you up who may not be in on the latest form of this debate, what I want to do is to indicate briefly the broad outline of the debate between Jack and myself, to indicate the contribution my book can make, and maybe to add a few new wrinkles.

### CRITICAL MODERNISM *v*. POSTMODERNISM:
### THE STATE OF THE QUESTION

As I see it, the main issue between us, moving from abstract to concrete, are four: self-referential consistency, descriptive adequacy to experience, hermeneutical justice to the western, modern philosophical and political tradition, and political efficacy. Which approach, critical modernist or postmodernist, is most adequate on these issues? Which approach most represents a move forward in philosophy and social theory?

Critical modernism, I argue, answers these questions better than postmodernism, even a version of it as brilliant as Jack's. Critical modernism, then, represents a third stage, transcending but retaining valid aspects from both triumphalistic modernism and a skeptical postmodernism that seems nihilistic in its implications. Critical modernism retains the modernistic commitment to rationality, critique, and evidence, but listens to and learns from its postmodern other about mediation, the fallibility of reason, the nefarious political uses to which reason is often put, and the pathology of the modern. Critical modernism rejects triumphalistic modernist tendencies toward a totally apodictic truth and is critical of postmodernism on the four issues already mentioned.[3]

The question concerning self-referentiality is this: can one criticize and transcend western rationality, as the postmodernist wishes to do, while using the resources of that rationality, using argument to transcend argument as such? In such attempts, is not one inevitably forced onto the horns of what we might call the performative hook? Either I arbitrarily state, without argument, that one should transcend metaphysics or I use argument. In the former case, I am guilty of arbitrariness, and what is arbitrarily asserted can be rationally questioned or denied. In the latter case, I am guilty of self-referential inconsistency, a contradiction between performance and content. The performance is rational, metaphysical; the content is anti-rational in the traditional sense of that word, anti-metaphysical. Dialectical phenomenology, because it is committed to a western evidential rationality, does not have such performative problems. It may have others, but it doesn't have these. What I am appealing to, then, is a performative, communicative, cognitive praxis, which has been developed by Lonergan and Habermas and which I incorporate and develop in my book. If the postmodernist agrees with me, that is fine. If she disagrees with me, then she has to employ transcendental method: experience, understanding, judgment, and decision. She hears the words being said, she understands the terms and propositions of the argument, she judges the truth or falsity of the argument, and she chooses to reject modernism and to pursue postmodernism. Self-referential consistency then, is not merely an issue that is formal, logic-chopping, trivial, but rather bears upon the *authenticity* and *integrity* of the postmodernist's praxis of philosophizing. Is she at odds with or in conformity with the fundamental transcendental structure of experience, understanding, judging, and choosing?

As spontaneously operative, such a transcendental method gives rise to four transcendental precepts corresponding to the four levels: "be attentive," "be intelligent," "be reasonable," and "be responsible." These precepts measure the authenticity of my own cognitive praxis of philosophizing. If I wish to say with Caputo, for example, that the only truth is that there is no truth or that truth is merely a useful fiction, I mean and imply that it is true that there is no truth and that it is the non-fictional case that truth is only a useful fiction. Again, an implied reference to truth emerges when I distinguish between "really useful" and "apparently useful," as the postmodernists must.

If we stress in a Habermasian manner the communicative as opposed to the cognitive aspects of philosophical praxis, then a similar point arises. The four validity claims—clarity, truth, sincerity, and appropriateness— are spontaneously operative and presupposed in any dialogue between people. Imagine the way the conversation between Caputo and me would come to a screeching halt if it became apparent that one of us was unclear, mendacious, insincere, or assuming authority illegitimately or dogmatically. In spite of his explicit claims, the postmodernist is involved in such communicative praxis. Derrida, when he complains about being misunderstood by Habermas, is engaged in such praxis. Derrida is on the horns of a dilemma: either Habermas is right or he is not. If Habermas is correct, he is *truly* correct. If Habermas is wrong, then he is *truly* wrong. If Habermas has misunderstood Derrida, then he has not gotten at what is truly presented in the Derridean text. In either case, to make his point and to carry on his argument, Derrida presupposes the validity claims of a communicative praxis.

Habermas, according to Derrida, is guilty of bad will, of violating the "ethics of discussion," the possibility of which Derrida questions coming metaphysics, however, the performative problem reappears, using argument to overcome argument, using metaphysics to overcome metaphysics.

Now within the Derridean text, there are several strategies of evasion available: aesthetic reductionism, a purely descriptive approach, and an ambiguous outside and inside stance, which I will discuss later and which we heard about tonight. A recent strategy used by Jack Caputo at a conference last December is that of pure description. One can avoid the performative hook by not taking a position, merely describing what is going on in the text. What is deficient in the strategy, I think, is, first, that it is textually inconsistent. Derrida and Jack certainly do, in other parts of their text, take positions on the evils of logocentrism, for instance, and affirming various infrastructures such as *différance,* and you also heard Jack affirming the "quasi-transcendental" tonight. The stance of pure description is performatively inconsistent in that I am presenting my description as a true description of what is going on in the text: sincere, clear, appropriate. The attempt to deny that I am taking a position is itself a position.[6]

On a more concrete, descriptive level, we can, from the perspective of my book, ask the following questions: Is rationality as we experience it simply or primarily logocentric, repressive, coercive, covering up Being, excluding difference, or are there various kinds of rationality, some of which or most of which are liberating and disclosive? For example, I distinguish in my book between coercion and an appeal that is free, noncoercive, open to the further question, self-critical, exemplified in a Socratic discussion or a conversation between friends. I distinguish among eight kinds of objectification, only one of which is alienating and repressive. Whistling at a woman as she walks down the street or insulting someone is qualitatively, essentially different from objectifying an idea in a work of art, seeing a visible object, or philosophical thematizing; the latter are liberating, disclosive forms of objectification. There are different kinds of rationality, each with its own appropriate criteria and methodology, perception, science, philosophy, art, ethical-political activity.[7]

The question, then, is this: Is postmodernism guilty of what we might call a loose, antiphilosophical philosophizing from on high, similar to and yet different from Descartes, Hume, and Kant, whom Husserl accuses of philosophizing from on high, not grounding in a prior description of experience conceptions about certainty, mind-body

or denies elsewhere. Understood in our terms, "good will" would s
ply mean observance of the transcendental precepts and valid
claims.[4] How can Derrida be legitimately angry at Habermas if g
will, as Derrida suggests, is equal to a nefarious metaphysics of s
jective will, will to power? Performative inconsistency and textual
consistency join hands here.

Now to state this case against postmodernism is only the beginnir
As we have seen tonight, postmodernism has various sophisticat
ways of dealing with this objection, what I call strategies of evasion f
getting off the performative hook. And this itself has a history to it, t
latest version of which you have seen tonight, I think, from the tv
people on my left.

Late Heidegger's dominant strategy, to which Jack was committed
his first two books, is what we might call prophetic esotericism. He
"Caputo I" says that the Heideggerian thinker is beyond metaphysic
in touch with and listening to Being, not subject to the requirements of
logic and metaphysics. He is beyond consistency requirements, th
hobgoblin of little, metaphysical minds. The problem, however, for th
Heideggerian thinker who wishes to convince us is the following: hov
does he persuade us on this side of the ontological divided line, mired
in the ontic and the metaphysical, to move into the realm of *Denken*
Here the dilemma reappears: either one asserts poetically and prophetically or he argues. If he merely asserts, then he is arbitrary. If he
argues, then he is self-referentially inconsistent. He is similar to Wittgenstein at the end of *Tractatus,* asserting that metaphysical propositions are nonsense and yet claiming that they are a necessary ladder to
get where he wants to go. This is the paradox of the broken ladder, necessary to bring me somewhere but unable to do so.[5]

Accordingly, there are two kinds of Heideggerians, those who are
prophetic at the price of arbitrariness and those who are argumentative
at the price of self-contradiction. Now Caputo, to his credit, was, dur-
ing his Heideggerian phase, an argumentative Heideggerian. He always got down into the ontic mire and argued with us. I respect that
about him. Richardson, I think, was more esoteric. So we have those
contrasts in the Fordham experience. Caputo in his recent book is even
more straightforwardly rational and argumentative and renounces
Heideggerian prophecy and authority. "Caputo II," we might say,
goes from being an argumentative Heideggerian to being an argumentative Derridean. Since Derrida and Caputo are still committed to over-

dualism, and atomistic conception of perception? To pick up a theme of De Nys's, is dialectical phenomenology or radical hermeneutics the truer friend of difference?[8]

On a more concrete hermeneutic level, we can ask the following question: Is the most comprehensive nuanced view of the western, modern philosophical and political tradition one that transcends it *rejectionistically* as a progressive darkening growth in domination and obfuscation, or one that sees it *dialectically* as a contradictory unity of light and darkness, truth and error, liberation and domination? Is the tradition to be transcended and rejected or to be recovered and redeemed dialectically? Is there not a rhetorical and conceptual negation of the modernist other, a refusal to be open, a refusal to listen, that belies postmodernism's own proclamation of tolerance, respect, and openness—in Caputo's words, "fair play"? Here the contrast between Heidegger's and Derrida's postmodern discourse, which puts all of western rationality under the rubric of calculation and logocentrism, and Husserl's dialectical critique in the *Crisis,* criticizing but ultimately fulfilling the modern philosophical project, is salient. Is there not, in such postmodern discourse, an ironic suppression of difference that belies its own proclamation of difference? Does not dialectical phenomenology here too emerge as the true friend of difference?[9]

We can note in postmodernism—and here's a new wrinkle on the self-referential argument as I've thought about it in relation to communicative, cognitive praxis—a hermeneutical, self-referential problem not present in critical modernist discourse: the problem is one of attempting to transcend the tradition of western rationality while using the resources of that tradition. Caputo and Derrida attempt to escape this hermeneutical, performative hook by resorting to what might be described as an ambiguous "inside/outside" stance. That's the latest strategy of evasion. They cannot be outside the tradition simply because they use the resources of that tradition. Therefore they are both inside and outside that tradition. Here again there is confusion and ambiguity between a dialectical and a rejectionistic version of being inside and outside. The dialectical, critical modernist version, because it uses the resources of the tradition to criticize it and fulfill it, is self-referentially consistent. A postmodernist, rejectionistic version is not. How can one consistently use concepts and arguments and insights from an essentially bankrupt tradition? Consequently, postmodernism's owning up to being inside and outside only intensifies the contradiction; it does not remove it.[10]

The dilemma is this: either I become so much a part of tradition that I approximate critical modernism (and that's what Jack sounds like at times tonight, a kind of "moderate Caputo-Derrida"), or I remain inside and outside in a contradictory way. Either I criticize as a whole a bankrupt tradition with a part of that tradition that is equally bankrupt, or the part that is used is not bankrupt and the tradition as a whole is not logocentric. I move into a dialectical rather than a rejectionistic critique of tradition. It is no answer to this dilemma, therefore—rather, a confirmation of it—to say that Derrida is committed to rationality within the tradition. I have never denied that point. Such a response misses my point that Derrida is rational and irrational in a contradictory way. The performance is rational; the explicit content is often postrational, postmodernist. Postmodernist rationality is a rationality at odds with itself, as the dialectic of performative praxis suggests.

On the most concrete, political level, the conflict between critical modernism and postmodernism is this: which version offers the best chance of transcending alienating social structures in late capitalism and state socialism? The argument with postmodernism here is that the picture it presents is so bleak on the first three levels—self-referential, descriptive, and hermeneutical; and western rationality and western institutions are so bankrupt, that there are no positive leverage points of transcendence, no criteria to indicate whether or why we should move forward, no groups identified whose position in the social structure presents a possibility or probability of transcendence, no identifiable crisis points within the system. The difficulty with postmodernism here is similar to that of the early and middle Frankfurt School thinkers such as Marcuse and Adorno. The affirmation of one-dimensionality seems to lead to a stance of pessimism and quietism.

Critical modernism, I argue, because it is less negative on the first three levels, can supply critical leverage points of transcendence, such as the resources of critical rationality or institutionalized democracy in the West; criteria for critique such as authentic subjectivity, the distinction between coercion and appeal, and the ideal speech situation, plausible agents for social change such as labor, women, blacks, environmental groups, anti-war activists, and anti-nuclear activists (here I am just summarizing points argued for in the book); and new points of crisis such as motivation crisis and legitimation crisis within the system. In contrast to an apparent political impotence in postmodernism, critical modernism claims a possible political efficaciousness. Critical modernism can offer a positive, constructive ethics and politics; postmodernism cannot.[11]

On the political as well as the hermeneutical level, one relevant contrast is between postmodernist deconstruction and critical modernist suspicion. I agree with Caputo and Derrida that the tradition has to be criticized for possible forms of class and group domination and marginalization, but would insist, as well, on a receptive, Gadamerian openness to tradition and a descriptive eidetic account of experience. Suspicion, I would argue, more adequately links positive to negative, description to interpretation, interpretation to critique. Dialectical phenomenology emerges as a unity of description, interpretation, and critique.[12]

Here the most controversial, but perhaps also the most interesting move I make is the use of a phenomenologically transformed and chastened use of Marxism and critical theory. The argument here has several stages: the description in chapter I of individualism, reification, and scientism as alienation, the argument in chapter VI for suspicion as a legitimate, necessary movement of phenomenology, the phenomenological critique in chapter VIII of capitalism as essentially contradicting the imperatives of democratic dialogue, the interpretation in chapter IX of individualism, reification, and scientism as forms in the West of obfuscating, mystifying capitalist ideology. Ideology critique emerges as a legitimate and necessary form of phenomenology itself. A merely descriptive or hermeneutically receptive phenomenology, a safe, bourgeois phenomenology, is a truncated, inconsistent, incomplete phenomenology.

My use of Marxism and critical theory meets the postmodern critique of modernity in several ways. First, critical theory takes seriously the pathology of the modern in a way that does justice to the postmodern critique. Here, I think critical modernism has something to learn from postmodernism. Such pathology cannot simply be washed or wished away in the waters of a bland reformism. Second, such critique saves modernist rationality by showing how the pathology of the modern is a betrayal of such rationality. Science is not wrong, but the exploitative capitalist use of science is. Third, rather than locating the cause of such pathology on the level of subjective spirit, reason, or on the level of absolute spirit, Being, critical theory locates it on the level of objective spirit, class or group domination. A Marxist account thus overcomes a mystifying element in the postmodernist critique, valid as that is up to a certain point. Fourth, Marxism and critical theory constitute the final step in giving a dialectical rather than a rejectionistic account of modernity and politics. Marx uses and endorses as valid such bourgeois values as freedom and equality to show the way those values are violated in the sphere of production. Critical theory is thus more able to supply criteria of critique than is postmodernism. Capitalism is hoisted on its own petard.[13]

We could say, then, that in one respect dialectical phenomenology is more conservative than radical hermeneutics and in another respect more radical. More conservative in that I hearken back to the very beginnings of the western philosophical tradition, all the way back to Plato, and claim to be enhancing, fulfilling, and redeeming that tradition. More radical in that the ethical-political critique is more pointed and determinate—capitalism is defined more explicitly and critiqued more fully. If full philosophical enlightenment means transcending the Cave theoretically and practically, and capitalism in the West is the Cave, systematically produced and reproduced illusion, domination, and injustice, then full enlightenment means transcending capitalism theoretically and practically. Dialectical phenomenology points beyond capitalism as a way of life. Capitalist reification is incompatible with the demands of authentic subjectivity, capitalist individualism with the social individual affirmed in phenomenology, capitalist scientism with the full range of rationality.

The issue between Jack and me then is the following: What counts as a forward move in philosophy and social theory? If performative consistency, descriptive adequacy to experience, hermeneutical adequacy to the tradition, and political efficacy are the criteria, then it may be that dialectical phenomenology is the better way to go. One might say that these are not the only criteria; maybe there are other criteria, maybe there are no criteria. But either the postmodernist simply makes these claims in an arbitrary manner, or he argues for them in a speech situation that presumes the legitimacy of rational, evidential communicative praxis. If he enters into conversation and argument, as Jack, to his credit, is wont to do, then he is presuming necessarily the very modernistic rationality he wishes to overcome and deny.

One major consequence of our disagreement of these four points is our differing conception of the transcendental, that is, universal, a priori structures of experience. Jack and postmodernism, I think, tend to conflate the Cartesian, early Husserlian version of the transcendental with the transcendental as such. I, on the other hand, argue for an existential phenomenological—as opposed to transcendental phenomenological—rehabilitation of the transcendental: fallibilistic, rooted in the body, tradition, and history, qualifying claims to clarity, having no pretensions to a totally presuppositionless account. The difference between Jack and myself on the transcendental constitutes a fifth area of disagreement.

A second major consequence of my disagreement with Jack on the above issues, which consequence arises as a sixth major area of disagreement, is our differing conceptions of the self. Both of us reject the naïve, immediate Cartesian ego. Jack is typically postmodernist in his willingness to minimize or deny the reality and value of the self. I, on the other hand, argue for a de-centered self, rooted in the body, the social life world, tradition, history, the psychological and sociological unconscious. Postmodernism equates the Cartesian ego with ego or self as such; I deny the legitimacy of such an equation.

Here again there are implications resident in communicative, cognitive praxis. If I must affirm the transcendental precepts and validity claims, then I must affirm a temporally and structurally unified self as the source, origin, and carrier of norms. If I try to deny, as postmodernists are wont to do, such a transcendental structure and criteria, then the ground is laid for denial of self. Selfhood becomes an issue, however, when they complain about being misunderstood—Derrida by Habermas, Caputo by Marsh. No death of the author here—"I am misunderstood." There is something approaching a Kierkegaardian dialectic of the comical here—questioning of or rejection of the self contradicted by a performance of angry or assertive self-expression. Kierkegaard's questioning of a Hegelian indifference to ethical decisiveness is now supplanted by a questioning of a postmodern indifference (not *différance*) or aestheticism. Postmodern irony gives way to critical modernist irony, a dialectic of the comical.[14]

## COMMENT ON DE NYS

Now I wish to comment on Marty's clear, finely wrought piece. In responding to his criticisms and suggestions, as well as to Jack's and Mark's, I am reminded of Ricoeur's comment at last fall's SPEP Conference that his inclination upon hearing his critics is to agree with them. Nonetheless, let us see what can be said.

I am inclined to resist Marty's suggested emendation that I dissociate
what I am doing from representational thinking. That move may concede too much to Heidegger's negative assessment of such thinking,
his tendency to equate representational thinking with alienating objectification and thus to ignore differences between and among kinds of
representational thinking, some of which are legitimate. Heidegger's
account here is an example of what I call an ironic suppression of difference in postmodernism, which is both bad phenomenology and bad
hermeneutics.[15]

Second, Marty's comments about the dangers of conflating "being"
and "life-world" are well taken, but I am here again politely going to
resist his suggestion. What I had in mind, first, in making the distinction was something like Lonergan's distinction between proportionate
and transcendent being. Second, to the extent that Marty's formulation
is Heideggerian, and more specifically late Heideggerian, there is the
difficulty in verifying it. This difficulty is rooted in what I perceive to
be the inadequacies of postmodernist methodology as opposed to critical modernist methodology. Can the distinction between being and
life-world be verified in a vigorous, descriptive, phenomenological
fashion? If not, should the distinction be made at all?

At a certain metaphysical, explanatory level, of course, I make the
distinction between Being and life-world. To offer a promissory note
for future work, I indicate these steps in developing the initial perceptual sense of Being as the life-world, the reflective intention of Being
as the object of the pure desire to know, existence within a thing as
distinct from essence, Being as processive and known as such through
genetic method, God as an unrestricted act of understanding and love,
God as processive, Christ as liberator. The most appropriate conception
of God and Christ in crowning and completing a phenomenology of
self and a critical theory of society is a God and Christ that are historical, processive, involved with and identified with the oppressed.[16]

Marty has indicated the way in which I do not affirm dissemination
of meaning to the extent of denying a legitimate presence and weak
apodicticity. What needs to be stressed, I think, in the context of tonight's dialogue is the extent to which dissemination of meaning is possible within the purview of dialectical phenomenology. My emphasis
on ambiguity, on the contextual and hermeneutical context of meaning,
on the differential play of meaning (nothing means simply itself), on
the way in which dialectical phenomenology points toward a future

theoretical praxis all are examples of legitimate disseminative play. Here the relevant contrast and comparison is between the "writing" of radical hermeneutics and "discourse" of dialectical phenomenology. The concepts are similar in that both are committed to mediation. They are different in that "discourse," as I use it, is linked to presence, weak apodicticity, limited transcendental structures, and legitimate openness to tradition.

The similarity and difference between writing and discourse reappears in other pairs of concepts such as *différance* and difference, deconstruction and suspicion, dissemination and dialectical play. My argument here is that dialectical phenomenology can account for what is valid in the postmodern concepts. To the extent that the concepts differ, I resolve that difference in favor of critical modernism for reasons indicated under my discussion above of the six major areas of disagreement between myself and Jack. Something of postmodernism escapes my incorporation or integration, as Jack insists, but what escapes is indefensible. In a sense, the challenge here playfully put to postmodernism, is: anything you can do *validly*, we can do better.[17]

Finally, I agree very much with Marty that Husserl and Hegel, as well as other thinkers such as Lonergan, are important influences and presences in my thought. The very term or concept, "dialectical phenomenology," indicates the blend of Hegelian and Husserlian perspectives in my work. I would also agree with Marty that Husserl's legacy has yet to be exhausted; unfortunately, his remains almost a forgotten voice in a contemporary philosophical discussion dominated by postmodernism and critical theory. But he will come back.

## RESPONSE TO CAPUTO'S CRITIQUE

Now I wish to turn to Jack Caputo's reflection on my book. He criticizes me for giving in to reprehensible intellectualizing tendencies, not really and fully and consistently owning up to phenomenological or hermeneutical ambiguity in my practice of philosophizing, not really doing justice to the way language influences and limits any attempt to do transcendental philosophy in any strong sense. All of these problems come to a head on page 252 of PCM, where I argue that dialectical phenomenology is a reasonable candidate to fulfill the telos of modern philosophy toward fully reflective and critical thinking and living. Here, Caputo argues, all fallibilism, ambiguity, indeterminacy, and situatedness have been left behind in favor of a scholasticizing intellectualism too much in debt to Lonergan and Habermas.

Caputo's critique here is rhetorical as well as logical, phenomenological, hermeneutical. Has the fallibilistic, chastened modernism that I am arguing for finally been subverted by the triumphalistic modernism I am attempting to transcend? I admit to some verbal exuberance on page 252, perhaps excessive, expressed in the heat of philosophical discovery, but the essential, substantive point I would defend. That that point is in a context of fallibilism and indeterminacy is indicated in another phrase at the top of page 252: "dialectical phenomenology is at least one reasonable candidate to fulfill this telos." When one considers this claim in relation to other points made earlier in the book about the ambiguity of experience and language, the necessary play between ambiguity and objectivity, the necessary openness of any philosophical claim to revision in the future by a community of inquiry,[18] then the claim appears far less outrageous. Full attention to the nuance and complexity of my own position, "making its opponents stronger in hermeneutic fashion" (supra, 7), an attention that Caputo and Yount rightly insist we give to Derrida, would reveal the plausibility of such a claim.

"Can" and "should" mean, then, that in my opinion dialectical phenomenology is defensible and preferable to other accounts in the history of modern and contemporary philosophy such as Husserl, Heidegger, and Derrida. If I wish to defend my interpretation of modernity as true, such preferability would seem to be a necessary implication of my argument. In this respect, Caputo's argument in RH is far closer to mine formally than might initially appear. Radical hermeneutics is preferable as an interpretation of modernity to others, Husserlian, Heideggerian, or Marshian. There is a progression in Caputo's argument from Kierkegaard and Husserl to Heidegger and Gadamer to Derrida and his own position: radical hermeneutics as the secret, hidden telos of modern philosophy.[19]

Even though I perhaps overstate the point rhetorically, page 252 simply follows up on the implications of the argument of the whole book. Caputo, on the contrary, has trouble with truth, as I already indicated in my initial reflection on RH. On the one hand, there is the affirmation of radical hermeneutics as preferable to all other accounts, a gesture and a judgment similar to mine. On the other hand, the only truth is that there is no truth; truth is but a useful fiction, and there are no privileged standpoints in the history of philosophy. PCM simply owns up to the implication of a truth claim in a way that RH does not.[20]

Caputo's critique, then, is only plausible through a subtle but massive begging of the question. If one accepts his postmodern interpretation of ambiguity as true, then, of course, my version is flawed and self-contradictory. But I have already offered in my book, in my comments on his book, and in this essay an interlocking set of arguments—self-referential, descriptive, hermeneutical, and political—indicating why the critical modernist version of ambiguity is preferable. For example, "full," as I use it on page 252, means, among other things, an attempt to do justice phenomenologically, hermeneutically, and critically to the relationship between ambiguity and objectivity. "Full" does not imply full apodictic presence.

Now Caputo uses various detailed claims and arguments to support his general logical-rhetorical point. One is that I demolish opponents by making them appear absurd through such devices as self-referential arguments. Such a claim itself rests upon a gross oversimplification amounting to a caricature of my position. First, I state explicitly on page 255 and again in my comment on RH that postmodernism is not arguing for irrationality, but for a more adequate account of rationality. Second, self-referential arguments are one form of critique among others. Someone guilty of self-referential inconsistency can be quite enlightening in other ways. Indeed, my reading of RH, critical of it on self-referential grounds but sympathetic and open and laudatory in other ways, bears out this point; the demolishing and disrespect I fear here are in the eyes of the beholder, Caputo, not in my intention or performance.

Third, that hermeneutical fairness is not only stated as an ideal but consistently practiced in the book is indicated by extended dialogues with such thinkers as Sartre, Heidegger, and Derrida, allowing them to state objections to my position, my criticizing them in certain places and positive using of them in others and my considering other interpretations. Thus, for example, I criticize Heidegger on objectivity but later use his insights on authentic temporality. I criticize Derrida on his conception of the self but later use and appropriate his conception of deconstruction. PCM, while admitting to the multiplicity of possible interpretations of a thinker, does come up with one that is preferable to those of thinkers like Derrida. Caputo's practice here is no different.[21]

What more can one do? Part of what offends Caputo here is my use of argument—formal, logical, self-referential. Caputo expresses an antipathy here, but because he gives little or no argument for this antipathy, what is dogmatically asserted can be rationally questioned or denied. I am reminded here of the distinction that used to be made in the 1960s between analytic philosophers who argue and phenomenologists who describe and interpret. That sterile dichotomy has been overcome by the best philosophers on both sides of the Atlantic— Searle, Rorty, and Bernstein over here, Gadamer, Habermas, and Ricoeur over there—philosophers who use the resources of both argument and description, logic and interpretation, rigor and rhetorical power. One of the virtues of dialectical phenomenology as a method is its blending of dialectical argumentation with description, interpretation, and critique. Argument without description-interpretation is sterile and empty; description-interpretation without argument lacks certainty and rigor.

Without the dialectical argument, for example, that strict determinism and indeterminism are both self-refuting, there remains the outside possibility and doubt that a description of a situated freedom is merely illusory. Through a rich battery of methods—dialectical, descriptive, hermeneutical, and critical—dialectical phenomenology aims to achieve as much certitude and comprehensiveness and determinateness as possible, as much ambiguity and undecidability and indeterminacy as necessary.[22]

The difference between us on the status, meaning, and value of ambiguity comes out in other ways as well. The primacy of perception and the mediation of language are not incompatible if one recognizes that perception itself is already mediated and interpretive. If, as Caputo argues, language on Derrida's account is not locked up inside itself but can be and is referential, then the implication is that reality will be revealed in language, not in some kind of immediate look taking place prior to language. If we arrive at certain necessary universals in our account of perception, expression, reflection, freedom, and intersubjectivity, then that account does not simply reveal the limits of our language but the limits and structure of reality as well. There seems to be a tension here between Caputo's rejection of essence and his assertion that language is referential, as well as his rejection of essence and his affirmation of the "quasi-transcendental." Are not *"différance"* or "metaphoricity" universals that are both linguistic and referential?

Perception, then, is primary even though it is mediated by language. Perceptual contact with things already interpreted as "red," "blue," "white," or "black" is presupposed by science if it is to do its proper work; scientific knowledge, however, is not similarly presupposed in order to perceive things. Both science and perception are mediated encounters with the external world, but perception is more privileged than science, more fundamental; perception has, to use the language of PCM on page 65, a relative, not an absolute primacy.

Again, I do not find the conflict between expression and constitution that Caputo asserts. To express in the way I mean it is to constitute, in the sense that I render explicit what is merely implicit: "this towel is green" or "that person is arrogant" or "F = MA." Some forms of constitution, such as artistic creation, are more creative with respect to the perceived world than is perception, but even these at times can be referential. Thus, Picasso's *Portrait of Wilhelm Uhde,* abstract as it is, reveals something of the real man: prissy, nervous, precise, snobbish. In any event, artistic creation is founded on perception; otherwise we would not know if the portrait resembled him or not.

Caputo seems to find a contradiction between my rejection of the transcendental ego as distinct from the empirical ego and my admitted use of transcendental method. In making this point, he misses the distinction I make on page 39 among the transcendental ego as distinct from the empirical ego, transcendental as referring to the correlation-constitution between meanings and conscious acts, and transcendental as referring to a priori noetic and noematic structures. As I argue in the book, the second and third of these meanings do not imply the first. The self can be embodied, worldly, linguistic, intersubjective, and historical and still be transcendental in these last two senses.

I would concede that the distinction between coercion and appeal is metaphysical, but that is not a term of opprobrium for me as it is for Caputo. His criticism misses the qualification I make on pages 150–51 that any concrete instance of appeal will fall short of the ideal; there will always most likely become elements of coercion. There are, however—as the contrast between kidnapping and Socratic dialogue indicates—instances that approximate the ideal and others that do not. Also, I would insist on a verifiable, essential difference between coercion and appeal: domination is not dialogue. The four validity claims, while not the whole story, seem to me to illumine part of what distinguishes appeal from coercion. Caputo must presuppose the validity of this distinction in making his criticism of me. Presumably he is trying to say something that is clear, true, sincere, and appropriate. If he is merely trying to coerce or manipulate or dominate us, then we need pay him no heed. Once again the issue of authentic philosophical praxis arises.

Finally, I agree, as I indicate in footnote 21, page 232 of PCM, that the Soviet Union is engaged in its own form of technocracy, reification, and domination. I would also agree that in some respects the two versions of domination, capitalist and state socialist, approximate one another. Habermas in a recent work talks about this approximation as two different forms of colonization of life-world by socio-economic-political systems. Nonetheless, differences between the two forms of domination remain. Under one form, the capitalist, domination takes a primarily economic form; in the other, the state socialist, domination takes a primarily political form. The danger in a Heideggerian account, to which Caputo remains indebted here, is that of missing class or group domination, whether economic or political, as the main source of the pathology of the modern and making rationality or the Enlightenment or technology the villain.

The Heideggerian account of technology as *Ge-stell,* or enframing, confuses in an undifferentiated fashion at least four different realities—two legitimate and two illegitimate. The first, technology, is valid as a form of knowledge and praxis, and the second, technocracy, is an incorrect equating of technology with all knowledge and praxis. The third is a beneficial uncoupling of system from life-world; the emergence of a market economy in the modern era allows for production, distribution, and consumption of goods and commodities that is much more efficient and universal than the old economic mechanisms. The fourth is the colonization of life-world by system; the inappropriate intrusion of economic models and criteria into political, social, and cultural spheres is an example of such colonization. In western capitalist democracies, election to political office does not depend on political talent or wisdom but on money. The program that makes it into television is not aesthetically the best, but that program that makes money for the sponsor. The intrusion of the role of money into spheres whose own internal structure or phenomeno-logic is alien to such rule is the basic colonization or alienation present in late capitalism.[23]

The basic thrust and intention of PCM is to defend the first and third senses of technology and to criticize and reject the second and fourth.

Heidegger's and Caputo's account remains "de-differentiated": differences are flattened out and the pathology of the modern is ascribed to reason or technology rather than to class or group domination. Postmodernism obliterates difference in the process of proclaiming it; dialectical phenomenology, if I am correct, emerges as the true friend of difference.[24]

## CONCLUSION

To conclude then, Caputo has raised an important kind of issue in his rhetorical-logical-hermeneutical critique of me. While admitting that my rhetoric may occasionally flirt with an illegitimate triumphalism, I think the argument, if one reads it with the appropriate hermeneutical sympathy and sensitivity to nuance, complexity, and difference, avoids that trap. The question that divides us is how to interpret the mediating role of language with regard to human experience. Is language basically ambiguity in my sense or dissemination, discourse or writing, *différance* or mediation, suspicion or deconstruction? One advantage of my interpretation, I claim, is that it is more comprehensive and nuanced. Not only can it do justice to the moment of ambiguity in language, but also to its objectivity, not only to undecidability but also to decidability, not only to critique but also to receptive openness, not only to the particular but also to the universal, not only to rupture but also to unity. Also, rather than obliterating significant differences in a postmodern "all cows are black," my account of language does justice to different forms and kinds of language use: common sensical, scientific, philosophical, technical, ethical, aesthetic. Or so it seems to me.

There is thus a movement in PCM from language as use to language as object, conceived in structuralist or poststructuralist terms, to language as discourse. Language as used in ordinary linguistic contexts has a validity that can never be entirely overcome or transcended but is breached and shown to be limited by language as objective system, as a differential play of meaning—nothing means simply itself. De Saussure formulates this structuralist insight, and Derrida, while accepting its truth up to a certain point, is surely correct to insist on the impossibility of full systematic closure and presence. The play of *différance* breaches any attempt at full closure and presence.[25]

Language as object or system, whether conceived in a structuralist or poststructuralist manner, also reveals itself to be limited. Such a conception ignores and eliminates too much of the historical and ethical and political and existential and hermeneutical; it does not do full justice to the reality of the text and to interpretation as conversation, someone talking to someone else about something. Language one-sidedly conceived either as use or as system must give way to discourse as a unity of understanding and explanation, interpretation and suspicion, reconstruction and deconstruction. In such a conception, reflection passes through the systematic and asystematic, Derridean moments and attempts to do full justice to these moments, but comes out on the other side. Deconstruction shows itself to be a quite legitimate moment but not the whole story; a moment within a more comprehensive account of language. Deconstruction must give way to discourse.

With Caputo I say "yes" to ambiguity, but ambiguity conceived in such a way that we do not reject the basic reality of the hermeneutical situation as conversation, someone saying something to someone else about something. In this way I deny with Caputo the total validity of any strictly immediate relationship in ordinary language to the other person or text. Even ordinary language and conscious speech are mediated by a systematic and asystematic differential play of meaning, "writing" in Derrida's sense, never fully available to the consciousness of the participants. As such, then, we can affirm not an immediate but a mediated immediacy; the text that I am interpreting and the person with whom I am talking are present to me in a way that others are not. If they were not, then the conversation could not go on.[26]

Coming back to the point of common ground between Jack and myself, what we both share and, I think, what is present in both of our books, is a prophetic, critical, radical conception of philosophy, a sense of philosophy as disturbing and upsetting and subversive. And here I'm going to use one of my favorite postmodern texts by Deleuze. I think this is a good way to end because it sums up an underlying spirit present in both my book and Jack's.

Philosophy does not serve the State or the Church. . . . It serves no established power. The use of philosophy is to *sadden*. A philosophy that saddens no one, that annoys no one, is not a philosophy. It is useful for harming stupidity, for turning stupidity into something shameful. Its only use is the exposure of all forms of baseness of thought. Is there any

discipline apart from philosophy that sets out to criticize all mystifica-
tions, whatever their source and aim, to expose all the fictions without
which reactive forces would not prevail? Exposing as a mystification the
mixture of baseness and stupidity that creates the astonishing complicity
of both victims and perpetrators, finally turning thought in to something
aggressive, active and affirmative, creating free men, that is to say, men
who do not confuse the aims of culture with the benefit of the State,
morality or religion, fighting the resulting *ressentiment* and bad con-
science which has replaced thought for us, conquering the negative and
its false glamour. Who has an interest in all this but philosophy. Philosophy is at its most positive as critique, as an enterprise of demystifica-
tion. And we should not be too hasty in proclaiming philosophy's failure
in that respect. Great as they are, stupidity and baseness would be still
greater if there did not remain some philosophy which always prevents
them from going as far as they would wish, which forbids them, if only
by "yea-saying," from being as stupid and base as they would wish.
They are forbidden certain excesses but only by philosophy.[27]

NOTES

1. For the distinction between Heidegger I and Heidegger II, see William Richardson, *Heidegger: Through Phenomenology to Thought* (The Hague: Martinus Nijhoff,
1967). See RH, pp. 153–206.

2. For my reviews of Caputo's two earlier books, see *Modern Schoolman*, LVIII
(November 1980), 53–55 for a review of *The Mystical Element in Heidegger's
Thought*; and *International Philosophical Quarterly* XXV (September 1985),
200–206, for a review of *Heidegger and Aquinas*.

3. See PCM, pp. 200–58, especially pp. 254–57. Even though political efficacy is
very strongly present in these pages, it is not listed on pp. 254–57 as it is so listed in
"The Post-modern Interpretation of History: A Phenomenological-Hermeneutical Critique," *Journal of the British Society of Phenomenology* 19 (May 1988): 112–27.

4. PCM, pp. 109–114, 143–57. Bernard J. F. Lonergan, *Insight: A Study of Human
Understanding* (New York: Longmans, Green and Co., 1957), pp. 319–32. Jürgen
Habermas, *The Theory of Communicative Action, I: Reason and the Rationalization of
Society,* trans. Thomas McCarthy (Boston: Beacon Press, 1984), pp. 1–42.

For Caputo's difficulties with truth, see RH, pp. 145, 155–56. For Habermas' critique of Derrida, see his *The Philosophical Discourse of Modernity,* trans. Frederick
Lawrence (Cambridge: MIT Press, 1987), pp. 185–210. For Derrida's critique of
Habermas, see *Limited Incorporated,* ed. Gerald Graff (Evanston: Northwestern University Press, 1988), pp. 156–58, footnote 9. I am indebted to a student colleague of
mine, Martin Matustik, for pointing out and developing the performative implications
of Derrida's complaint. See his "Habermas on Communicative Reason and Performative Contradiction," *New German Critique* 47 (Fall 1989): 165–66, footnote 4. On

Derrida's questioning of or denial of good will, see his "Three questions to Hans-George Gadamer," *Dialogue and Deconstruction: the Gadamer-Derrida Encounter,* ed. Diane P. Michelfelder and Richard Palmer (Albany: SUNY Press, 1989), pp. 52–54.

5. Ludwig Wittgenstein, *Tractatus Logico-Philosophicos,* trans. D. F. Pears and B. F. McGuiness (London: Routledge and Kegan Paul, 1961), p. 151. James L. Marsh, "Strategies of Evasion: The Paradox of Self-Referentiality and the Post-Modern Critique of Rationality," *International Philosophical Quarterly* XXIX (September 1989): 339–49.

6. John Caputo, "Gadamer and Derrida on Interpretation," Metropolitan Round-table, Iona College, New Rochelle, New York, Dec. 8, 1988. Jacques Derrida, *Grammatology,* trans. Gayatri Chakrovorty Spivak (Baltimore: Johns Hopkins University Press, 1976), pp. 1–73. RH, pp. 3–4, 185. "Strategies of Evasion," 339–49.

7. PCM, p. 75–89, 148–57.

8. PCM, p. 256. Edmund Husserl, *Formal and Transcendental Logic,* trans. Dorion Cairns (The Hague: Martinus Nijhoff, 1969), p. 278.

9. See my "The Post-Modern Interpretation of History," 119–23, for fuller development of this argument.

10. See PCM, p. 119–23, for the discussion with and about Derrida concerning this issue.

11. See my "The Post-Modern Interpretation of History," 123–24, and PCM, pp. 200–58, for fuller development of this argument.

12. PCM, pp. 160–80, 239–58.

13. Marsh, "The Post-Modern Interpretation of History," 122–25. Marx, *Capital,* I, trans. Ben Fowkes (New York: Vintage, 1977), pp. 279–90.

14. RH, pp. 289–90. PCM, pp. 106–22, 183–97. On Derrida's anger at being misunderstood, see footnote 4 of this essay. On Caputo's complaints about being misunderstood by me, see *supra,* pp. 54–55. On Kierkegaard's dialectic on the comical, see his *Concluding Unscientific Postscript,* trans. David Swenson and Walter Lowrie (Princeton: Princeton University Press, 1968), pp. 53–55. On the dangers of aestheticism and indifference in deconstruction, see Fred Dallmayr, "Hermeneutics and Deconstruction: Gadamer and Derrida in Dialogue," in *Dialogue and Deconstruction,* pp. 89–92.

15. See my "The Post-Modern Interpretation of History," 119–23; also my "Heidegger's Overcoming of Metaphysics: A Critique," *The Journal of the British Society for Phenomenology* 16 (January 1985): 55–69.

16. Lonergan, *Insight,* 348–74, 431–37, 458–79, 634–86. David Tracy, *Blessed Rage for Order* (New York: Seabury Press, 1975), pp. 172–91. Leonardo Boff, *Jesus Christ: Liberator* (Maryknoll: Orbis Books, 1978).

17. PCM, pp. 23–39, 116, 211, 245.

18. PCM, pp. 23–39, 121–22, 131–33.

19. See RH, especially pp. 1–186.

20. *Supra,* pp. 17–20. RH, pp. 144–45, 156, 180.

21. PCM, pp. 76–81, 87–88, 90 footnote 14, 91 footnote 32, 96–99, 113–14, 119–22, 139–42, 144–48, 158 footnote 28, 245.

Concerning the offending footnote on Busch, I fail to see why there is anything illegitimate in noting that, even if his interpretation of Sartre is true, such an interpretation supports my position, especially since it is my own position I am developing in

PCM. Such a move is only illegitimate if trying to state the truth is illegitimate. Once again, Caputo's problems with truth show up.

22. PCM, pp. 92–99.

23. For Heidegger's account of *Ge-stell,* see *Question Concerning Technology and Other Essays,* trans. William Lovitt (New York: Harper & Row, 1977), pp. 3–35. Jürgen Habermas, *The Theory of Communicative Action, II: Life World and Systems,* trans. Thomas McCarthy (Boston: Beacon Press, 1987), pp. 153–97.

24. For the term and concept of "de-differentiation," see Jürgen Habermas, *The Philosophical Discourse of Modernity,* trans. Frederick Lawrence (Cambridge: The MIT Press, 1987), pp. 87, 94–95, 112–13, 136–37, 336–41.

25. For language as use in PCM, see pp. 23–39, 54–61, 148–57; for language as object conceived in structuralist or poststructuralist terms, see pp. 117–22; for language as discourse, see pp. 117–18, 161–64; for language and interpretation as conversation, see pp. 164–69. See David Tracy's *Plurality and Ambiguity* (New York: Harper & Row, 1987), pp. 47–65 for a charting of the path from language as use to language as object to language as discourse. See Paul Ricoeur, *Interpretation Theory: Discourse and the Surplus of Meaning* (Fort Worth: Texas Christian University Press, 1976), pp. 1–23, for his definition of language as discourse.

26. For Derrida's conception of writing, see *Grammatology,* pp. 27–73.

27. Gilles Deleuze, *Nietzsche and Philosophy,* trans. Hugh Tomlinson (New York: Columbia University Press, 1983), p. 106.

# Open Forum

BALESTRA: This is addressed to Jack Caputo, a question which needs a little more discussion or elaboration—this question of "quasi-transcendental": I find it a tease!

CAPUTO: The claim is that that in virtue of which one is able to make claims or assertions is also simultaneously that in virtue of which it is impossible to make those claims incontrovertible. The system of signs, the constellation of signifiers and of meanings, which is the condition of the possibility of discourse, is such that it does not allow the meanings and the assertions that are formed by it to harden and acquire immutability. Derrida works that out in detail in his earliest works and in his account of *différance* when he is, in particular, describing de Saussure and the Copenhagen linguist Hjelmslev. The point at which deconstruction arises is a critique of the move made by the Copenhagen school of structural linguistics. At a certain point, after critiquing the primacy of speech over writing in de Saussure, Hjelmslev says language is a formal operation. It is a deployment of formal differential signs, and it makes no difference whether you speak or write. And then he says that the task of structural linguistics is to formulate the rules, the structural and a priori rules, that govern the formation of well-formed formulae in any possible natural language. Derrida intervenes at that point and says that whatever those rules will be, they will be possible in virtue of *différance,* that is to say, they will be possible in virtue of the fact that signs already are significant to begin with, so that the rules of formal linguistics will be subsets of the play of signifiers or of the differential sign-making quality that all signifiers have. Consequently, they presuppose already the ability to make signs. Consequently, it is impossible to close the system. The corresponding demonstration outside of structural linguistics is Gödel's theory. It is the same kind of argument. So the claim is that it is possible to make arguments, possible to reason, possible to form meanings and make assertions, but it is not possible to close the system. The mistake of people like Marsh is to think that either all signs are arbitrary or everything is a formal system. Marsh gives you two choices: you've got to take one of those, whereas Derrida has deconstructed this kind of oppositional scheme. Then you get this kind of obstinate objection against what's going on. (I know that I am not supposed to comment on other people's papers but Dominic asked me to.)

_____: This question is directed to Mark Yount. When Dr. Marsh was talking about the paradox of the broken ladder, you sort of threw your hands up in disbelief. I was just wondering why.

YOUNT: I think I sort of like the paradox of the broken ladder. I like it as a motif for explaining certain moves in Zen Buddhism, that you use reason in some context to get to a point at which reason is no longer the regulative framework for understanding, that you use it but that in some sense you kick the ladder away. But of course it's the sort of ladder that won't get you there. I think that the broken ladder was kicked away before we were through with the broken ladder, that we hadn't gotten to where the broken ladder was supposed to get us even as a metaphor. And I think that was what my body involuntarily signified.

_____: I want to ask something about the historical content of the dialectical side of dialectical phenomenology (addressed to any volunteer) and what the concept of postmodernism is. I just want to be clear on the historical content and the connection between dialectical phenomenology and postmodernism as a temporal historical reference.

MARSH: That sounds like it might be addressed to me, at least as one of the volunteers. "Dialectical" in dialectical phenomenology has many different aspects to it. It refers, first of all, to the unity of opposites which I think is discovered by a careful phenomenological description of the experience. Perception and reflection, for example, passive and active, receptive and active moments in freedom. It refers, second, to a sense of dialectical progression in history and dialectical critique of history. And so what I did in the book, where I briefly outlined the stages of capitalist development according to Marx, is to discuss forms of contemporary alienation and then to show how those are explained by an analysis and critique of capitalism.

As to the relationship of postmodernism and dialectical phenomenology, I would view that progression dialectically. It seems to me that you can chart a history in modern philosophy, a movement starting from what we might call triumphalistic modernism, examples of which might be Husserl and Descartes in certain respects. This modernism has its own kind of nihilism built into it and leads to dead ends. Post-modernism draws out those dead ends in a negative, skeptical moment. The claim here is that critical modernism or dialectical phenomenology is more comprehensive, that it does not have the deficits of a trium-phalistic modernism and it listens to and learns from postmodernism about fallibilism and the non-apodictic character of eidetic claims.

What I find interesting about Jack Caputo's presentation tonight . . . it's a different Caputo. Is this the wild man of radical hermeneutics who is going to overcome metaphysics? The discourse at times comes very close to approximating critical modernism. Derrida is a safe fig-ure who throws a bomb every so often at the metaphysical enterprise. But what got the academic community concerned, the radical project of overcoming metaphysics—that's absent or de-emphasized tonight.

I think you see also a good example in Jack's discourse of the sup-pression of difference within postmodernism. Mine is not triumphalis-tic modernism, but a different brand entirely. And one indication of that, I think, is that the kind of transcendental claims I make in my book are very, very close to what he was describing just now as the quasi-transcendental. There's a very interesting question here, I think. If postmodernism insists that it avoids the problem of performative contradiction, how much is it within the tradition, how rational is it (and I think that is in Derrida), what is the difference between that kind of discourse and a critical modernist discourse such as you have with Kant vis-a-vis the tradition, Merleau-Ponty vis-a-vis Husserl, Ha-bermas vis-a-vis all sorts of people—what is the difference between those two kinds of discourses? In Jack's presentation tonight, there seems to be very little. So I wonder what all the shouting is about.

KOBOLAKIS: I have a two-tiered question addressed to both sides. Dr. Caputo's book talks about playful thinking vis-a-vis the seriousness of rationality, while at the same time the book begins with "life is hard; life is suffering." I would like to know, spelled out in more detail maybe, how exactly the philosopher can be playful in the face of suf-fering. Mr. Marsh ends up saying that philosophy saddens. In your ra-tional view of philosophy do you have a moment of playfulness? Does your reason laugh?

CAPUTO: First of all, what's interesting to me about play and serious-ness is precisely the inability to keep those two things apart. The move-ment of deconstruction is to show the way in which opposites bleed into each other. There are differences of degree rather than differences of kind. It would never be possible, if you think deconstructively, that there would be no amount of seriousness in play and vice-versa. The way in which I could concretely illustrate how they come together comes from Nietzsche. Nietzsche says that the ability of a spirit or individual to *suffer* almost determines its order of rank (#270). And then a few aphorisms later (#294), in *Beyond Good and Evil,* he says the ability of the spirit to *laugh* does determine its order of rank. What happens in the figure of Zarathustra is that it is precisely in virtue of the looking into the abyss, the understanding of tragic suffering, that one comes up affirmatively. One comes up with the laughter of the shepherd boy who bites off the head of the snake—this horrible passage about the snake that crawls into the throat of the shepherd who bites it off. Then there's laughter. Zarathustra says "Oh how I long for that laughter." Or look at the end of the book *The Name of the Rose.* What's the whole book about? That damned monk found Aristotle's book on comedy and old Jorge wanted to hide it because Jorge thought comedy was unholy. But we know the gods laugh.

MARSH: What I tried to do in the book is to show, through a phenomenology of reason, the link of preconceptual and conceptual, question and answer, pre-reflective and reflective, playful and serious. I think that one of the best examples of playfulness in philosophy is the person with whom we all begin and then forget: Socrates. The dialogues, I think, hermeneutically are a beautiful manifestation of the playfulness in seriousness of philosophy, which is also linked to a seriousness of the concept. He goes after Meno for describing, in a postmodernist way, just particular kinds of virtue and not virtue itself. So you don't need to go to Nietzsche to do it; it's already in Socrates. Again the claim: anything you do we can do better.

BETROS: To Caputo: I would like you to pursue further one of Marsh's criticisms. One of the things he hits you over the head with is that you and your line are anti-evidential. Sticking to just that criticism, could you respond to it? I mean, do you want to distinguish different types of evidence; do you want to say there is ambiguity in evidence? For Marsh: this is a question that comes out of your book and didn't come up this evening. One of the things in reading your book that comes to me as a little jarring is the transition from the earlier part of the book, where you develop quite well a clear epistemological standpoint to the critique of capitalism. One of the things you said, a provision you made maybe in a footnote, is that there is some sort of similar criticism of state socialism, but we can't do everything in one book. I think there is a problem with taking capitalism as your central critical category. If you are going to have a similar criticism of state socialism, aren't you really criticizing something deeper?

CAPUTO: I wonder if that deeper thing is technology. I think that it is technology that does these things that capitalism is being criticized for, and this is just as true of socialism. Socialism is just as much committed to raping of the earth, raping of social relationships, as capitalism. Nothing is innocent.

Yes, the characterization that the position that I hold is anti-evidential goes hand in hand with saying that I want to overcome rationality, overcome argument, overcome evidence, overcome tradition, and throw these things out. This is simply a misrepresentation, a caricature of positions that have been very carefully nuanced by Derrida from the very start. This business of the "inside/outside" distinction has been the ongoing constant position that Derrida has held since 1967. He has not budged on that point for well over twenty years. It is not a bit new. Maybe Jim is just now beginning to hear it.

The position that I hold was elicited by Dominic Balestra's question: one operates within evidential, rational, discursive systems with a certain tentativeness. That is, we all think we're getting things right. The account I have of getting things right is "watch out because it may well come down on top of you." The sense in which we are getting it right may well rest on excluding some other things that we're making wrong. It is never the case—what Jim says is just simply untrue; I know of no text in Derrida in which Derrida would hold that—that we think there is a choice between throwing out reason, argumentation, evidence, tradition, philosophy completely, or holding to a hardline Cartesian system. What we think we're dealing with are assertions, propositions that we put forward for which there are good reasons. What you hear from Jim is a lot of methodological rumbling. And when you plow it out of the way and you find out that the arguments—e.g., against apartheid— are about the same arguments that most sensible people have against excluding and marginalizing black people in societies with white minorities. The choice between what I do and what he does is a choice between inflated rhetoric and just saying things that appear to be the most reasonable position you can take given the amount of evidence that you have.

MARSH: I think that's a very sensitive and very good question on your part and it shows a very careful reading of my book. In my book I move from descriptive criteria that are operative in eidetic variation to hermeneutical criteria that include comprehensiveness, parsimony, relevance, consistency, and the canon of residues. I use those to develop a hermeneutical interpretation and critique of capitalism. Now because the context of the book is Cartesian and western, I did not develop a full analysis of all the forms of alienation in a way that finally has to be done. I traced the various stages of capitalism: early dominance of exchange value over use value, the movement to absolute surplus value, acquisition of profit by lengthening the working day; relative surplus value, acquisition of profit through decreasing the value of labor power; then moved into an analysis of late capitalism, with science functioning as a form of ideology. I think that a next step, a full analysis and interpretation of the twentieth century, would be to move into an analysis, as PCM does in a footnote to which you refer, of state socialism as another form of class domination—political rather than economic class domination. Contrary to what seems to me to be a mystifying critique by Heidegger, that's the pathology and not technology as such. The pathology consists in the misuse of technology in the service of class or group domination.

One brief comment on your comment about my criticism being unfair to Caputo: I never said Caputo was non-evidential, or if I did, I didn't mean that simply. Caputo, like all the major postmodernists, is bright and intelligent; he is evidential, but it is an evidentiality that does not own up to itself. That's the point. And that's the point about Derrida. Concerning the comment that our Derrida is not the real Derrida, the movement to transcend metaphysics is there in the text. I think one place where it is present is in the first 80 pages of *Grammatology*. I would like to read just a few sentences. This is not hermeneutically decisive, but it is an indication at least of the possibility of this reading. "On what conditions is a grammatology possible? Its fundamental condition is certainly the undoing of logocentrism" (p. 74). So we have the western tradition, conceived as a whole, and some kind of desire to get beyond it. Again, on page 83, "through all the recent work on that area, one glimpses the future extensions of grammatology, called upon to stop receiving its guiding concepts from other human sciences, or what nearly amounts to the same thing, from traditional metaphysics.'' Derrida here is arguing for a transcendence of western tradition as a whole. Now in these pages as well, there's also a recognition by him of the necessity of operating within. My claim is that he cannot square the circle of attempting to negate the tradition as a whole with the admitted necessity of working within it as a whole. That's the problem.

TIRONE: This is for Dr. Caputo. We see Marsh reading Derrida right now. You already talked about how Marsh and people like Marsh have a tendency to misinterpret deconstruction, to misinterpret radical hermeneutics, to tend to see it as an attempt to completely overcome metaphysics, rationality, throwing ourselves into absolute arbitrariness. This is pretty much American deconstruction in conflict with Derrida. I am fascinated by why Americans tend to interpret deconstruction this way. And now that you've described Dr. Marsh's interpretation, why do you think Dr. Marsh has to interpret deconstruction in this way? What is it about his position that leads to this?

CAPUTO: Do you want me to ''psychoanalyze'' him? I think that Jim has uncritically bought into exactly what you described: the image of deconstruction that has been popularized by the literary, and I must say also the theological, appropriations of deconstruction.

WESTPHAL: And Rorty.

CAPUTO: And Rorty. That's true.

WESTPHAL: Which is neither literary nor theological.

CAPUTO: (This is what you call subversive intervention.) The key to overcoming these misunderstandings of Derrida is (this is a very territorial thing to say, but I would say it here because we're pretty much in the same territory) to read Derrida philosophically, and to have a background in Husserl and Heidegger. And you do need structural linguistics. Then one can see the operation of delimitation, which is a much better way to describe what Derrida is doing. If you call it ''overcoming,'' then you're translating Heidegger's word *Überwindung,* and Heidegger had a tendency to talk like this. At the very end of the *Mystical Element of Heidegger's Thought,* of which Jim did a very balanced and incisive review, I said it made me very uncomfortable to talk about leaping beyond the principle of reason and leaving reason behind. I said we have to come up with a better idea of what reason is as well as opening ourselves to the splendor of this nonrepresentational thinking that Heidegger, Zen Buddhists, Meister Eckhart, and lots of people have come upon. So the short answer is: Derrida is delimiting. He is not "overcoming" in this sense that Heidegger sometimes suggests. And then at a very critical point, even Heidegger drops the word *Überwindung*. He says it suggests *über,* that we get beyond something, and he puts in its place the word *Verwindung*. What does that mean? You are sick and you're able to deal with it. You've got a bad cold and you're able to survive. You're paralyzed and you're able to cope with it. *Verwindung* means knowing how to cope with something that "has" you and you're not going to get beyond it. He contrasts that critically with the notion of *Überwindung*. So even Heidegger, who is rather prone to do the sort of thing that Marsh is saying, in his more critical moments got straight about it. One of the great advantages of Derrida is that he almost never got into that thing. The closest he did was when he talked about the "end of the book" and then in a very short term he took that right back.

It really is surprising to me that Jim keeps pushing this misconception on Derrida. You might be able to make it stick on some texts of Heidegger, but even Heidegger gets to be more careful at a certain point. Derrida is always careful.

WESTPHAL: Thanks for coming. Thanks to our four panelists. The conversations can continue on their own.

# A Philosophical Dialogue:

## James L. Marsh, John D. Caputo, and Merold Westphal

WESTPHAL: We might begin by trying to focus on some broad areas of agreement, identifying the larger philosophical movement within which the debates among us take place. One could say that it is the postfoundationalist movement in philosophy. And here it might be helpful to borrow from the introduction Thomas McCarthy wrote for the volume *After Philosophy*, seeking to identify some of the common themes among the postfoundationalist philosophical traditions. One of them is repudiation of what he calls strong conceptions of reason by emphasizing contingency and conventionality over against necessity, plurality over against universality, and fallibility and fragmentation over against totality and certainty.

A second theme he gives is the critique of the notion of the sovereign, rational subject as a disengaged and disembodied self-transparent entity. All of the philosophical perspectives that will be represented in this discussion repudiate that Cartesian notion of the subject.

A third theme he mentions is the repudiation of immediacy, the idea that there is a naked given, or a linguistically free access to the world, and by contrast to that, the emphasis on the fact that the subject belongs to the world that is being interpreted or understood.

And finally, the fourth theme is the repudiation of the neat distinction of philosophy as conceptual thought from rhetoric and poetics and so a questioning of the standard oppositions between *logos* and *mythos*, logic and rhetoric, literal and figurative, concept and metaphor, argument and narrative. Such oppositions are, if not completely undermined, seriously qualified.

I take it that both of you, Jack and Jim, would agree with these four themes. I think it would be interesting to see if there are any further agreements that you wish to ferret out between the two of you, between your two books, before we get on to discovering how it is that you disagree with each other even when you agree.

MARSH: Well, one additional agreement between Jack and myself is a shared political radicalism that I think deserves exploration. Some of my favorite passages in *Radical Hermeneutics* occur in the discussion of "Toward a Postmetaphysical Rationality." Jack, for example, says on page 230:

> But the power exerted *within* the university is dwarfed by the power exerted *upon* the university from without. For the university belongs to a technico-political power structure. It is part of a social system which has increasingly technical and pragmatic expectations of the university and, hence, of what is "rational."

And you have on the next four or five pages discussions of the way various kinds of power come into the university to inhibit or negate a free, critical play of rationality. I resonate with the passages in those pages. But I think after a certain point there is a disagreement emerging from that agreement, because I have a different account of where the pathology is and what's going wrong.

CAPUTO: You mentioned political radicalism. I wonder if a mark of agreement among the three of us is not a concern with radicality—that is, from the very beginning of the phenomenological movement the aim has been to become radical. And that, of course, is in one sense a foundationalist metaphor and quite Cartesian. That was the sense in which Husserl was using it. But it also has another sense, viz., of the inextricability of the roots of our existence. Then the "root" metaphor is not that of a single, central "tap-root" that we can go back to, but rather a sense of the enormous complexity of our existence and of what Heidegger, back in the '20s when he was beginning to appropriate Husserl's phenomenology for the first time, called our "facticity."

I take it that we three are all very much committed to the notion of the facticity of human existence. And that the "post" in postmodern and in post-Cartesian arises from the desire to come to grips with the factical situatedness of the predominant themes of modern philosophy: of subjectivity, consciousness, and freedom. Although Kierkegaard had done this before, what Heidegger did vis-a-vis Husserl was to situate phenomenological consciousness in being-in-the-world. Then the rootedness of this consciousness was no longer the root of a pure foundation, but the rootedness of a being which, as you say frequently, Jim, in *Post-Cartesian Meditations*, puts us in a situation where something is always going on behind our backs. There is a mark of radicality in recognizing the radical facticity of our situation.

And so the radical politics that I want to pursue is of a piece with the radicality of the whole hermeneutic project. Heidegger once said that hermeneutics means the hermeneutics of facticity and facing up to the radical facticity of human existence.

Now that, I take it, is something that we are all agreed upon. And the differences that emerge among us may very well be a function of our different understandings of facticity.

WESTPHAL: The way in which I've tried to express that agreement, in the briefest way, is to pose the question, "Who is the transcendental subject?" That way of posing it, I think, has a lot of usefulness in that it hooks up posttranscendental philosophy with the transcendental question. Now one of the things we would want to talk about is the meaning of the transcendental.

I find that a useful question, because it suggests that whatever the function of transcendental subjectivity may be, an adequate analysis of the transcendental subject is going to have to be based on exploration of just those themes you mentioned, Jack, of the situatedness, the root-edness of whatever subjectivity there is in complexity, and context, and opacity that keeps transcendental subjectivity from ever having the character that Descartes and Husserl had hoped that they might be able to develop for it.

We probably don't have, among the three of us, a common under-standing of the transcendental. I think we do have a common notion of what it isn't, of what it is we are seeking an alternative to.

MARSH: I think there again there's an interesting approximation, at least, to agreement between Jack and myself which came out a bit in the initial presentations of the symposium. I would describe my version of the transcendental as a qualified or chastened transcendental, interacting with the hermeneutical but nonetheless making eidetic claims. I even talk about it as being relatively, as opposed to absolutely, apodictic.

The part of Jack's treatment that approximates that version is, I think, this notion deriving from Derrida of the quasi-transcendental. So I take it that notions like *différance*, suupplementarity, and meta-phoricity would be notions that approximate without equaling my version of the transcendental. Both accounts, I think, have in common again a rejection of a straightforward Husserlian transcendental. . . .

CAPUTO: When Merold said, "Who is the transcendental subject?" my first response was, "The subject who never quite was." I mean that seriously. The transcendental subject is the subject that philosophy has aspired toward and yearned for since the onset of modernity. And I think that the "post" in post-Cartesian and postmodern is the recognition that such a subject never quite was. That is to say, there always has to be something like a transcendental structure. I think that in the twentieth century, anyone who has inherited the tradition of modern philosophy finds himself inevitably committed to some kind of notion of the transcendental. It is inescapable. The transcendental is the way that we philosophize, whether we like it or not. And the notion of a quasi-transcendental is the notion of a transcendental that is a certain kind of transcendental, but not the transcendental which modernity expected to find. This probably is what we share.

You know, there's this famous letter of Heidegger to Husserl back in 1927 where he says: You and I agree about the notion of constitution; but we differ about the nature of the constituting subject, the constituting agency, the being that constitutes. And Heidegger said that Husserl thinks that what constitutes is transcendental consciousness whereas he (Heidegger) thinks that it is factical *Dasein*.

I think that something like that is the case, that in fact, we are talking about a world, to use Husserl's word, that has been constituted by a being that is radically factical. Now that presupposes a certain kind of transcendentality. But it also undoes it in the same gesture, because it disallows transcendentality in some strong sense. And I see postmodernism as pursuing that opening created by Heidegger against Husserl, and by Kierkegaard against Hegel.

WESTPHAL: Let me pose this question to see if I can ferret out some disagreement in the agreement. If we talk about the situatedness of the transcendental subject so that it never quite is, there are various themes that could be emphasized. One could emphasize the embodied character. And I take it that while none of us wants to deny that, that's not primary for any of us. What tends to be primary for us is linguisticality or social historicality. I think that in a sense you, Jim, would be more inclined to emphasize the social historicality of the transcendental, and you, Jack, are probably more inclined to emphasize the linguisticality.

I want to argue that in the final analysis, the two have to be taken together, that they are inseparable. I'm not sure that either of you disagrees with that. But it seems to me that your emphases are different on that point in terms of what the crucial rootedness of the transcendental subject is: social structures or linguistic structures.

I think that it would be helpful to talk about a difference of emphasis, because it seems to me that when the two of you go at each other, it's often because you want to emphasize different things, rather than because you finally disagree on substantive issues.

MARSH: I think they both imply one another, and therefore, in a sense I agree with you. Here again, re-reading the discussion that you, Jack, have on the person in RH, I find more agreement with my position than I thought was there initially. In my own book, I would describe the argument as a movement from the bourgeois ego to the post-bourgeois self. There is a great deal of mediation, presence interacting with absence, consciousness interacting with the psychological and social unconscious.

The equivalent movement in your book, in different terminology, is from the ego or the self to the person. That's the term you use a lot on pages 275 to 277. And it's not just absence. It seems to me that a kind of presence is affirmed when you talk about dignity and the face of suffering. For example, on page 277 you say, "and not just absence, but the interplay of presence and absence, of the self-giving which is also self-withdrawing. . . . " When I first read RH, I thought you were denying selfhood in any sense. But now that doesn't seem to be true. Would you agree?

CAPUTO: That's why it's radical hermeneutics. The title was in part produced at the urging of the editor, who didn't like the first title. She was right. The first title was "Coping with the Flux." The editor seriously objected to that. And when I went back to the drawing board in the process of rewriting it, I came up with this title, with which I'm much more satisfied. There's a sort of a genus and difference in the title; there's a commitment to the generic operation of hermeneutic inquiry and I'm perfectly happy to be aligned with a version of hermeneutics. I take myself to be pushing a hermeneutic point to its limit, following it to its ultimate implications, which is the sense of radicality. That means that there is some theory of something like the self.

Now the word "person" I chose because it seemed to me a pre-Cartesian word in some way. That is to say it is a classical and medieval word, and I thought perhaps it would not be as subjectivistic as the notion of self or subjectivity itself. And it preserved for me this alethic notion, that is to say, the notion of a mystery that withdraws, which is a very Heideggerian and a very hermeneutical idea. So I am committed to some idea of something like a self, I mean, a certain self in the same way that there is a certain transcendental. There is a certain self, or maybe many selves or too many, as Nietzsche says.

But that for me is a moment of mystery and of consternation, not just simply a moment of skepticism, that is, it is not an attempt to simply write off in a kind of skeptical way the notion of the self, but rather to be confounded all the more deeply by the experience of the self.

If I had to reduce to a formula what I take all of us to be committed to, I would have said it is just these ideas of embodiment, linguisticality, and historicality. And it might be possible to rank-order these ideas, and to take one to be more fundamental than the other. It's to Merleau-Ponty that we owe that of a genuine phenomenology of embodiment, to Heidegger the notions of historicality and linguisticality.

WESTPHAL: But isn't it the case that while we all acknowledge with gratitude a debt to Merleau-Ponty for his phenomenology of the body, none of us really makes that very central to our own philosophical project, in relationship to the other two themes?

CAPUTO: The only time I do is at the very end of RH, where I raise the question of suffering, and then the question of the face and of suffering becomes very important to me. But it is not preceded by any adequate phenomenology of the body, that is true. It is not thematized until that point. I find myself coming back to it at that point.

WESTPHAL: Isn't it the case that the phenomenology of suffering at the end of RH presupposes a phenomenology of the body but is at best tangentially related to the Derridean themes that you have developed previously?

CAPUTO: No, absolutely not.

WESTPHAL: I thought you'd say that. But I'm not convinced from reading RH. So maybe you could say something about how that phenomenology of suffering is an integral part of the deconstructive process.

CAPUTO: Well, this comes back to Jim's point when he singles out the question of political, or let us say more broadly, the ethico-political. The account of factical existence needs to be radicalized in the direction of the ethical and the political. That's what's wrong with Heidegger—his failure to do that. And what's interesting about the particular kind of postmodernism that interests me, namely, the kind that I find in Derrida, is exactly this ethico-political streak. This arises in Derrida, if I have to attribute it to a source, from Levinas, where there is a very rich and deep phenomenology of embodiment; a close connection with Merleau-Ponty, and perhaps the most salient ethical voice in contemporary continental philosophy. That's very much a part of Derrida's agenda. It's becoming very plain recently that that's an important part of Derrida's whole position, because his writings have taken a twist in the last ten years or so in which that thematic has been emphasized. And so when I turn to suffering at the end of RH, I am picking up on something that is latent in the particular kind of postmodernism that I am interested in, that is, a phenomenology of the oppressed and the excluded.

WESTPHAL: Let me push my question, then, back from you to Derrida, because insofar as there are those motifs in Derrida, derived as you say from Levinas and Merleau-Ponty, they seem to me *ad hoc*. They seem to me themes which he has picked up which represent perhaps his Jewish origins and his political preferences but which don't have any clear relationship to his poststructuralist critique of logocentrism. So that if somebody just took the emphasis on the excluded and said, "Well, let's move in political directions with that," then somebody might say, "Well, the neo-Nazis are excluded in the United States and maybe we need to do something about that." Neither Derrida nor you are very interested in getting the neo-Nazis included, but it seems to me that the notion of exclusion that's operating in deconstruction, as a poststructuralist critique of logocentrism, is so formal that it doesn't have intrin sic linkage to the Levinasian Judaeo-Christian motifs that you articulate in your phenomenology of suffering, that they're just sort of juxtaposed as historical, biographical facts about you and Derrida, but not very closely related to the argument of deconstruction.

MARSH: I just want to chime in by saying that's a point I made in my initial reflection on RH about the excessively formal character of deconstruction. There's a question about the ethico-political implications that you want to draw from a theory too thin to be able to do that.

CAPUTO: We really need to get to the bottom of this because I think that the question is very important, very central, and if we can sort it out we would have made some progress.

The connection of the ethical and political with Derrida's whole project could hardly be less *ad hoc*, although in a flip-Derridean mood, I could say: to be *ad hoc* is good because the opposite of that is metaphysics. He would call it his good chance that he came upon this idea. But it goes directly to the heart, to speak in traditional categories, of his project because he says at the very beginning that his (Derrida's) whole thought turns on this notion of difference. The philosophers of difference for him are Freud, Heidegger, Nietzsche, and Levinas. Levinas is the fourth of these figures.

You could put it this way (I will have to retract this at some point), but you could say that deconstruction arises from a hermeneutic source. That hermeneutics is the hermeneutics of the other. Derrida is always on the tracks of the other that is being excluded or repressed or silenced or mutilated in some way.

Levinas says that he is interested in the other to philosophy, the other of philosophy, that uniquely Judaeo-Christian thing that got silenced by the Hellenic. Levinas also recognizes that he is a philosopher and therefore is Hellenic. Derrida takes account of that. Derrida quotes Joyce's remark that Jewgreek is Greekjew. That's a fair way to describe deconstruction, too. I see him speaking in a philosophical voice that is also aware of what is other than philosophy, invoking an issue which in its background is Judaeo-Christian, which is ethical, which is other than Hellenic ontology, and systematically, if we may speak like that, reintroducing that other into philosophical deliberation so that his philosophic work is always inside/outside philosophy.

MARSH: I'd like to pursue that issue. I guess the question would be— and here we would be getting into a possible difference on the political-ethical level—whether you and Derrida (even though I'd agree that Derrida is a man of the left as you are, too) can justify or sustain or maintain the distinction between legitimate and illegitimate marginalization. This is a point I made about the difference between a Barnett and a Wallace, on the one hand, versus some of the people whom we support and defend and aid. So I think we would all recognize as really illegitimately marginalized: African Americans, women, labor. One kind of question that I have concerns your resources to make that distinction. A point I made is that you can only do that by drawing implicitly on certain resources of western tradition that deconstruction wishes to call into question or negate.

CAPUTO: I welcome the chance to address that. That's why I spoke just a moment ago of a hermeneutics of the other. I think I'm speaking for Derrida; if not, I'm certainly speaking for myself, although I do think this is good Derrida. What lies behind the particular version of postmodernism that interests me, the impulse which moves it along, is an experience of exclusion and of otherness. Now I am willing at this point to go so far as to say "experience," to use the classic vocabulary of phenomenology, which has been in other places attacked by Derrida and by postmodernists, in order to make this point. Deconstruction depends upon an experience of otherness.

What I think lies behind this kind of postmodernism of mine and, I would say, of Derrida's, is what I would call, to use a word that you've used in PCM, appeal, the appeal of the other, the call of the other. This thematics of call and responsibility is very, very important to Derrida, and, I think, separates Derrida from people like Deleuze who are expressedly critical of the notion of responsibility. My version of postmodernism is very interested in the idea of responsibility as a responsiveness to the call of the other.

Now, I do not believe that it is possible—and I believe that PCM suffers from this illusion—to offer apodictic justifications and legitimations of our political and ethical views. I think that those things are rather second-order elevations and abstractions which derive from an embodied, linguistic historical experience; and that is the experience of the excluded one.

What I would go back to, when pushed in the way that you're pushing me, is a hermeneutics of the other, the appeal issued by the oppressed, and ethics as responsiveness to that other. It is a little bit like Kant, like the notion of responding to an imperative. But the imperative can't be categorical; it's not purely rational and respect is not a feeling of pure reason.

MARSH: I wouldn't want to say that when I get to the political, which for me in the book is hermeneutical, that the arguments are apodictic in any strong sense. I would argue for qualified apodicticity for certain eidetic claims.

But I wonder whether we can't do better. For example, one of the differences between your account of reason in the university and the kind of account I would give is that it isn't the principle of reason as such that is problematic, but what I would call a bad reason that one can criticize in the light of a more adequate version of reason. What I would argue for is a more adequate conception of reason that is broader, more nuanced, more pluralistic. And the kind of pathology that you're talking about with reason as a function in the university is due to a large extent to the deformation of reason. Habermas's term for it would be technology and science as ideology, functioning in the service of class and group domination. The difference here between you and me, then, is between a use of the tradition of Marxism-critical theory in order to make a distinction between justified and unjustified exclusion, inadequate and adequate versions of rationality, and a method of deconstruction that cannot make such distinctions. There would be reasons within my tradition that one could give to make those distinctions. The kind of exclusion that workers suffer under capitalism, for example, can be described as illegitimate because capitalism violates its own criteria of equality and freedom. That's the kind of distinction I don't see you making sufficiently.

CAPUTO: I do expressly say that I am not questioning reason as such but reason whenever it erects itself into a principle. It's when it puts on princely airs, the airs of the *principium*, that I become nervous about it. I'm as interested in rationality as the next person. And I do think that radical hermeneutics is an attempt to find what I call a more sensible or a more reasonable idea of reason. To be reasonable with someone is to say, "Well now look, neither of us is God, neither of us has dropped from the sky." What we're interested in doing is to come up with a more sensible way of adjudicating our affairs.

Now, I think that in matters of ethics and politics, that always comes down in one way or another to dealing with the issues of suffering, oppression, exclusion, degradation, humiliation, matters of the other, matters of excluding the different. When you start rationalizing, that makes the university happy. If it pleases you, I suppose it's all right. But it is inflation. And inflation is always dangerous, not only in economics but also in philosophy. And I think that inflation is what you get out of Habermas, and that a good deal of the formulations in PCM are inflated. You don't have any more access to universal *a priori* principles than I do. Our mutual commitment to linguisticality, embodiment, and historicality cuts that off. All we can do is proceed as sensibly as we can, with the aim of minimizing the suffering we inflict on one another.

WESTPHAL: I wonder if there isn't another danger, and maybe Mark Yount's comment is helpful here. He says that what's in question is not Caputo's rationality but his account of it. What I don't find, Jack, in your attempt to give a politically viable defense of the other as excluded, is, if you like, a metaaccount of how this works. The kinds of things that Jim appeals to when he says, well look, Habermas and Rawls are willing to spell out procedures and say these are the kinds of things we ought to do, this is the way in which we construct arguments which would entitle us in a very limited way (no finality, no apodicticity, no immediacy, no absolute certainty) to speak in a tentative way, but nevertheless to put forward a claim that claims some significant level of justification. They give an account of how you get to that place and sort out who are the excluded people that should be included.

Now, when I look in your project for a metaaccount of how one gives justifications, what I find—and here it seems to me you and Derrida are together—is a lot of negative accounts about what you can't do, about what you can't have. Negative accounts that Jim and I, I think, for the most part would be fully in agreement with. No absolute, nothing drops from the sky, and so on. What I don't find is a positive account, a metaaccount of how it is that one could do a phenomenology of suffering that would entitle one to make some political judgments with some limited level of justification.

I'm not sure whether the reason I don't find that is because it is there and I don't see it, or because it's not there because you thought it's not necessary, or because you think it's much more important to emphasize the negative moments.

CAPUTO: It's not there. But it's not there because it seems to me that the preoccupation with that is precisely the Cartesianism and modernism and epistemologism of Jim's position. I'm very much taken by what Kuhn points out in *The Structure of Scientific Revolutions*, and that is the inability of scientists in the midst of scientific crises to set forth a metaaccount or procedures which would offer anything more than vacuous generalities in the way of guidelines which would resolve the crisis at hand. My notion of rationality is very, very Aristotelian. It's that moment of reason in Aristotle, the moment of intellection or simple understanding, where reason is at its best and at its most difficult, where it has to take a first cut into uncharted waters. One builds up a tradition and a community of practices by trial and error over a long period of time. Only afterwards can one provide a metaaccount. And that will last only until the next crisis.

I think of rationality as the ability to cope just at that point when our guidelines and principles are wavering. And so I am wary of this epistemological preoccupation with procedure and metaaccounts. I am more interested in forging ahead and doing the work of—let us say, for the sake of agreement here—some kind of postmodern ethics and politics.

MARSH: Where does one find out whether one is coping well? And I guess another question would be, aren't you running the risk, in talking that way, of emphasizing so much what I describe as the preconceptual moment of reason, the moment of questioning, that you don't give sufficient emphasis to the conceptual, methodological side of reason? Isn't the full story of reason the interaction or the interplay between question and answer, between the moment of coping when systems break down and method? Have you really answered, therefore, my argument—and that of Habermas and Rawls—that claims to be a third way between the Scylla of an absolute Cartesianism and the Charybdis of postmodernism that just leaves you with coping but with no methodology, no criteria for telling whether you are doing it well or not?

If we assume, as we did at the beginning of the discussion, that there isn't a solid, hard Cartesian ground, can't we, nonetheless, do a little bit better than just mere coping? Isn't there a third way?

WESTPHAL: I'm a little nervous about the notion that this methodological metareflection will tell me whether I'm doing well. That sounds to me a bit too reassuring, and it seems to me to not take seriously enough the notion that that metatheory is going to be utterly tentative and have all the complications that the original theory has.

So, the way I would prefer to put it is that the need for metareflection on what the criteria are that are being involved and what the procedures are and so forth, is not to provide me with reassurance, but to make clear to myself and to those whom I address what I mean when I say, "I think this is a better argument than this." So when we talk about it and debate, I will have laid out explicitly how I am proceeding, and that can be taken up in the conversation. When Gadamer says that the purpose of dialogue is to put your prejudices in question, among the prejudices that need to be put in question are the methodological, criteriological prejudices. And the only way, it seems to me, to get a good discussion of those is to render them explicit. That's why it seems to me important to have the kind of methodological metarereflection that I find in a Rawls, or in a Habermas, or for that matter in a Gadamer, and in a Ricoeur, but not, as you acknowledge, Jack, in the politics of radical hermeneutics. And I wonder if your way of trying to salvage the excluded other wouldn't be enhanced if you were willing to engage in that kind of reflection.

CAPUTO: First of all, let me say that I don't take the sorts of things that I say about ethics and politics to arise from caprice or personal opinion or personal circumstance . . .

WESTPHAL: That's why I quoted that thing from Yount. An issue here is not Caputo's rationality but his account of rationality.

CAPUTO: The non-capricious character of what I want to say I think comes back to this notion of a hermeneutics of the other, a hermeneutics of the excluded. The other acquires a particular pointedness, I think, in the case of suffering. I believe that there are ambiguities about suffering, and I believe that there are some kinds of sufferings that need to be endured, some kinds of sufferings that need to be stopped at once. Suffering is sometimes necessary and unavoidable, and one ought to discriminate among the kinds of sufferings and one would have to work that out with some care. But I think that ethical and political rationality takes a hard look at the kind of order that is in place, looks for the people who are groaning under the order of things and seeks remedies, seeks some better way. I think once someone has come up with something better, it would then, after the fact, be possible to formalize it. I think that is really all there is.

Look at Jim's example in PCM. At one point you talk about kidnapping, and your objection against kidnapping is that it violates the third or fourth condition of rationality or something like that. I must say that I read that with some amusement. What is the status of an observation like that? What is it doing other than explicating in some very formalistic and, pardon my saying so, rather artificial way something that everyone knows, whether there ever was a Habermas or a theory of the validity claims. All you are doing is formalizing something which in human experience is experienced as an abomination and as a violence.

MARSH: Well, I would to a certain extent agree with you, at least about the fact of formal analysis. I don't think the formalization was the whole story, but the question I was preoccupied with there was why do we experience such coercion as an abomination? What is it in our interaction with one another that makes us dislike kidnapping and experience that as degrading? And one of the ways I tried to get at that phenomenologically—and I think this is the point of Habermas's position too—is that operative implicitly, even when we are not explicitly reflecting on it, is this sense of the violation of truth, appropriateness, sincerity, comprehensibility.

Now in PCM that's accompanied with reflection on the level of content as well, the sense of domination, the sense of using the other. I would supplement Habermas's analysis with my own kind of content analysis coming out of a direct phenomenological description, too. I don't know whether that's precisely what you would describe yourself as doing—that is, trying to articulate phenomenologically an experience of suffering that distinguishes it from other kinds, that distinguishes illegitimate from legitimate suffering. That's precisely what I am trying to do here. What is it in the experience, in this case, of kidnapping that would cause us to condemn it? And part of the answer is the validity claims.

CAPUTO: So we both agree that what we need to do is to explicate an experience, an experience which in fact we both agree is one of violence.

MARSH: Yes.

CAPUTO: Now, one of my objections to PCM is that the explication you give is intellectualistic and it's at odds with your own commitment to phenomenology and to hermeneutics. What we're always treated to in PCM, in very critical moments, is a formalizing rationality, an abstract rationality which is, I think, very deeply Cartesian, Habermasian, and Lonerganian. I really think that I hear an awful lot of Lonerganian proceduralism here. And there's no unpacking of the experience. What would Merleau-Ponty have done with that? He would have unpacked in a very rich way and made phenomenologically manifest the violence of that situation. That seems to me the phenomenological procedure and the hermeneutic way, not this intellectualistic course that you've embarked upon.

WESTPHAL: Let me express a different framework for expressing that distinction. What you are doing now, Jack, is giving the metatheory that I was looking for, partly by saying that you don't like Marsh's metatheory. You find it too formal. It seems to me that you're saying that Marsh is a Kantian, that he is looking for these abstract universals. By contrast, you're a Humean, that you want to base ethics on a phenomenology of sympathy rather than a formalism of universality. The appeal you just made now to Merleau-Ponty, who would give a phenomenology of sympathy, seems to me to fall in the Humean tradition rather than in the Kantian tradition. I don't know how comfortable you are with that particular description of it. But I find it helpful to get to the place where we can say that one of the things we have to talk about is the relative merits and demerits of a Kantian metastrategy, very broadly speaking, over against a Humean metastrategy, in a context where everyone is agreed that neither of those is to be understood in a Cartesian way. We're not looking for apodicticity. We're not looking for certainty. We're not looking for self-transparency. But there is a clear difference beween moving toward a relatively abstract universality and, in a different manner of which Levinas would be another good example, appealing to a very concrete, almost intuitionist strategy. That seems to me an important difference between the two of you. And the question I pose to both of you is: Why should one have to choose between the two? Why shouldn't we try to develop an account of our rationality that would draw on both of those strategies and see to what degree we can integrate them and make them mutually corroborative?

MARSH: You're stealing my best lines from me, in a way, because that is precisely the point I was going to make. That's what I am trying to do in the book. There is, I think, an undoubted formal, intellectualistic dimension to PCM.

CAPUTO: Did we get that on the tape?

MARSH: I think that one of the things that's going on is an interaction between Lonergan's influence and phenomenology. But I would argue that the form is interacting with content, mediation with intuition. So I describe the cognitional structure of experience, understanding, and judgment that emerges in the book very concretely, in the descriptions

of perception, freedom, embodiment. I am very conscious of comple-
menting and supplementing these descriptions with hermeneutical retrieval and political critique. So in a Hegelian manner, I move to an
integration of form and content, universal and particular. And one of
the ways that integration comes out is in the sense of dialectical phenomenology itself as a method of moving back and forth between
universal and particular, the eidetic universal and hermeneutically en-
countered particular.

CAPUTO: Some of the best hermeneutics in this century have been destroyed by the Hegelianism of its practitioners. That's true of Ricoeur
and Gadamer, and I think it's also true of Marsh.

Let me start back at what Merold said about Hume versus Kant. First
of all, giving a certain metaaccount of what one does is always possible
after one does it. I don't think it is possible before you've done it,
which is why I think this kind of methodology is barren. Second, there
is something to saying that it's more Humean than Kantian. But I
would like to qualify that in two ways—first, by showing the sense in
which it is not Humean, and second, by showing the sense in which it
is Kantian.

It is not Humean inasmuch as phenomenology has been a very eloquent critique of Hume's conception of experience and perception.
Husserl and Merleau-Ponty have displaced Hume, I think, with a very
much more rich and ample account of what it is to have an experience.

WESTPHAL: But Hume, of course, disregards his theory of experience
when he does moral philosophy.

CAPUTO: Well, that's another sense then in which I am not a Humean at
all, because I don't see that there's any way out of accounts of experience when you talk about ethics and politics. This, I think, is an Aristotelian point; that is to say, practical reason is driven by affectivity and
empirical experience. And so rather than Hume, I would point to
people like Merleau-Ponty and Levinas as providing me with the
wherewithal to talk about the ethical.

Second, the sense in which it is Kantian. I'm not interested in Kant's
preoccupation with transcendental rationality or issues of legitimation
or justification, but I am very interested in the second version of the
categorical imperative. That is the element of Kant that I am most taken
with. That is, the notion of the respect for the other in the second ver-

sion of the categorical imperative. The first one seems to me utterly vacuous and formalistic, and I think has been amply refuted again and again. But the second version, which talks about treating the other as an end in itself, is one which, although it is vitiated by a preoccupation with the notion of the law and treating the other merely as an instance of the law, is, I think, a very rich idea for ethics. To tell you the truth I don't know what other ethical idea there is. Where else can we come back than to this notion of the other?

MARSH: There, it seems to me, you're doing something that I had picked up a bit on in the initial reflection on RH. And that is, to bail yourself out on the question of how we distinguish between legitimate and illegitimate marginalization. The problem arises from what both Merold and I were describing as the excessive formal character of Derrida. In a certain sense I am accusing you of being excessively formal, too, in a different way from me. On the other hand, at certain points you're deep in tradition; you try to find some supplementary content— a tradition, to which in RH you're pretty unkind in different ways. This use of tradition leads to the problem of both textual and performative inconsistency.

CAPUTO: There never is a moment when I take myself to be outside the influence of tradition. We began, the three of us, by agreeing on this notion of facticity, that is to say, the inextricable roots of philosophizing in the historical, linguistic tradition in which it finds itself. And so there's nothing else but the tradition. What else, other than tradition, can one turn to for a resource? Now, my relationship to the tradition is not one of trying to erase or destroy or negate it, but of loosening it up. What has always interested me, for example, in the religious tradition are precisely the marginalized figures in the religious tradition—like Meister Eckhart, one of the greatest but (until quite recently) most silenced voices of the late Middle Ages. So, my notion of the tradition is not that we can somehow ahistorically extricate ourselves from it, but rather that it is an enormously complex and complicated thing with all kinds of strands. There are things in the tradition that don't have the right to speak in the name of the tradition. There are many silenced voices and repressed subtraditions within the tradition that I call upon. When I call upon Kant, I call upon someone in my tradition. It is a fundamental mistake to think that deconstruction means leveling, erasing, destroying, and then moving beyond as if there were some pure break.

MARSH: I know we're here in the double gesture. But let me just read something to you from RH, page 185:

> Metaphysics launches an all-out assault upon things; it is a power play on the part of human conceptuality, and the critique of humanism was meant to counter its pretentiousness and will-to-power. The history of metaphysics is the story of so many attempts on the part of metaphysics to capture in its net, to see to it that things are subdued by the will-to-know, by power-knowledge.

Now there are a number of issues that arise from that kind of claim and that course throughout RH. One of them would be: Isn't the conception of other people as ends in themselves precisely coming out of this tradition? Therefore, to the extent that you're denying validity to the tradition as a whole, wouldn't that concept be just a power-play, an assault upon things? Yet on the other hand, at a certain point to complement an excessively formal analysis on the part of Derrida, you're deep in that tradition. You come up with human beings as ends in themselves. Isn't that textually and performatively inconsistent on your part?

CAPUTO: No. I don't know how to say it more plainly that neither I nor Derrida nor Heidegger, when he's somewhat carefully read, deny the tradition as a whole. What we deny is the pretension of the tradition, the pretensions of metaphysics, and the metaphysicizing of human experience, which speaks as if it has some kind of knowledge from on high. That's what I am out to get: the "meta" in metaphysics, insofar as that takes itself seriously. But the whole point of a deconstruction or *Destruktion* is precisely to loosen the thing up. Its point is affirmative. Its point is to make space, to liberate. The very idea of facticity makes it inconceivable that one would think that one could step outside this tradition. The idea is not to step outside this tradition. The idea is to see how inextricably complex the tradition is, and how many things are going on in the tradition. So when I go back to the second formulation of the categorical imperative, I don't think I am merely going back to a very Greek, Hellenic metaphysical idea. I think that I am going back to the Judaeo-Christian element in Kant which is metaphysicized by his metaphysics of the law. Then what I want to do is deconstruct out from that metaphysical formulation of the second version of the categorical imperative the phenomenological experience which animates it. That, I think, is Judaeo-Christian, Levinasian, and certainly goes to the heart of what I mean by ethics.

WESTPHAL: Jim, I think that one of the helpful ways of identifying what unites us emerges at the end of your talk at the Fordham exchange, where you talk about the prophetic, disturbing character of philosophy as we see it. It seems to me—and I've tried to develop this elsewhere—that one of the characteristics of prophetic speech is that it is ad hominem speech. And so it seems to me that if one wants to speak prophetically, one is always going to have to be doing just exactly what Jack said, that is, drawing from a tradition in order to critique that tradition. It's like an inside job. That being the case, I think it's clear, both in RH and in the "inside/outside" presentation that Jack made, that his position toward the tradition is not, as you keep insisting, rejectionist. That's your word. Rather, it's dialectical. And Derrida also says this: I couldn't help but draw on the tradition in order to critique the tradition.

Now, one of the things I am puzzled about, and maybe you can help to clarify it, is that you seem to have almost a need for everything to be neater than that. I'd almost say that the view you want to attribute to Jack is a Manichaean view: the tradition is either evil and to be rejected or not. In a couple of places in the Fordham exchange, when Jack sounded a little too reasonable, you expressed dismay that he was so tame. And that puzzles me. Why isn't it possible simply to take at face value the notion that part of what our embeddedness is is that no matter what we call ourselves we are always appealing to the tradition against itself, that is, if we are not just blandly echoing it. If we are trying to be critical at all, we are always appealing to the tradition against the tradition, our speech is always ad hominem speech, and therefore we are always affirming that which we're critiqueing. I don't see why that is a problem for you. It doesn't seem to me, in terms of your own methodological commitment, that it should be.

MARSH: Well, I think that there is a dialectical relationship to the tradition that is quite valid and it's the one that I try to take in my book, and I think the one that Hegel and Marx and Habermas take.

WESTPHAL: And I would say Derrida and Caputo. I'm puzzled as to why you can't just say yes.

MARSH: I think they do and they don't. There are places where it sounds like they do, but then there are other places where they don't. I'd like to explore that a bit.

First, there is the difference between a dialectical approach and a deconstructive approach. I think a dialectical approach tries to recognize in a much more explicit way than I see Jack doing here the positive elements or valid elements within the tradition. It describes the tradition as dialectically complex. A dialectical approach would not make this kind of wholesale negation, wholesale attack on metaphysics. It seems to me a second difference is that my dialectical critique of the tradition is one that would be finally friendly to metaphysics. That is, the point of it is to help metaphysics to do its job better, to loosen it up. In some places of your presentation, you, Jack, sounded like that. There is really no attempt to overcome metaphysics in the sense of Heidegger. We're trying to introduce a Socratic moment of questioning into metaphysics to loosen it up. That strikes me as valid to the extent that it is offered as a moment in your approach. The value then of deconstruction, third, would be, to the extent that there is that friendliness to metaphysics built into it, the introduction of that Socratic moment into an enterprise that isn't necessarily in all respects an all-out assault upon things, or, as you say on page 3 in what seems to me another wholesale negation, just an attempt to escape the flux.

WESTPHAL: I wonder if that way of putting it doesn't push it too much on the semantic level. If you're reading Levinas, for example, you find out that the good stuff is metaphysics and the bad stuff is ontology. That's how he chooses to use those terms, and you don't have to read very carefully, very far, before you're clear about that. And then you're not worried about it anymore. Nobody else uses the language quite that way.

It seems to me very clear that for Derrida and Caputo metaphysics is the name for the bad tendencies that they want to resist. That's how they use the term. And in so far as they explicitly acknowledge their drawing on the tradition to do this, that there are things within the tradition that they find helpful and useful, they couldn't possibly be just outside of it; they're always inside it in order to be outside of it and so forth. They are in some sense meeting your expectation of being friendly to metaphysics, as you use the term. Why should they be asked to use the term "metaphysics" in that way if they find it useful to use it as the name for the bad tendencies that they want to resist?

MARSH: Well, you're reformulating it in a way that I find acceptable, but I don't see either Jack or Derrida doing that. For example, within Derrida the wholesale critique that seems to be going on in the first 80 to 100 pages of *Grammatology*, the characterization of metaphysics as logocentric, seems to be at odds with such a distinction between good and bad tendencies within metaphysics. But if that's the way you want to move as a way of saving what Jack is trying to do in deconstruction, then I find that quite acceptable. I just don't see him doing that enough.

CAPUTO: Well, you can call the last three chapters of RH what you want. It is what it is. It is an attempt to do certain philosophical work which operates both inside and outside of the metaphysical tradition. I don't know what you want to call it. I know that some deconstructionists regard it as business as usual.

MARSH: Do they?

CAPUTO: They said, "Well, the result of RH must be, then, that we should now go on teaching the philosophy of science, ethics, and the philosophy of religion. And it is business as usual." I find myself sputtering to explain myself further. So I have the same reaction, on the opposite side, when you talk about a wholesale rejection of philosophy. I get it from both sides, which convinces me that I found a middle ground.

Merold is absolutely right. I use the word "metaphysics" rhetorically to nail just what it is about philosophy that makes me nervous. Just when philosophy gets to be transcendental, just when it gets to be pretentious, just when it thinks that it has nailed things down, that's just what I'm after. The word that I find, that Heidegger found, and that Derrida finds to describe that is metaphysics. You won't find me using "philosophy" that way. I don't think of myself as postphilosophical.

MARSH: You do, though, in places, talk like that. I'm not sure I can find the page where you identify metaphysics with philosophy.

CAPUTO: Well, if I ever said that I retract it. It's probably in the course of an exposition of Heidegger, who says it quite explicitly.

MARSH: One place is on page 3, end of the second paragraph: "For it does not trust (by "it" you mean radical hermeneutics) philosophy's native desire for the *Erleichterung*, its desire for presence . . .

CAPUTO: Yes, I don't trust that streak of philosophy. And I call that streak metaphysics. Now, if you want to have a very process-oriented idea of metaphysics so that every time you use the word metaphysics what you're going to mean is the fluidity, the mobility, the instability of things, then . . .

WESTPHAL: Or if you use the word metaphysics the way Levinas does.

CAPUTO: Yes, that's right. That's a very apt point Merold is making: Levinas's use of "metaphysics" and "ontology." What I like in Levinas is precisely what he calls "metaphysics," which he differentiates from "ontology." I think that he's taking this word "ontology" from Heidegger's critique of the history of ontology.

WESTPHAL: I think there may be another issue here. I'm not sure. But at one place, Jim, in your Fordham talk, if I remember correctly, you're asking Jack to sort out the good parts of the philosophical tradition from the bad parts, and say these are the parts I like and these are the parts I dislike. And we have sort of been talking along those lines the last few minutes. But that way of putting it makes me a little nervous — as if the parts are so discrete from each other. I suspect that part of what the deconstructionist project is up to, and the part of it that I am very sympathetic to, is the notion that the parts are not that discrete, and that the bad stuff has contaminated the good stuff. Just as persons aren't just good or evil, and they aren't just additions of good parts and bad parts, but rather, our virtues are contaminated by vices and our vices are mitigated by our virtues, and the two sort of blend together in ways that are not neatly separable, I suspect that part of the deconstructionist view of the tradition that I would want to affirm is this notion that you don't have clean lines there. And that where, in the Derridean-Heideggerian sense, metaphysics has entered in, it has in fact affected everything, so that precisely those tendencies on which one calls in trying to overcome these have been corrupted or domesticated or in some other way contaminated.

CAPUTO: I think that's a lovely way to describe precisely what Derrida means by undecidability. That is to say that there are no simple notions.

This word "contamination" that you're using I think is important. There are no uncontaminated ideas; there are no uncontaminated principles. That is an indictment of the facileness of dialectical thinking which thinks that the thesis and the antithesis, the good and the bad, can be brought into balance, taking this from this one and that from that one. That is terribly unphenomenological and insensitive to the ambiguity (a word with which you begin your PCM) of experience. I see a very close affinity between ambiguity and undecidability, and the connection is well expressed by speaking of contamination.

I think that we constantly find ourselves in a situation of undecidability. We're not sure what's going to happen if we do this or what's going to happen if we do that or what it is that we should do or what the situation is, and we've got to move ahead. That is like *phronesis*, because it's got to be a practical judgment, but it is in a sense more difficult than *phronesis* in its classical mode. This is what I call "metaphronesis" in RH, which always lacks an established framework. I think the situation of what we call postmodernity, just to use it descriptively and not normatively, is that we've lost a common framework, we've lost a common horizon, so the question has become not how but what to apply. We don't know what to apply; we don't know what paradigm to invoke. We're in a situation of deep consternation, deep ambiguity, and very profound undecidability. It is not with the aim of skepticism or escapism or apoliticism that I speak of undecidability. It is precisely in order to sharpen our hermeneutic sensitivity to the situation in which we have to decide that I want to insist upon undecidability.

MARSH: Two things. First of all, I don't want to sound or be interpreted as saying that you can distinguish between good and bad aspects in an atomistic way. I agree with your point. I think they are relational, that at best we are talking about aspects, internally related aspects, but what I am insisting on in a way that, I fancy, is more clear is those good aspects, admitting that they may be contaminated by other aspects.

Second, I think that what PCM is trying to do is something very similar to what Husserl is arguing in the *Crisis* and Habermas is arguing in *A Theory of Communicative Action* and that is to affirm a fundamental validity to the western philosophical project and to complete that project. And I don't see Jack doing that. And this may be another difference amid all the agreement between us. I see you as wanting to contest in a certain way, both phenomenologically and hermeneutically, the validity of that project, and thus to engage in wholesale illegitimate condemnations of the tradition.

Would you agree with that as a difference between us? Is that fair?

CAPUTO: No. I do not agree to that formulation of my position. I am not—and I insist on this—engaged in wholesale condemnation. That is the opposite of what I mean by undecidability. I look upon the western philosophical tradition as, first of all, my life's work and as the source of quite extensive and profound resources for dealing with the issues that confront us all. I also regard it with considerable distrust. I worry about it. And I really don't trust it. I don't like the way that it rationalizes and intellectualizes. I don't like its tendency to erase its own Judaeo-Christian element. The thing that I most dislike about Heidegger is the story that he tells, the history of philosophy that he makes up, that he contrives, which begins with the Greeks and ends with the Germans, and which treats the medieval Christian moment as what he calls a distortion of the primordial view. He ends up in the long run erasing the Judaeo-Christian, and that's not accidental to his politics. I think that there are other things going on besides Greek philosophy and the Greek philosophical tradition. I am extremely interested in the resources of religion to illuminate our existence and I want to incorporate them into my story. I think that philosophy tends to erase these elements.

You've been quoting at me, so I'm also going to quote at you. Here's something in which I think every trace of ambiguity, undecidability, and contamination has just simply been erased. This is intellectualism let loose, unconstrained. On page 252 (PCM): "What I have done in the book is to show how phenomenology, and by implication the whole of modern Western philosophy . . . [a totalizing gesture] . . . can and should lead to . . . [a teleological gesture] . . . dialectical phenomenology if . . . [philosophy can reach its telos, it can become Marsh, on a condition, if] . . . it is faithful to itself. . . . [So if it is purely authentic and faithful to itself, then it can become Marsh]. . . . Only with the final step into critical social theory does one achieve. . . . [Now here's what you get if philosophy becomes Marsh. If it achieves its telos, that is to say, becomes dialectical phenomenology, the paragraph begins by saying "What I have done in this book," so that if philosophy reaches this stage of this book, then here's the pay-off] . . . full rationality [that is to say, rationality which is not contaminated, which is not partial, which is not undecidable, which is not ambiguous. One does] . . . full justice to the phenomena . . . [so that the phenomena are no longer distorted or they have been completely saved. We've done "full justice" to the phenomena. There's no injustice to our account; the phenomena have been saved.] . . . and reconcile . . . [this dialectical balancing act] . . . theory and practice . . . [fantastic juxtaposition] . . . fully." It's been fully reconciled, this opposition! So we get full justice, full reconciliation. Philosophy becomes faithful to itself and becomes dialectical. Short of this move, that is, if we don't do this — and here is the warning from the judge — then we have not asked crucial questions and cannot explain crucial contradictions.

Now, I would say that that is western philosophical intellectualism going out of control. It has erased its debt, its expressed debt, to ambiguity, embodiment, linguisticality, historicality, finitude, intersubjectivity.

MARSH: Well, I think I say before or after that page that this is one possible story. I don't want to back away from that. Part of what I mean by "full," to be taken in the context of the whole book, is the interaction between objectivity and ambiguity. One of the relationships that has been examined . . .

CAPUTO: But when something has become fully rational, how is it any longer ambiguous?

MARSH: It's fully rational in the sense that one of the polarities that I tried to do justice to is the relationship between ambiguity and objectivity, between eidetic universality and the hermeneutical situation. So it's not fully rational in the sense of being totally certain, in the sense of there being no unexamined evidence, nothing implicit, etc.

The point I'd want to make, though, is that anytime anybody articulates a position, he is making a claim that it is in some sense true. It seems to me that RH is making such claims. That is, you're doing something that is actually closer to PCM as a gesture. There is the claim that your account of the tradition — moving from Nietzsche and Kierkegaard through Husserl, Heidegger, Gadamer to Derrida — is the best, truest account of the tradition. But with your gesture, as with mine, there is no denying that there is ambiguity; evidence is not fully uncovered at all.

But isn't there, in any kind of argument — since both our books are not just historical studies but attempts to say what is true — a presumptive universality built into the accounts? In some way you're saying that RH is a better account of the western tradition of philosophy than, say, the *Crisis*. I would argue that I am just being more honest in owning up to that.

CAPUTO: But the difference is that my account says there is no metaaccount and you can never say things like this. I'm telling a story and trying to make a point, and I hope that I am right. All that is true and I hope to be getting something right. But if I'm right then you can never go around talking about the secret longing of modern philosophy, you can never talk about full rationality, you can never make these inflated claims. So, my account is to stick it to accounts that claim to be *the* account. I would say that you're very fond of telling me about my performative contradictions. There's the performative contradiction of Marsh. All the talk about ambiguity and, by implication, a certain undecidability is systematically undone by an over-intellectualized, rationalistic account of the phenomena which then culminates in this sort of Habermasian, Lonerganian inflation. It is performatively at odds with its own commitment to ambiguity. Now I don't like this formalistic kind of objection, but I must say I can't resist it.

MARSH: What's sauce for the goose is sauce for the gander. Sure, make it. I agree. I go as far as I can with philosophy in terms of trying to get as full an account as possible. That move seems to me to be valid, with the proper qualifications on ''full'' and with what I just said about any account, even that of RH, that is in some sense saying that it is truer or more adequate than other accounts. And that's basically what I'm saying here.

CAPUTO: You're saying this is the teleological fulfilment of the longing of western philosophy. And that's the sort of systematic claim that philosophers make that I reject.

MARSH: Isn't that by implication what you're saying here?

CAPUTO: No.

MARSH: There's no way in which you want to defend your account as being a better and more adequate account than Husserl's?

CAPUTO: Sure, I would. But I would not say that this is the secret longing of modern philosophy, that it fulfills the telos of modern philosophy or western philosophy in general. I would never make such claims at all. What I would say is, look, here's a way of being sensible and reasonable about the issues that face us. What can I know? What should I do? And what can I hope for? Here is something which, I think, is pretty good, and I am willing to argue about it. That's all.

MARSH: But it is nonetheless superior to other accounts—to Heidegger's, to Husserl's, to Marsh's . . .

CAPUTO: I'd like to raise another question at this point and it has to do, Jim, with your discussion of eidetic phenomenology and your notion of essence in general. I have a sense that you've given a very overly essentialistic portrait, for example, of Merleau-Ponty, and that the implications of a radical phenomenology, of a phenomenology which is truly caught up in the facticity of the human situation, is such as to undo this notion of essence to a considerable extent. There is a radical, historical contingency to these essences or essential structures. My own approach to a radical hermeneutics is very much of a non-essentialistic sort. I am very much inclined to believe that we have to do not with essences but with certain contingent unities of meaning that hold together for a bit and then waver. Hence, there is a much more deeply contingent and linguistic structure in the things that you are calling essences.

MARSH: Well, I think that's maybe one of the differences between us, although I'd want to say right away that I wonder whether in yours or Derrida's position that's the way things like *différance*, metaphoricity, and others function. It seems to me that there's a necessity to those structures. But my own approach is to argue, in contrast to Husserl, that an eidetic claim and the essence discovered through an eidetic claim would be fallibilistic, would be qualified by the kind of claim that Merleau-Ponty makes about the rootedness of thought. What the reduction shows is the impossibility of a complete reduction. So there would be a putative universality to any essential claim. And part of what makes that putative is the present and future verification that would go on in the community of inquirers. I say toward the end, in the last chapter, that the hermeneutical qualifies and tests the eidetic also. That is, it seems to me there's a form of historical, hermeneutical inquiry into the particular gestalt—psychological and social—that always raises a possibility of certain essential claims themselves being historically rooted and therefore contingent and possibly untrue. The

Cartesianism that I reject, for example, is rooted in the historical structure of capitalism. But I do want to argue for other essential, and in a certain sense, non-contingent, necessary, universal claims. I would say those are in Merleau-Ponty too—the claim, for example, that all perception is perspectival, the foundedness of thought on perception, the motivated character of freedom.

CAPUTO: Well, I think that by the time of the *Visible and the Invisible*, that is greatly weakened. I really think they've lost their essentialistic meaning.

I think that there's a danger in taking notions that have sedimented in our language, that we've become used to, as if they were essences. If one takes into account the linguisticality of experience, then I would just be suspicious of using the notion of essence any longer. I don't think that it's a question of revisable essences or essences with a kind of tentative status. I think what you have instead are certain linguistic constellations, a deep part of our vocabulary. But this vocabulary can always undergo a Gestalt switch. It's not a question of essences; that's a piece of modernism.

WESTPHAL: Isn't it the case that the closest thing that Derrida has to a theory of essences, if I could put it that way, is his account of iterability. When he talks about iterability, he is giving his account of what other philosophers often discussed under the notion of essence. And it's what one might expect, a yes and a no. We couldn't function without iterability. If there were not a sense in which we could come back to the same, we'd be completely lost; whereas on the other hand you can never fully come back to the same. So the condition for the possibility of coherent speech is the condition for its impossibility at the same time.

That account, perhaps, is more closely expressed, Jack, by your notion of contingent unity of meaning. Even yours, Jim—putative universality, if you build into it the notion that universality is always something that is being strived for and never achieved, surely never possessed. If you really take seriously those kinds of qualifications and add them in, then it seems to me that the differnce that you're fond of drawing between the eidetic level of analysis and the hermeneutical level of analysis collapses and that everything that would come along under the heading of eidetic is going to be hermeneutical. It will be a specifically historical interpretation of historically generated structures in their historical contingency and transcience, not just temporality. I wonder if the language of essences is still helpful for talking about iterability under those conditions.

MARSH: I want to say that there are at least two differences between the eidetic and the hermeneutical. One of them is that the object of the hermeneutical is rooted in and part of particular psychological, social structures. So, for example, the development of a particular psyche or capitalism as a particular historical gestalt must be distinguished from the intention on the part of someone making an eidetic claim to reach something that is universally human, that is common to all human experience.

The second difference would be the kind of certainty which I think is present hermeneutically, a kind of certainty that is probable at best. Whereas with the kind of essential claims that I want to make—and this gets me into something problematic that I don't see any way to avoid—there is relative apodicticity. I've toyed and played around with that a lot, but part of what Husserl is describing in the experience of eidetic variation is this experience of running up against the impossibility of something being otherwise than what it is. So, for example, in thinking about particular examples of perceptual experience and considering actual and possible counter examples, we finally see that for something to be perception, it can't be otherwise than to be figure against the ground, presumptive, all of the things that Husserl and Merleau-Ponty want to ascribe to perception.

But the reason I say that such claims are apodictic is that I want to do justice to that experience that I think one has when one does eidetic variation. But I want to say it's relative because it is open to correction. It's open to the correction of the hermeneutical. It is open to other eidetic insights that might challenge it.

So there are at least those two differences between the hermeneutical and the eidetic that I wish to articulate.

CAPUTO: That is deeply Cartesian. I mean, the notion of the universal and common features, the notion of some kind of apodicticity, is precisely to resist the whole tendency of phenomenology and hermeneutics. There are many moments in this book that are not post-Cartesian at all, but simply Cartesian. Like the talk about the experience of the invariable that we can't vary away. It seems to me that the invariable means nothing more than running up against the limits of one's language and of one's historical horizon. That's all. Once you've conceded, as you do again and again, the linguisticality and historicality of experience, I don't see how it's possible to fend that off.

WESTPHAL: I am in agreement with what you, Jack, say about Husserlian essences. But isn't there a sense in which for all the talk about undecidability, it is also the case that we have already decided, that part of what it means to be situated is that in the midst of undecidability we have always already decided? And the relevance of that to this discussion is that in the midst of the contingency of any unities of meaning that we may invoke, isn't it always the case that we are always helping ourselves to what we take to be essences? That's to say that we always unavoidably end up thinking as if we had possession of some Platonic or Cartesian essences. That's part of our situatedness and we need to be reminded that they aren't what Plato and Husserl would tell us that they are, but that account is a fairly good description of what we always more or less immediately take ourselves to be in possession of and use as coinage.

CAPUTO: I think that that's very true. We are constantly making use of things that we ourselves have made questionable, deciding in the midst of undecidability, using something we know better than to trust too much.

WESTPHAL: It's as if we were using the currency of a government whose legitimacy and survival was seriously in question. And when we take it to the store, there's always the question of whether it's going to be accepted.

CAPUTO: That's exactly right. That's really a very good image. And so consequently it seems to me that the task of a good phenomenology, of a radical phenomenology, is to put us on the alert, to be a kind of whistleblower about these things rather than embracing them in what I think to be frankly the uncritical way that characterizes the tradition from Descartes to Husserl and which I don't see Jim resisting.

WESTPHAL: Why not both? Why not blow the whistle of undecidability while acknowledging the unavoidability of our use of the problematic currency? If we do both simultaneously our embrace of essences cannot be uncritical.

MARSH: As I think of the history of phenomenology, there are at least three stages: transcendental, existential, and hermeneutical. There's the

Husserlian transcendental stage, there's the stage of existential phenomenology which, I would argue, includes Merleau-Ponty, Heidegger, Ricoeur in *Voluntary and Involuntary*, Sartre in *Being and Nothingness*. Now it seems to me the theoretical, qualifying move vis-à-vis discussion of essence and the eidetic universalism occurs right there, and it seems to me what Merleau-Ponty does in the *Phenomenology of Perception* is to retain the notion of essence, but to put a qualifier on it. You can still make eidetic claims.

CAPUTO: I agree that he's still doing that in the *Phenomenology*. I don't think he's doing it in *Visible and Invisible*.

MARSH: Well, we'd have a difference of opinion on that. But it seems to me that when Ricoeur and Gadamer move to a hermeneutical stance, there's a focus on interpretation of particular historical gestalts.

I think what I am arguing for is actually in Ricoeur. What I wish to do is to make the retention of that eidetic moment, even with regard to the doing of hermeneutics, more explicit than it is in his work, to talk about a fruitful interaction or interplay between the two.

CAPUTO: Well, that's the dialectical balancing act that I reject throughout.

WESTPHAL: But why?

CAPUTO: Because you can't have it both ways. It won't come to grips with the radicality that's imposed upon one by conceding linguistic and historical facticity.

WESTPHAL: Is it not more faithful to Derrida, who emphasizes the unavoidable character of iterability, to say, look, here is the contingent unity of meaning I am working with. I am going to try to spell out, to articulate, to make as clear as possible what the unity of meaning is that I am working with, and say at the same time the things that I need to say to keep me from lapsing, as I am always inclined under ordinary circumstances to do, if you like, into the natural attitude. I always lapse into some sort of Platonic-Cartesian interpretation of that. But I remind myself precisely of the impossibility of doing that and still recognize the value of identifying the "essences" that I am working with at any given time.

MARSH: Isn't that what in fact *différance*, metaphoricity, and what you referred to earlier as the quasi-transcendental are?

CAPUTO: Well, that's the self-referential argument. *Différance* must be something, it must be itself, or else . . .

MARSH: I'm not saying that now. I'm just arguing that it seems to me that they function transcendentally, don't they, in Derrida?

CAPUTO: As it were. Almost. A quasi-transcendental.

WESTPHAL: But Derrida gives an account of dissemination and then he says, "Now I'd better move on lest somebody think this is an essence; I'll give an account of supplementarity or I'll give an account of *différance.*" The way in which he keeps reminding himself that these essences, that these unities of meaning that he uses, can't have the Cartesian and pre-Cartesian meaning that he wants to deny them, is by moving on quickly from one to another and never staying very long with any one of them. That seems to me a perfectly good Derridean strategy: giving an account of the conceptual unities he is using and then doing something to keep those from encrusting and becoming the sort of thing that he's worried about . . .

CAPUTO: Yes, I think that's a fair point. But we want to distinguish between the unity or identity which *différance* is—or supplement, etc.; all of these are key words—and the unity which *différance* produces. Now, there are two different problems. Derrida, deconstruction, radical hermeneutics want to take account of the relative unity one has to have in experience; otherwise it will just simply degenerate into chaos. We have a discourse and an account of relative unities which avoids the language of essence in order precisely to avoid self-delusion. We talk about meanings in terms of production of relatively stable unities of meaning which are always being produced by *différance*, rather than the reproducing of some kind of independent essence, a pre-existent essence. An essence is not something out there, it is not something self-identical which then gets expressed. It is, on the contrary, to the extent it is anything at all, something that's generated by the historical deployment of *différance*, the use of language. We generate unities. That's what language is. And it has only that much unity.

So it is a produced unity, a constituted unity. Then there's the second question of the status of *différance* itself. Is that an identity? Well, it's a quasi-identity. It's not either identity or difference because it's a condition of possibility of these things. But it is not a self-identical condition of possibility because it is that condition which says that you'll never get self-identical meaning. So it's a quasi-condition of possibility which is not subject to the same questions and demands and requirements as the effects that it produces.

Now, all of that, it seems to me, is a much more vigilant discourse than the discourse of PCM, which, I think, on this point has not broken with Descartes. It is faithful to Descartes and early Husserl.

MARSH: Well, the ''post-Cartesian'' in PCM takes off from and retains the legitimate elements in Descartes. But I really wonder whether essence by any other name is not as sweet. And it seems to me that when you make the qualifications that I made about essence and admit the putativeness of it as open to further correction, there's an approximation in the way I use it and the way Derrida uses *différance*. I mean, again—referring to our talk about the agreement between us, both of us rejecting any kind of naïve immediacy, naïve unity, unmediated unity—I could say as well of my notion of essence that we're not talking about something that's simply itself but something that's always mediated by its other.

CAPUTO: But the goal of an overarching universal essence remains in place.

MARSH: I don't see that . . .

CAPUTO: The difference between the eidetic and the hermeneutic as you just spelled it out is that the eidetic ought to have a universal commonness and ought to have a relative apodicticity. So it is being defined teleologically in terms of universality and necessity. That's the regulative idea behind it which remains in place for you.

MARSH: I agree. But the question would be: What's wrong with that regulative idea?

CAPUTO: It's undone by any commitment to language, history, ambiguity. And the experience of a certain common unity, I think, is in terms of experiential adequacy, better accounted for by a theory of *différance*.

MARSH: But that has also, does it not, a universality to it. I mean, that's an attempt to get at what is universally present.

CAPUTO: Well, in a way that I described it before—as a quasi-universal. It is a quasi-universal because it is something that undoes the idea of universality in the very process of explaining how you can have universals. It performs both those operations at once.

WESTPHAL: Maybe one way to get at the question that's haunting me as to whether there is really a disagreement between you other than one of semantics and emphasis (there clearly is a semantic difference and there clearly is a difference of emphasis) is to ask what you see as the implications of this for the conception of the self. Do you see what you say about universality having a very direct bearing about what we can say about the nature of the self?

MARSH: Well, wouldn't you have to talk about the kind of use you make of Kant, for example, that we talked about before—the second formulation of the categorical imperative? And the extent to which you use that to distinguish between human suffering and animal suffering? Isn't there a universality that's built into the use of Kant and the notion of the person as an end in herself?

So it seems to me that once you move to the ethical, if you're going to generate any kind of ethics out of deconstruction or postmodernism, PCM or critical modernism is much more honest in owning up to the universality necessary to make those kinds of ethical, political claims. Aren't you affirming, implicitly at least, a universality in that use of Kant?

CAPUTO: The notion of the self as an end in itself, it seems to me, is a notion of respect toward the other in the other's almost unlimited capacity for novelty, newness, difference, and ability to surprise me. It's precisely the ideas of universality and necessity which become oppressive. The ethical for me has to do with the radically singular, not the universal. I mean, universals become defining and normative and people are told that they are unnatural and abnormal because they don't abide by these conceptions of universality and normality. In the notion of the end in itself, the universal is not a universal, but what is always singular. That is to say, the one thing that I want to say about others is that it is always true that they are different.

MARSH: But they're different in a way that is common across the board. We distinguish them from an animal, dog, Fido. It seems to me that there is a universality that you have to own up to there. Certainly with the use of Kant.

CAPUTO: I think that thinking in those terms is "humanistic" in a bad sense. Derrida is right about Heidegger on this point. Heidegger thinks in those terms himself. And even though there is an overcoming of metaphysics in Heidegger, he retains the most classical metaphysical idea that man is a rational animal and that animals are just brutes. There is an insensitivity to animal life in Heidegger. And it's part of Derrida's critique of Heidegger's humanism that he is so preoccupied with the human species. I would rather think of a spectrum of life and to think of forms of life that are quite close to us. So when I raised the question of suffering, that also is a question of animal suffering for me, too.

WESTPHAL: In suggesting that the boundary between other animals and humans is not an absolute boundary from an ethical point of view, you are emphasizing the contingency and the ambiguity of the universality. But aren't you at the same time, both in theory and in practice, making a distinction between animals and humans, so that, as I was suggesting a few moments ago, you have working for you what Marsh calls an essence, a contingent unity of meaning, one that you don't take to be absolute and final and clean, but nevertheless one that is operative.

CAPUTO: One would have to be mad to think that there's *no* difference between human beings and animals. It would be bizarre to suggest that. What I'm saying is that this way of casting it, this classical language of a difference of essence, makes me very nervous. And it also has resulted in extraordinary brutality toward animals and a willingness to cause them the most excruciating torment, because it serves our purposes, because they are just simply separated by an abyss, the abyss of essence. Why not think of them as simply other forms of life which are not as complicated as ours, but which also deserve respect. This notion of essence, it seems to me, is a dangerous one.

MARSH: I think it can be misused. I think a lot of the cruelty and brutality that you are talking about is the effect of a misuse of essence. But it seems to me that ethically and politically you come up against questions where finally you do have to make choices that presume some kind of difference.

CAPUTO: Sure. I just don't want to describe it in the language of essence.

MARSH: This is putting Merold's point in a different way; aren't you, equivalently, doing that? Aren't you making use of the notion without calling it that? If you have, for example, a community of people who are starving and what can help them out is killing a few deers, cows, or pigs, there would be no hesitation on our part to doing that, would there? And it seems to me right at that point you're saying, implying, and making use of a notion implying that human beings as human have something that differentiates them from animals.

CAPUTO: I think that there's a difference between human beings and animals. I distrust the language of essence in order to describe it. So we come back to this question of descriptive adequacy.

MARSH: What language would you use to describe it?

CAPUTO: Different forms of life.

MARSH: Doesn't that imply the notion of essence?

CAPUTO: No. There are other and better ways to describe our experience than that. The idea of essence has no a priori claim on me. I don't feel committed to preserve it, so that my position then is described as having a modified notion of essence or weakened notion of essence. I find the notion questionable. And I think the momentum of phenomenology is to undo the idea of essence, *pace* Husserl. And I think that's exactly what happens to the major phenomenologists. I think it's what happens to Merleau-Ponty and to Heidegger, that they start out with this Husserlian attachment to the idea, but the idea drops out.

I am very interested in the idea of the self. But I don't want to have to talk about the self in terms of the essence of humanity or a notion of human nature, because I think those ideas produce at least as much trouble these days.

WESTPHAL: Even if we don't talk about the self in terms of human nature or the essence of humanity, aren't we going to have pretty much the same conversation we've just had when we talk about the identity of the self? We're going to be in a conversation one side of which is emphasizing the absolute indispensability of self-identity to any notion of selfhood, and the other side of which is going to be nervous about the implications that have been drawn from that and is going to be talking about the dangers of the language of identity, and it's going to be talking about how we have to keep reminding ourselves of difference.

And I wonder if we're not going to have the same deadlock over the nature of the self that we have over the notion of essence.

CAPUTO: I think we will. I mean, I think that the notion of the self is an idea of our own identity and unity. But when we become more attentive to it phenomenologically, what we discover is a tremendous complexity, multiplicity, many selves—the self that we have with one another, the self we have with our children or spouse, the self we have in different contexts. There are many selves, which are various functions of the circumstances in which we find ourselves, the change of ourselves in the course of time. It seems to me that there is a plurality of selves. It's not that we don't have a self, but that we have too many selves.

I like to think of the self in terms of the notion of mystery, that is to say, the unplumbability of the self. The very notion of *the* self, Nietzsche says, is a grammatical fiction, a necessity of grammar.

WESTPHAL: So you want to say that each of us ends up saying, My name is legion, and there is no possibility of reducing that to a unity. I can't imagine, Jim, that you would want to deny that. And yet I have a feeling that you're not comfortable with that emphasis.

MARSH: What I want to say, I think, is that you can talk about different levels of selfhood. On the level of conscious experience itself, there would be the unity of the self experienced over the course of the process of knowing, moving from an experience to understanding to judgment to decision. But it seems to me, more to Jack's point, that in the very saying that there's a legion of selves in me, there's someone saying that, and that saying in itself functions as a conscious unifying of that legion. The legion that I unify—I'm saying that about myself—is different from the legion that someone else articulates. What I do in Chapter 7 of PCM is to try to talk about the experience of the recovery of self. I think we do all have an experience on a conscious level of being inauthentic, of trying to move from inauthenticity to authenticity, so that there is a movement from sheer dispersion, alienation from self, which Heidegger articulated in *Being and Time*, to unity of self. But it seems to me both in psychoanalytic experience and then in experience of critical theory, there is an experience of recovering aspects or parts of the self that are split off from myself. That's really the definition of psychoanalytic cure that Freud talks about. Where id was, there ego shall be.

So my own position I think would imply, yes, there is legion. But legion is not and doesn't have to be the final word. There's also the experience of recovery of self, of moving from multiplicity to unity in multiplicity.

WESTPHAL: One of the ways in which you want to make that point is to say that whenever someone says my name is legion, someone is saying that and that is a unifying act.

MARSH: Yes. The very saying itself is a unifying act.

WESTPHAL: But isn't it the case that it's always an open question "who" it is who is saying that?

CAPUTO: Or what it is, or whether it has but one source.

WESTPHAL: What comes to my mind here is Derrida's attribution of Searle's reply in "Signature Event Context" to Sarl in order to suggest in a rather playful and not entirely charitable way that that was written by a committee, written by many voices, not all of whom are Searle's. Isn't there something universal about that? Isn't there a sense that whenever I speak it is always somewhat of a question as to which of the many voices within me is the one that's saying that?

MARSH: Sure. But they're still within you, in a sense, aren't they? For example, if you're interacting with someone in a love relationship and you fall in love with a woman and the question arises, "Am I doing this for the reasons I think I am or is it part of the Oedipal formation from my own past that's unconsciously feeding into the relationship?" Psychoanalysis can help us to recover and to distinguish between those two voices. But they're still, it seems to me, voices that are resident in me. It's my body, it's my psyche, my consciousness which can integrate them in reflection of psychoanalytic theory.

CAPUTO: But Nietzsche has a pitiless critique of this as a structure of grammar. In every case what you appeal to is a grammatical structure, a grammar which is cast in the language of the first person. Now one could imagine alternative grammars in which the language of the first person isn't there. There are anthropological studies in which the first person plays a very diminished role. Who is saying it . . . or what's saying it? "What" desires, what does it want?

Here is a way to encapsulate the difference between these two approaches to language. I think that we're united in our commitment to the notion of diversity, plurality, and historicity, etc. But your approach to it is always dialectical, that is to say, you always situate diversity within an overarching unity.

MARSH: Or try to.

CAPUTO: You always end up doing that! There's never any sign of defeat here. I think this is true also of Ricoeur. I would say that the real voice behind this approach is Paul Ricoeur. There are many voices in the book; PCM is rich in the plurality of voices that it brings together. But there's one that has a kind of organizing power in the book, and that is the voice of Paul Ricoeur. And that's a Hegelian voice because it is a voice that is willing to permit unity to be diversified. There's always difference in unity, but this always ends up being unity in difference. There's a deep overarching unity. There's always recovery after alienation, there's always return after exile. That dialectical moment is precisely what I challenge. That, it seems to me, is a metaphysical presupposition in just the sense of metaphysics that I question. That is, it is an unquestioned presupposition. I don't mean that you don't argue for unity, that you don't point to unity, or give evidence for unity. But there is an unquestioned presupposition that underneath diversity, there is an overarching, reconciling structure of unity. Whereas I think that I am more prepared, and this is the thrust of the movement of post-Husserlian philosophy, more willing to look into the abyss and to recognize that the arguments against unity don't go away. They can't be re-incorporated, re-inscribed, circumscribed, contained, and have a fence built around them. There is a kind of unhealable wound in the self, in us . . . in the "we" who cannot say we, as Derrida would sometimes put it, I who cannot say I. And there's no way around that. There's only a certain dealing with it or facing up to it or coping with it. And that's not nihilism but it's not Hegelianism.

WESTPHAL: That challenge to Ricoeur seems to me to have a dogmatic character to it, because what Ricoeur is saying is not what metaphysics has traditionally said, namely, that there is that underlying unity and I have got it and I can put it on display, I can demonstrate it, I possess it and control it. He is making a statement as an act of faith, as a declaration of faith with all of the very self-conscious awareness of the limitations of that. He does not possess it, he cannot demonstrate it. He nevertheless believes that there is an underlying unity that precisely he can never possess nor demonstrate. Kierkegaard is another example. If Ricoeur's faith or Kierkegaard's faith is going to be lumped together with Husserlian-Cartesian-Platonic metaphysics, then it seems to me that deconstruction ends up as a kind of dogmatic unbelief on the opposite side, contrary to its claims. If deconstruction is not going to be dogmatic, then it seems to me it ought to recognize that kind of faith for the kind of thing it is, which is neither metaphysics in your sense of the term nor surely deconstruction, although it comes accompanied, in the case of both Ricoeur and Kierkegaard, by lots of deconstructive moves to remind faith that it is not knowledge. It seems to me that that kind of faith needs to be left with its integrity, aware of the fact that it is over 70,000 fathoms of water, that it is without foundation, but not dismissed as being indistinguishable from Husserl.

CAPUTO: That's a fair point. First of all, I think that Ricoeur does try to demonstrate that unity again and again. That is, he repeatedly, when faced with the question of difference, integrates it into unity—in all of his books, from the very beginning, from the discussion of *Freedom and Nature* all the way through the book on narrative. Over and over again we see the same gesture in which he begins with an idea from the tradition, a classical metaphysical idea, points out its naïveté in its classical form, and then incorporates into it a negative moment. The very best example of this is the discussion of the masters of suspicion. But to treat or talk about suspicion as suspicion is to situate it in a context of trust, and then to reintegrate it with a regained innocence or a no longer quite innocent faith, so that we move from a kind of innocent faith to suspicion to a modern faith. He does this repeatedly. He not only has a certain faith in unity, but he constantly thinks he can demonstrate it. The book on Freud is an attempt to balance out the claims of Hegel and Freud. He is repeatedly balancing out claims, opposing claims. Take his discussion of the "masters of suspicion." I want to say, look, Freud, Marx, and Nietzsche have pointed to a wound in our consciousness which can't be healed. What's valuable about these writers is that they show that we are wounded in some unhealable way. And to "believe" or to press forward on any front is always to press forward with the sense of radical insecurity. I don't know whether I believe in God or not, as I say in RH. Not if I am radically honest. If the believer is honest, he or she doesn't know whether he or she believes in God—because of all the things we've been saying, that the self is a corporation, not an individual; because of the unconscious, and so on. It seems to me that the important thing is to deal with the wounding of consciousness and not to hasten on in this dialectical manner to the reconciliation. That's ultimately where you and I differ.

MARSH: It certainly is at least part of our basic disagreement. I think I would agree with Merold's characterization of Ricoeur as also characterizing what I'm doing. I think there is a faith and reconciliation which is continually being tested, continually trying to reflectively justify itself as a faith. It doesn't seem to me that there's anything particularly vicious about that if one rejects as I do the idea about Cartesian presuppositionlessness. It becomes as it were a presupposition which is unfolded and justified progressively over the course of the work.

CAPUTO: It doesn't read as faith. It reads as a highpowered intellectualistic refutation of all disagreement. Every person, every philosopher, every position that is disputed in PCM is reduced to absurdity. Every position is self-referentially inconsistent except the one which proclaims itself the telos of western philosophy. You use that argument on every major figure in the book. There are always only two choices: one is capriciously affirmed and therefore can be capriciously denied (that argument must be in the book twenty times) and then the alternative that is set up as the only one that is rational. So there is no hesitancy to speak in the name of rationality and of a relatively strong theory of rationality. There is a *reductio ad absurdum* of everybody else. And there's the apocalyptic claim at the end. There is very little faith there. It is a strongly intellectualistic, metaphysical argument.

WESTPHAL: I'd like to defend faith here in Marsh, and so for the purpose of discussion, let us concede that everything you said is true. Isn't it still the case and isn't it in fact entailed by your opening discussion in "Inside/Outside" that part of what it means to be situated is that, willy-nilly, we have already trusted? We already come with a faith of one sort or another. What reflection does is to remind us of the need to be suspicious of our trust. And that is an important move. Trust must not be naïve, trust mustn't be uncritical, trust must be introduced to suspicion. But isn't it just as important to say to highly reflective folks like ourselves that suspicion needs to be reminded, not just of the need for trust, but of the absolute inescapability of trust? So, to say in response to Ricoeur that he has situated suspicion in the context of trust doesn't seem to me to be an objection. It seems to me that the strength of Ricoeur's is that he says with equal conviction that trust must be put through the fires of suspicion. Suspicion can never become something that cuts us off from trust. Not only couldn't we do that if we tried, but just to the degree that we did succeed in moving along that line we would turn ourselves into cynics. And I don't take it that that's a project of any of us—to be cynics.

MARSH: Here you're talking about a kind of dialectical reconciliation, it seems to me, of trust and suspicion.

WESTPHAL: That's my view of a really radical hermeneutics.

MARSH: The necessity of a revival of the Gadamerian moment, the necessity of that moment of trust, that moment of reception, both to tradition but I think also to the nascent rationality and the desire for intelligibility that we experience within us. That is nourished by the metaphysical tradition.

CAPUTO: It is precisely a metaphysical presupposition to think that trust and suspicion work nicely together in a balanced way. That's just what I find unjustified.

WESTPHAL: That's not what I'm suggesting. I think it creates a ferocious tension to try to hold to both of them with equal seriousness. I don't think they balance and harmonize easily. I think that's what generates fear and trembling.

CAPUTO: Well, even if it is difficult to harmonize trust and suspicion, the effect of what Ricoeur does, and I think the effect of PCM, is to balance them every time—Freud and Hegel balance, Husserl and Merleau-Ponty balance—there's an endless juxtaposing of opposites. It is driven by a deep sense of unity, a metaphysics of unity which will always be unshaken by diversity. It has predetermined diversity as a "moment" within a larger totality.

WESTPHAL: If you're Kierkegaard, then your deepest commitment, your deepest faith is that there is an underlying unity. And if you're Nietzsche, your deepest faith is that there is not. And it seems to me that a philosophical methodology ought not to be one that a priori excludes the possibility of either Kierkegaard or Nietzsche, but one that ought to leave open the possibility of both of them so that they can join in the discussion.

CAPUTO: But you must be careful. The moment you say that the two ought to be able to work together and that a good philosophy is one that has both, then you've effectively negated Nietzsche. I would rather say, as I do in RH, that we are caught in an irresoluble oscillation between Nietzsche and the religious, e.g., Augustine or Kierkegaard.

MARSH: But supposing you try to argue this way: you try to show, as Gadamer does, for example, with regard to Husserl on the whole business of the Enlightenment, that the very attempt to be free of presuppositions itself depends upon presuppositions, and derives from the Enlightenment. The very attempt at a total suspicion presumes, in its actual operation, the reliance on and trust in tradition. That would be a way, it seems to me, of moving beyond the naïve trust in reconciliation to actually showing how it functions in the very act of suspicion itself. In order to distrust, I have to trust. So the two function together in the actual act of suspicion. If that argument works, that's a way of taking it beyond a mere faith in the possibility of reconciliation.

# The Cheating of Cratylus
## (*Genitivus Subjectivus*)

### *Merold Westphal*

THERE ARE REASONS, I think, why one does not get from this conversation between conflicting philosophical positions, as one does from the so-called Derrida-Gadamer and Derrida-Searle encounters,[1] the impression of ships passing in the night. Mutual respect and a willingness to be questioned as well as to question are foremost among them. And yet there is one respect in which this conversation is like those less-than-successful attempts at dialogue. Gadamer and Searle (Austin, Sarl), while acknowledging the impossibility of ever eliminating finitude, ambiguity, and infelicity from our attempts to come to mutual understanding or to perform speech acts successfully, focus their attention on what is possible, on the ways in which we do come to understand what we previously misunderstood and in which we do manage to make promises and even to get married. Derrida, by contrast, focuses his attention on what is not possible, on the structural barriers to communication, or, to put it differently, on language as a barrier rather than as a bridge.[2]

In a strikingly similar way, Marsh is the optimist and Caputo the pessimist in the conversation before us. One sees the glass half full, the other half empty. If we ask them what percentage of the glass has water in it, they will give the same answer: 50%. This could mislead us into thinking that they are perhaps in substantive agreement, the apparent differences being, perhaps, merely semantic or rhetorical. But one does not have to be very sophisticated in Gestalt psychology to know that the perception of a glass half full is very different from the perception of a glass half empty. What is merely apparent is the formal agreement expressed in the answer, 50%. It is not difficult to find any number of philosophical theses to which both Marsh and Caputo subscribe. What is difficult is to determine how much real agreement this represents and what the differences are that get obscured by it.

In his Fordham symposium paper (*supra*, 95–96) Marsh suggests that these differences may arise from different levels of analysis, one operating at the level of subjective spirit, the other at the level of objective spirit. I find it more helpful to see the difference between an optimism that emphasizes what can be accomplished intellectually and a pessimism that emphasizes what cannot as rooted in different fears. Just as Hegel was afraid that the center wouldn't hold and that social and intellectual anarchy would prevail, while Kierkegaard, confident that the center could take care of itself, was afraid that an artificial and idolatrous center was holding all too well, so Marsh, the Hegelian in this scenario, and Caputo, the Kierkegaardian, philosophize out of different fears.

If there should prove to be good reason to take both fears seriously, that will be good reason to take both Marsh and Caputo seriously rather than simply choosing between them. I hope that that reference to Hegel and Kierkegaard as well as the optimist/pessimist paradigm will make it clear that by taking them both seriously I don't mean anything like a happy, harmonious, dialectical synthesis, but rather a dialectical juggling or tightrope walk full of difficulty and danger. To use a theological metaphor, it is like trying to take the biblical themes of creation and fall with equal seriousness in reflecting on the question, Who am I? or Who are we? The one affirms the goodness of being human, the other the corruption. No one who has ever felt the need to take Hegel and Kierkegaard or creation and the fall with equal seriousness will minimize the challenge such a task entails.

But what are the different fears? What leads Caputo, for example, having affirmed that we are always, inevitably and simultaneously, both inside and outside of truth, to focus so singlemindedly on the outside part of the story? He affirms the inside part so clearly in his Fordham symposium paper that Marsh finds him disturbingly reasonable, but his tone of voice in doing so is one of making a concession that cannot be denied but that invokes no passion. It is the voice of duty that says we are inside the truth, but the voice of inclination says we are outside. Caputo's heart is clearly in the outside, negative part of the story. Far from wanting to reassure anyone, he wants to ''take some of the steam out of the rhetoric'' with which philosophy comforts (*supra*,

52) and to "just keep breaking the bad news to metaphysics, for which a lot of people want to kill the messenger" (*supra*, 53).

Surprisingly, perhaps especially to Caputo, the fear that motivates this one-sided emphasis bears the face of Foucault, and one might say that it is Foucault who drives him to Derrida. Caputo tells us that he sides with Galileo against Bellarmine (*supra*, 55), and he suspects "that we are being followed by the police of truth" (*supra*, 62). Sensitive to the linkage between knowledge and power, his version of Lord Acton's adage is that absolute knowledge poses the same danger as absolute power, namely, absolute corruption. Like Arthur Schlesinger, Jr., he suspects that "the damage done to humanity by the relativist is far less than the damage done by the absolutist."[3] His fear is that a reason too confident of itself will be, as it has been in the past, the instrument of both social oppression and psychological repression, the domination of others and the deception of oneself. His fascination with the flux is grounded in his suspicion of the solid and stable. From his fear grows a touch of the cynicism of Diogenes and more than a touch of the iconoclasm of Kierkegaard.

By contrast Marsh is less afraid of the absolute than of the arbitrary. He agrees with postmodernism that foundationalism in all its various forms is dead, that facticity and situation, linguisticality and historicality, finitude and mediation all make the Platonic-Cartesian-Husserlian ideal of rationality a pipe dream. For him, if not for Husserl, the dream of philosophy as rigorous science is over. But he fears that if that idea is repudiated too vigorously the result will be an intellectual anarchy in which all beliefs and pratices are equally unjustified and thus equally justified. In response to a postmodernism he sees (or better, needs to see) as throwing the baby out with the bath, he calls for a chastened rationality that will abandon the pathologies of modernity as betrayals of reason, thereby preserving reason in its true integrity. Without some place for evidence and justification, he fears that intellectual and social life will revert to a Hobbesian war of all against all. Like Caputo he is afraid of oppressive power that masquerades as reason (hence his hermeneutic of suspicion), but what he fears most (at least in his methodological reflections, if not in his concrete social theory) is not the power of arrogant reason but the arrogance of power unconstrained by reason.

Given his fear of reified rationality, it is not surprising that Caputo sees Marsh's formal agreement with him about being outside as well as

inside truth, about the finitude and facticity of reason, as merely a concession that cannot be avoided, ultimately submerged in a project of
damage control (*supra*, 3), seeking to save as much of the modern ideal
of rationality as possible. Given his fear of arbitrariness and decisionism, it is not surprising that Marsh sees Caputo's formal agreement
with him about being inside as well as outside truth and his repudiation
of the view that each belief or practice is as good as any other as merely
a concession that cannot be avoided, ultimately submerged in an unre-
lenting guerilla war on all forms of evidential rationality, even finitist
versions. It is no accident that of the three whom Ricoeur identifies as
masters of suspicion, Marsh (like Habermas) identifies with the two
whose project retains the scientific ideal, Marx and Freud, while
Caputo (like Derrida) identifies with Nietzsche, the one who most vigorously challenges that ideal.

    To repeat: suppose they are both right. Suppose neither fear is neu-
rotic but is a sober response to the realities of today's world. Suppose
even that Weber and MacIntyre, among others, are right in suggesting
that the two fears belong together inasmuch as irrationalism, subjec-
tivism, emotivism, decisionism, and such are but the convex side of a
curve whose concave side is Enlightened Reason. In that case neither
would turn out to be adequately fearful, and each would lose by win-
ning the debate with the other. For that which is truly to be feared
would remain essentially undetected as long as opinion oscillates between two opposite but equally partial diagnoses of the crisis of modernity. I do not pretend to know just what it would mean to take
Caputo and Marsh with equal seriousness. I only share my suspicion
that it is to such a task, far more difficult than the task to which either
of them calls us, that the dialogue between them may be calling us.
With that confession I turn to specific issues in the debate.

One of the most central, if not always to date the most fruitful, of these
issues is the question of performative contradiction or self-referential
inconsistency. The argument that postmodernism cannot state its position without undercutting itself is important both because Marsh loves
it so much and because Caputo hates it so much. Caputo does not hate
it because he finds it a telling and damaging argument against him but
because he finds it to be entirely beside the point. In corresponding
with me he recently praised an essay on postmodernism, one rather

sharply critical of his own work, because "it drops the stuff about performative contradiction and actually addresses the issues."

The question of self-referential inconsistency has a place in philosophy going back to the Megarian discussion of the liar paradox.[4] Suppose I say to you, "What I am saying right now is false." Paradoxically, it seems that if my statement is true, then it is false, and if it is false, then it is true. The problem arises most inconveniently in formal theories that are intended to be free of ambiguity and paradox. It becomes necessary for set theoreticians to decide what to do with the set that includes all and only those sets that are not members of themselves. If that set is not a member of itself, then, by definition, it is a member of itself, but this can only be because it is not a member of itself. Gödel's theorem, to the effect that any formal system rich enough to embody the first-order functional calculus could be complete only at the price of being inconsistent, in the sense of generating both 'p' and 'not-p' as theorems, is a similarly awkward appearance of the self-reference problem.[5]

The issue came to be more than a curiosity of paradox lovers or a curse of formalists in the debate over logical positivism. The positivist criterion of cognitive meaning was that only formally tautological (analytic) propositions or empirically verifiable (falsifiable, testable) propositions can be cognitively meaningful and thus candidates for truth or falsity. The problem was that this claim itself is neither analytic-tautological nor empirically verifiable and thus, like the metaphysics and the ethics the positivists were glad to ban from the kingdom of the cognitive, not so much false as not even a proper candidate for being true. Because positivism presented itself as a scientific philosophy this was an extremely awkward result, and it was a major defeat when Carl Hempel had to acknowledge that the principle was a proposal and not a truth.[6] The performative contradiction in positivism had been the assertion as true of a proposition whose content precluded the possibility of its being true.

Because postmodernism scarcely presents itself either as a formal system or as a scientific philosophy, it is not self-evident that the issue will turn out the same in this context. That is what we have to explore. Sometimes Marsh formulates this charge as the claim that postmodernism (Caputo included) contradicts itself when it uses argument to transcend argument and when it appeals to the tradition of western rationality in order to reject that tradition (*supra*, 18–21). All this gets us is the consistent denial from Caputo that this is what he is up to. Speaking for himself and Derrida, he calls the view that "we want to overcome rationality, overcome argument, overcome evidence, overcome tradition and throw these things out . . . simply a gross misrepresentation, a caricature of positions that have been very carefully nuanced by Derrida from the very start" (*supra*, 115). Or again, "We are not out to deny truth but to take some of the steam out of the rhetoric about life, world, the things themselves, living presence, being, pure truth and all of the other lures and comforts of philosophy. . . . The denial of the transcendental signified is not the denial of reference but of reference without difference. . . . This is not a denial of truth, but a more merciless account of what truth is like" (*supra*, 52–54).

I find these denials convincing. I do not find either Derrida or Caputo seeking to eliminate argument and evidence as such, but rather, challenging claims traditionally made (at times only implicitly) about argument and evidence that they find untenable. Similarly, I do not find them adopting a rejectionist posture toward tradition. Both are fully candid that the resources they draw upon in criticizing the tradition are drawn from the tradition itself. Thus far, in my judgment, the charge of performative contradiction simply fails to make contact.

But Marsh has another formulation of the charge, more interesting if for no other reason than that it rests on a direct quotation from Caputo. In his reflection on *Radical Hermeneutics* Marsh quotes, not once but three times (*supra*, 17–21), these eight words from Caputo's own mouth: "The truth is that there is no truth" (RH 156). Now isn't this a proposition about which it can be said that if it is true, then it is not true?

First we need to notice that these words are not from Caputo's own mouth, but from his pen, his typewriter, his word-processor. Even if speech has all the features of full presence that Derrida wishes to deny it, we are dealing here with writing and all of its ambiguity. Caputo might say that if we read carefully we will find that he is merely summarizing Derrida's summary of Nietzsche. But neither Caputo nor Derrida are likely to disown these words and slough them off on Nietzsche. Both are too committed to hearing Nietzsche and learning from him, not just from his easy sayings but especially from his hard sayings. So I assume that Caputo will own these words as his own. It is true that he does not quote them three times in a row, as Marsh does, but he does not run from them, either. What can he say to the charge that this doctrine of truth is self-referentially inconsistent?

First, he can (and does) make an *ad hominem* point against Marsh. "If I have counted right, every single position which differs from *Post-Cartesian Meditations* is declared self-referentially inconsistent and hence logically absurd. . . . Marsh's very sensible commitement to hermeneutics at this juncture in the text has been preceded by a series of chapters in which every position which differs from PCM is reduced to absurdity—quite literally—by being shown to be in performative contradiction with itself." This "excessive intellectualism," derived from Lonergan and Habermas, is incompatible with the hermeneutical flexibility and phenomenological ambiguity that Marsh also professes. "(Were it not for the fact that I consider the argument from performative contradiction to be for the most part completely barren, I would suggest that PCM is in performative contradiction with its own commitment to phenomenological ambiguity and hermeneutic plurality)" (*supra*, 6–10). This "it takes one to know one" argument is not without its point, but it distracts from the important question—one which might be formulated this way: What does it mean to say, "The truth is that there is no truth"? This formulation is not as innocent as it seems, for it almost inevitably reads as the equivalent of the following: What truth is proposed by the proposition "The truth is that there is no truth."? A more neutral formulation would be, What is the point of saying, "The truth is that there is no truth"? For that leaves open the possibility that the point is something other than proposing a truth, at least in the ordinary sense.

This is not an idle possibility. No doubt a major source of Derrida's interest in speech act theory is the realization that speech acts can be viewed in terms of their illocutionary and perlocutionary force, that the constative (truth asserting) function does not have the dominance in ordinary language that it has in the discourse of philosophical logicians. I cite two examples from Derrida. First, with reference to the opening essay in his (non)dialogue with speech act theory, "Signature Event Context," which he refers to as *Sec*, he writes, "Does the principle purpose of *Sec* consist in being *true*? In appearing true? In stating the truth? And what if *Sec* were *doing something else*?"[7] Second, in his essay on Freud's *Beyond the Pleasure Principle*, Derrida tries to discover a kind of writing that is unlike scientific or philosophical writing without being exactly fictional or literary. Since its purpose is not to transform its hypothesis into a thesis, it can be called "non-positional" or "a-thetic" discourse. Because of "the essential impossibility of holding onto any thesis within it," in such writing "The impossibility of a resting point pulls the textual performance along into a singular drifting."[8] I shall not pretend that there is anything self-evident about the notion of "a-thetic" discourse, or even that its meaning emerges very clearly from the entire essay devoted to exploring it. I only remind us all that for Derrida, writing that may have the appearances of "serious," "theoretical" writing can be concerned with something other than asserting true propositions. The question now is if this clue is of any help in making sense of Caputo's (Derrida's, Nietzsche's) famous eight words, "The truth is that there is no truth."

Here we are on the verge of a second response to the charge that postmodernism has a doctrine of truth whose assertion is a performative contradiction, namely that we are not dealing here with a doctrine (thesis, position) at all. In trying to make sense of this possibility I want to draw on the Austinian sense of a speech act's perlocutionary force. Suppose I say "The window is open." Normally, in making this statement I mean to assert a fact, to utter a true proposition. This is the constative or locutionary force of my speech act. But under certain circumstances I may also, and even primarily, be doing something else: suggesting, requesting, or even commanding someone to close the window. The illocutionary force of "The window is open" is more perspicuously expressed as "Close the window." Viewed in this way as a performative speech act, the question raised by my utterance is whether or not it is appropriate for me to address such a suggestion, request, or command to that person in these circumstances. The question of truth takes a decidedly peripheral role.

Finally, we can distinguish the act I perform (directly) in the very act of saying, "The window is open," such as making a suggestion or giving a command, from the act I perform (indirectly) by means of saying it. If my speech act is taken to be felicitous in its illocutionary force, the person to whom it is addressed just may close the window. It is the perlocutionary force of my speech act to which we refer when we say that by saying "The window is open" I got the window closed. Here the evaluative question about my speech act concerns effectiveness rather than appropriateness, and once again the question of propositional truth all but vanishes. There is no necessary connection between the perlocutionary force of a speech act and the propositional truth it asserts or implies. I may succeed in getting someone killed by saying "He betrayed us," even when, far from having betrayed us, he has become a threat to me because he is about to reveal my betrayal of the group in question.

What, then, might Caputo (Derrida, Nietzsche) get done by saying "The truth is that there is no truth"? Some kind of link between deconstruction and Gödel's theory has often been noted. Derrida himself introduces such a reference in connection with his notion of undecidability.[9] Gasché appeals to it in arguing that "undecidability" is preferable to "ambiguity" in speaking of Derrida's project.[10] And Caputo himself uses it in seeking to explain the notion of "quasi-transcendentals," the conditions of possibility which are at the same time conditions of impossibility (*supra*, 111–12). It is as if he, along with Derrida and Nietzsche, want to say of language, experience, writing, and textuality in general, what Gödel says of certain formal systems. The problem is this. Gödel can simply come out and assert that the systems in question have certain properties, for he has available to him the metalanguage not afflicted by the same radical undecidability. Or so he thinks. But what if one wants to challenge precisely that assumption? Then the language in which one asserts the deep incoherence or undecidability of the language as such is itself part of the language about which this is asserted. Precisely because of its sensitivity to problems of self-reference, postmodernism finds itself in need of saying what it cannot quite say. To resort to the language of ambiguity, it cannot unambiguously assert the ambiguity of all discourse.

What can it do? It can resort to what Kierkegaard calls indirect communication, using language in such a way as to evoke an awareness of what cannot be directly communicated because of a discrepancy between the *Sache* and the conditions of direct communication. It can try to show what cannot quite be said and it will look for things to say that will have that kind of perlocutionary force. One candidate for the desired kind of "statement" will be "The truth is that there is no truth." In this situation the paradoxical nature of such a claim, far from being its self-destruction, will be its genius, its point, its "message." It will exhibit the human condition as being inside/outside of truth. To read it and understand will be less a matter of observation than of self-discovery. Rather than a judgment that we compare to our experience, it will be a judgment that produces a certain kind of deeply disturbing and disorienting experience. The argument from performative contradiction is a defense against this experience. Worse yet, by insisting and assuming that postmodernism must have a doctrine of truth that is free of ambiguity and undecidability, it begs the issue that is at stake.

There are several other models that can serve as hermeneutical keys for reading "the truth is that there is not truth." Each, in its own way, I believe, points to the primacy of the perlocutionary force of the speech act in question. One is the Kantian antinomies. Postmodernism seeks to express the deeply antinomic character of reason, and this is not in terms of thesis and antithesis, since both thesis and antithesis lay claim to the Logos, but rather in terms of a thetic and a-thetic world. The conditions of the possibility of meaning, truth, experience, iterability, and so forth are at the same time the conditions of their impossibility. But if reason is antinomic in this way, how is that to be said? To say so, as a thesis, would indeed be to lapse into performative contradiction. It needs to be said in a way that gives equal justice to the thetic and a-thetic. Aha! Why not say, "The truth is that there is no truth"? Perhaps if this is read in the proper way it will generate the insight that cannot quite be stated as a thesis. In such a context, insisting that postmodernism choose between reason as *Grund* and unreason as *Abgrund* is like responding to the Kantian antinomies by repeating the argument for the thesis.

A second model, already hinted at in the reference to showing what cannot be said, is the Wittgensteinian ladder whose use and disposal as unusable are almost, but not quite, simultaneous.[11] Like the cartoon characters who remain suspended in mid-air until they notice that nothing is supporting them, the trick is to use the ladder to get somewhere before noticing that it is not quite adequate for that purpose. Both Marsh and Yount refer to this ladder, Marsh critically, Yount sympathetically. The latter way of taking this image depends entirely upon focusing on the perlocutionary force of the language that plays the ladder role and, in particular, on its ability to show what can't quite be said.[12] The difference between the Wittgenstein of the *Tractatus* and the logical positivists is that the latter thought, at first, that they were saying what could be said, while he knew better: "anyone who understands me eventually recognizes [my propositions] as nonsensical, when he has used them—as steps—to climb beyond them. (He must, so to speak, throw away the ladder once he has climbed up it.)" (6.54.)

What enables Wittgenstein to talk this way is his sense of *das Mystische*. "There are, indeed, things that cannot be put into words. They *make themselves manifest*. They are what is mystical" (6.522).

Thus it should come as no surprise that Yount mentions Buddhism in almost the same breath (stroke of the pen, typewriter, word-processor) as he mentions Wittgenstein's ladder (*supra*, 112) or that Caputo should pick up the reference favorably and add Meister Eckhart's name (*supra*, 118). Is Derrida a Buddhist? Michelfelder and Palmer suggest as much when they write, "The *Sache* of philosophical thinking for Derrida is not something that language can put into words."[13] Fred Dallmayr suggests the same when he writes of Derridean undecidability, "This abyssal structure is finally presented as the vortex in which being and non-being become interchangeable and where all distinctions or decidable issues vanish into nothingness."[14] After all, do not Derrida's lengthy writings have the character of the sophisticated Buddhist logic from the Abhidharmika to the Madhyamika in which language is used to show the limits of language?[15] And does not "The truth is that there is no truth" function enough like a koan to make Yount's reference specifically to Zen Buddhism quite appropriate?

Underlying the Buddhist philosophy of language, of course, is a metaphysics of radical flux. Yount suggests that 'flux' is the central metaphor of RH (*supra*, 24); and Caputo, for whom metaphysics is normally the name for what he distrusts in philosophy, acknowledges that it would be different "if you want to have a very process-oriented idea of metaphysics so that every time you use the word metaphysics what you're going to mean is the fluidity, the mobility, the instability of things" (*supra*, 140).

Elsewhere, he evokes Heraclitus. "We write from below, slowly and painfully forging unities of meanings from the flow of signifiers (or of internal time consciousness, or of perceptual multiplicity, or of the data of the senses, or of the Heraclitean stream), unities about which we keep our fingers crossed that they will get us through the day. We are always inside and outside the truth, unable to stop the rush of truth, yet unable too to hold truth in place and stop its rushing off. Inside/outside" (*supra*, 52).

It begins to look as if "The truth is that there is no truth" might be passed off as a long-lost fragment of the famous finger-wiggling Cratylus. In Book IV of the *Metaphysics*, Aristotle speaks of those for whom "to seek truth would be to pursue flying game." They held such views because "they saw that all this world of nature is in movement, and that about that which changes, no true statement can be made; at least, regarding that which everywhere in every respect is changing nothing could truly be affirmed. It was this belief that blossomed into the most extreme of the views mentioned above, that of the professed Heracliteans, such as was held by Cratylus, who finally did not think it right to say anything but only moved his finger, and criticized Heraclitus for saying that it is impossible to step twice into the same river; for *he* thought one could not do it even once" (1009b 37–1010a14).

Two observations about Cratylus, foremost of the pre-Socratic post-modernists. In the course of them, my attempt at a charitable reading of "The truth that there is no truth" will turn around, and I will be defending Marsh's critical modernism against Caputo's postmodern-ism. But this will be a qualification, not a retraction of the defense I have so far given of Caputo as Cratylus.

The first thing to notice about Cratylus is that he cheats. He does not think it right to say anything but only to move one's finger. Does any-one think that Aristotle and antiquity guessed this from watching his finger? They knew the point of his pointing only because of the words, spoken or written, in which he explained the futility of words by crit-icizing Heraclitus and by affirming that we cannot step into the same river even once. It is the genius of postmodernism to give us, if the term may be pardoned, a transcendental deduction of Cratylus, an account of why such speech, which makes its perlocutionary point by undermining itself, is necessary. My attempted defense of postmodern-ism against the charge of performative contradiction is a defense of Cratylus' cheating.

But it is not clear that postmodernism is willing to stay with its patron saint to the bitter end. To signify the inability of language to capture the flux, Cratylus is compelled to use language that has such stability that, millennia later, we can still read it. In spite of the seman-tic snow, rain, heat, and night to which signifiers and postal couriers are prey, somehow the message has gotten through, and nothing the postmodernists can say can convince us that we have not, with help from them, among others, reached a significant measure of under-standing with Cratylus.

Postmodernism doesn't exactly deny this. After all, doesn't Caputo put us inside as well as outside of truth? Similarly, in exploring the non-positional, a-thetic discourse he hopes to find in *Beyond the Plea-sure Principle*, Derrida writes, "In a word, from the first session on, it had been stated that a 'logic' of the *beyond*, or rather of the *step beyond*

[*pas au-delà*], would come to overflow the logic of the position: without substituting itself for this logic, and above all without being
opposed to it. . . . ''[16] In other words, unless only finger wiggling is
radical and all discourse reduces itself to the onto-theo-logo-centric
complacency of Judge William and his ideological cronies from Plato
to Husserl, the thetic has its rights along with the a-thetic, and the truth
is (also) that there is truth.

To repeat: postmodernism is careful never to deny this. My complaint is that it is equally careful to avoid talking about how it is possible. We might say that what's in question is not postmodernism's
rationality but its account of it. While both Derrida and Caputo place
us inside as well as outside of truth, their account is so one-sidedly
about the outside that its claim to radicality is placed seriously in
doubt. Unless, as at times they seem to suppose, but are careful never
to assert, radicality consists in being one-sided. They have tons to say
about how Cratylus (who's he?) could never communicate with us
(who are we?). But what is their account of how we do manage to understand him? They do not like Gadamer's account of how we are in the
truth. Fine. I have my problems with Gadamer, too. But at least he has
an account. Where is theirs? We have already noted the fear that leads
to this pessimism, to an account of thought and discourse so devoted to
the negative as to be all but completely silent about the positive.
Derrida has been so badly spooked by Husserl that he has never recovered, and Caputo is so wary of comfortable Hegelian synthesis as to be
frightened away from anything that could be accused of being balanced. But suppose there is a balance pole whose ends are named not
synthesis and comfort but danger and tension, the kind a tightrope
walker uses while crossing Niagara Falls. And suppose radicality consists in this kind of balance. Then postmodernism, for all its valuable
insights and in spite of all its flaunted wickedness, remains tame indeed, domesticated by the fear that keeps it from developing both sides
of what it promises, an account of what it means to be inside/outside
truth. Has Yount touched on something central when, for all of
Caputo's enthusiasm for Kierkegaard, he finds more confidence and
authority than fear and trembling in RH (*supra*, 38–41)?

Cratylus cheats. This puts him in the company of all the mystics of
the *via negativa* who talk endlessly about silence as the only home of
truth and who write endlessly about the futility of words. It puts him
especially in the company of the Buddhists, who ground their specific

*via negativa* in a metaphysics of radical flux. The second observation
to be made about Cratylus is that while the Buddhists and other mystics
have placed their negativism in the service of the religious life, there is
nothing to indicate that this is true of him. This question of service is
the question of ideology. From Marx, Nietzsche, and Freud, and before
them, from Bacon, Hume, and Schopenhauer, we have learned to ask
about any theory, not only what does it say and is it true? but also, why
does it say that and what is its function? What interests lead to its adop-
tion? What lifestyle is legitimated by this language game?

For any number of reasons it makes less sense to ask this question
about Cratylus than about his recent reincarnations. Needless to say,
the question has already been put, usually in the form echoing Kierkegaard's question: Does the System have an ethics? Can postmodernism
have a viable ethics? In the very passage, cited above, where Fred
Dallmayr suggests, in effect, the link between Derridean undecidability and Buddhism, he expresses a widespread suspicion. "It is (at the
latest) at this juncture that Derrida's key notion of 'difference' shades
over into a celebration of indifference, nonengagement and indecision."[17] Is not postmodernism's critique of logocentrism so formal as
a theory of language as to be compatible with virtually all ethical (or
unethical) postures?[18]

Caputo's response to this charge, it seems to me, is twofold. First,
he points to the substance of an ethics or politics he more or less shares
with Derrida, noting both that RH "takes the side of the marginalized
and excluded" (*supra*, 58) and that Derrida shares with Levinas a concern for the radically other. Marsh appreciates this fact about them, but
rightly finds it an unsatisfactory response to the question. For what is at
issue is not whether Derrida and Caputo, as persons, have a politics
that passes Marsh's muster. The question is whether their hermeneutics
(a term at least Caputo is willing to use) provides any support for such
a politics. To paraphrase an earlier point, the question is not about their
politics but about their account of their politics.

It is not enough to take the side of the "marginalized and excluded," since in the United States today, neo-Nazis fall into that category and it is clear that Caputo does not mean his book to provide
them with aid and comfort. So something must be said about how to
identify which excluded groups to champion and how much selection is
to be justified. Furthermore, it is not enough to talk about Derrida's
appreciation of Levinas, for while he may personally be sympathetic

with what we might call the Jewish ethical personalism of *Totality and Infinity* and may express that sympathy in some of his specifically political writings, it is not clear that there is any link between the critique of logocentrism that has come to be known as deconstruction and this sympathy, other than an entirely formal concern for otherness. Indeed, it might well be argued that the radically other with which deconstruction is concerned is radically other than the radically other with which Levinas is concerned, and the fact that both make Husserl a major target does not mean that they are shooting at the same enemy. For the other with *which* deconstruction has been concerned is the categoreally subordinate term in the many dualisms of classical metaphysics—for example, writing as distinguished from speech—while the Other with *whom* Levinas is concerned is the human sister or brother whom I encounter face to face. And I have yet to see how the rehabilitation of writing helps to undermine the defacing of the poor and the powerless, the stranger, the widow, and the orphan. The fact that Derrida and Caputo are not personally neutral on these latter matters does nothing to establish that the theory of undecidability is not neutral in a way that encourages indifference, as Dallmayr suggests, or even worse, the cynicism in which indifference becomes incorrigible.

Happily, this is not the end of the matter. Caputo recognizes the force of such objections and offers an account of his politics in the sense of telling us how it might be justified. Naturally, he is skittish lest talk of justification be read to mean something foundationalist. So his answer to the question whether he can justify his political choices is, "Yes and No: I am on the slash" (*supra*, 58).

Marsh is eager to give the Yes part, but Caputo insists on giving the No part first. In doing so he lapses into a dogmatism that sits poorly with (is in performative contradiction with?) his basic position. He wants to deny that we can find "cosmic support for our beliefs," and he writes, "The cosmos does not know we are here. That merciless fact Nietzsche calls the great cosmic stupidity. I do not know of any response to that objection. I have certainly never heard any from Husserl or Habermas, Marx or Marsh. 'Racism is unjust,' the critical modernist shouts from the surface of the little star, his hands cupped to his mouth. The cosmos yawns and draws another breath" (*supra*, 58). In direct violation of Caputo's own claims to ontological neutrality, radical hermeneutics here becomes indistinguishable from dogmatic atheism. For if there is a God of the kind that Augustine, Aquinas,

Kierkegaard, and Lonergan, for all their differences, point to, then surely the cosmos does not yawn at all in the presence of racism or the opposition thereto.

The tendency of Caputo's methodological negativism to lapse into ontological dogmatism seeps through, I fear, in another passage from Caputo's Fordham lecture.[19] He writes,"There is no *truth of truth*. . . . Truth is groundless. . . . Es gibt: that's all. . . . [W]e keep on responding to the claims which truth makes upon us, but when we ask about the source of the origin of that claim, about *what* is calling in the call which makes a claim upon us, we get no answer" (*supra*, 47–48).

No doubt it would be possible to give charitable interpretations in which, for example, "We get no answer" would turn out to mean "We get no unambiguous, definitive, knock-down answer" and "The cosmos yawns" would turn out to mean "Whether or not the cosmos cares about racism remains open for debate." But if this is what is meant, why not say so in the first place? These statements, unlike "The truth is that there is no truth," do not have the paradoxical character that makes them almost necessary vehicles for saying what can't quite be said. What is defensible in these cases can be said quite clearly, and since Caputo is capable of clear prose, the question arises why he speaks in these ways after claiming that deconstruction is ontologically neutral. I think the answer is that he is so frightened of metaphysical dogmatism that he falls, at times, into an equal but opposite dogmatism. If I understand him correctly, he wants to deny that we have any absolute guarantees, but he gives the wrong reasons why we don't. He would be more faithful to his own methodological commitments if instead of saying, in effect, with Nietzsche, There is no God, he were to say with Kierkegaard, We are not God.

Having explained the No answer to the question of justifying his ethical preferences, Caputo turns to the Yes part. In doing so he completes his reply to the challenge of showing that postmodernism has a viable ethics and does not foster the politics of indifference or even cynicism. The complete form of that answer is 1) to point to the substantive ethics/politics he shares with Derrida and 2) to show that it is not arbitrary but is as well-founded as such matters can be. He claims that some choices are better than others and that his politics is better than, for example, that of the neo-Nazis, for two reasons. First, with reference to Marsh, "the two of us are very much embedded in a Judeo-Christian facticity and we are both taken (impressed, persuaded) by the systematic preference that Jesus showed for the poor, the lepers, the lame, the prostitutes, the Samaritans, the tax collectors, and the prodigal son—in short the marginalized" (*supra*, 59). In addition, "we are both impressed by western ideas about democracy and justice" (*supra*, 59). Second, it is possible to point to what it is that calls to us from the marginalized by developing a phenomenology of suffering, and this has been done to a considerable degree in RH.

I see two difficulties with this reply. First, assuming that the traditions and the phenomenology to which Caputo appeals do the work he calls upon them to do, what has that to do with postmodernism, or more specifically, with the charge that the theory of undecidability is politically neutral at best and at worst tends to encourage indifference, even cynicism? The fact that certain postmodernists, even such distinguished ones as Derrida and Caputo, are not indifferent, cannot identify for us the political content, if any, of deconstruction. Surely, being impressed with Jesus is not part of the theory of undecidability.

Second, it is far from clear that the traditions and the phenomenology to which Caputo appeals can do the work he calls upon them to do. His own critique of Gadamer's uncritical appeal to tradition makes it clear that the facticity of being embedded in tradition is not self-justifying. After all, marginalization itself is a tradition, or to be more precise, is rooted in a variety of traditions, including the Christian tradition. I would not for a moment deny the presence in Christian traditions of a powerful impetus against racism of all kinds. Indeed, like Marsh and Caputo, I want to see American Christians revitalize that part of their faith. But surely Caputo would not deny that much of the worst anti-Semitism the world has seen has been perpetuated in the name of Jesus and that the racist elements of slavery and colonial imperialism have regularly drawn upon Christian tradition for their support. It is not enough to appeal to tradition to justify one's preferences. It is necessary to appeal to the right aspects of the right traditions. If postmodernism is going to reduce our relation to tradition to sheer facticity and reject the challenge of modernity to justify our use of it, then it does constitute a giant step backward and is the moral peril many have seen it to be.

Exactly the same point can be made with respect to the phenomenology of suffering. I like Caputo's treatment of suffering and so does Marsh. So what? There is also Nietzsche's phenomenology of altruism as weakness and decadence. Phenomenologies are like traditions. One

can find one for virtually any ideological purpose. Modernity has challenged us not simply to develop phenomenologies that will justify our
ethico-political preferences, but to develop an ideology critique that
will put our phenomenologies and our traditions to the test.

I do not see Caputo rejecting modernity's challenge on this point
outright. But neither do I see him taking it very seriously. And I do see
him rejecting out of hand the Habermasian element in PCM, which I
take to be one of Marsh's most important contributions.

It has to be admitted that there is a rhetorical barrier in the way of
comprehension. Just as Marsh has a hard time getting through "The
truth is that there is no truth" to what Caputo is trying to say, so
Caputo has a hard time getting through an amazingly purple passage of
philosophical prose which he is just as fond of quoting.[20] Marsh makes
triumphalist claims here that are quite contrary to the argument of his
book. Still, it is a momentary lapse and we would do better to focus on
the argument of the book. But instead of seeing the Habermasian element as an important part of the reason why Marsh is not entitled to
such a glorious climax, Caputo regularly identifies Habermas with the
abandonment of hermeneutical humility and with the exaggerated pretensions of a not yet post-Cartesian reason (*supra*, 7–8, 129–30). He is
as allergic to Habermas as Marsh is to Derrida—in both cases a pity.

What Marsh offers us through the Habermasian element in his book
is an attempted reply, missing in Caputo, to modernity's challenge to
be critical about our traditions, our phenomenologies, and so forth. In
addition to a theory of society, Habermas gives us a theory of reason.
It is anything but a foundationalist, triumphalist account, for its norm,
the ideal speech situation, is self-consciously counterfactual, a regulative ideal whose function is to guide rather than to guarantee, to provide a basis for critique, not comfort.[21] This is a theory of rationality
that takes our hermeneutical finitude seriously.

Can this position be reconciled with a postmodern posture? No. At
least not if reconciliation connotes harmony. It is one thing for Cratylus
to cheat. It is quite another to ask him to show that the lifeworld sup-
ported by his discourse is rational, even if only in certain specified
ways vis-a-vis certain specific alternatives. To accept such a task would
be, for Cratylus, to capitulate and become someone else.

But what about us? I think we can afford simply to be Cratylus with
Caputo, as little as we can afford simply to dismiss him, with Marsh,
as incoherent. The logical possibility of taking both Caputo and Marsh

seriously lies in the fact that the Habermasian account of reason, which precludes any final decisions, is formally compatible with the Derridean theme of undecidability. The psychological possibility of giving them equal import in our philosophical reflection lies in a willingness to live in the tension between poles that will not simply reconcile.

NOTES

1. These are to be found, respectively, in *Dialogue and Deconstruction: The Gadamer-Derrida Encounter*, and Derrida, *Limited Inc.* The latter only contains a summary of the crucial essay by John Searle, "Reiterating the Differences: A Reply to Derrida," which can be found in full in *Glyph* 2 (1977). Derrida does, however, quote very extensively from this essay in his reply to the reply.

2. See Gadamer in *Dialogue and Deconstruction*, pp. 27 and 106, for this contrast between optimistic and pessimistic views of language.

3. Arthur Schlesinger, Jr., "The Opening of the American Mind," *The New York Times Book Review*, July 23, 1989, p. 1.

4. See the index reference to the liar paradox in *The Encyclopedia of Philosophy* and "Self Reference in Philosophy" in Frederic Brenton Fitch, *Symbolic Language: An Introduction* (New York: The Ronald Press, 1952).

5. See Ernst Nagel and James R. Newman, *Gödel's Proof* (New York: New York University Press, 1958).

6. Carl G. Hempel, "Empiricist Criteria of Cognitive Significance: Problems and Changes," in his *Aspects of Scientific Explanation and Other Essays in the Philosophy of Science* (New York: Free Press, 1965).

7. *Limited Inc*, p. 43. Cf. 45. Derrida proceeds to suggest a couple of alternatives.

8. "To speculate—on 'Freud'," in *The Post Card: From Socrates to Freud and Beyond*, trans. Alan Bass (Chicago: University of Chicago Press, 1987), p. 261.

9. *Dissemination*, trans. B. Johnson (Chicago: University of Chicago Press, 1981), p. 219.

10. Gasché, *The Tain of the Mirror: Derrida and the Philosophy of Reflection*, p. 240.

11. It is interesting that Heidegger, along with Wittgenstein the fountainhead of anti-foundationalism in twentieth-century philosophy, speaks in much the same way. In the Preface to *Identity and Difference*, he writes, "In this realm one cannot prove [*beweisen*] anything, but one can point out [*weisen*] a great deal." *Identity and Difference*, p. 22. Cf. p. 84.

12. Precisely with reference to the problem of self-reference in Derrida, G. B. Madison writes, "If the 'truth' of his position cannot be argued for, cannot be *said*, it can perhaps be 'shown,' can be concretely instanced, made manifest, or pointed out (*demonstrare*) by means, precisely, of a particular usage of language." "Gadamer/ Derrida: The Hermeneutics of Irony and Power" in *Dialogue and Deconstruction*, p. 193.

13. Introduction to *Dialogue and Deconstruction*, p. 9.

14. "Hermeneutics and Deconstruction: Gadamer and Derrida in Dialogue," in *Dialogue and Deconstruction*, p. 90.

15. See Th. Stcherbatsky, *Buddhist Logic*, 2 vols. (London: Dover Publications, 1962) and T. R. V. Murti, *The Central Philosophy of Buddhism* (London: George Allen & Unwin, 1980).

16. *The Post Card*, p. 260.

17. *Dialogue and Deconstruction*, p. 90. in the context of pp. 89–92.

18. Marsh makes this suggestion in his reflection on RH (p. 19–20) and I raise the question in our three way discussion (*supra*, 124–25).

19. I first raised the question of this tendency in Caputo in a paper presented in March of 1989 to the Conference on Religion and Contemporary Interpretation at the University of Southern Mississippi. See "Postmodernism and Reading Religious Texts," forthcoming.

20. The passage is on p. 252 of PCM. Caputo takes it apart (*supra*, 9–11, 142–43).

21. While I have probably spoken with too much confidence at times about what Caputo means to say, I confess to being mystified by his attack upon regulative ideals (*supra*, 129–30). What a commitment to language, history, and ambiguity would seem to entail is only that a regulative ideal is one that by definition is never fully achieved. Would Caputo wish to dispute that political discussion in contemporary America, for all its faults, more fully approximates the ideal speech situation than that in, say, China or South Africa?

# A Final Word
# (Eight Famous Ones)

## John D. Caputo

MEROLD WESTPHAL'S VERY FINE ESSAY on the issues at stake in this debate makes reference to the "famous eight words" (*supra*, 168) in *Radical Hermeneutics*, words that seem to Marsh a sitting duck for his Habermasian can(n)on, one more bald performative contradiction, indeed *the* contradiction par excellence, the very definition of contradiction: "the truth is that there is no truth" (RH 156). Westphal proceeds to give a series of very illuminating, nuanced readings of that text, for which we all can be grateful.

But the truth is—and here I must own up to it—Westphal's first and most innocuous supposition is right: this remark (like so much else in Parts I and II of RH) is intended mainly by way of a commentary on a text from Derrida's *Spurs* which I cite on the same page. Caputo's famous eight words are not quite from Caputo's mouth but come as a paraphrasing, a telescoping, of Derrida's words: "For if woman *is* truth ["the truth is"], *she* knows that there is no truth" ["that there is no truth"]. So much for the *intentio auctoris*.

But as Westphal points out, I would never disown these famous eight words—above all, not after his own wonderful explanation of them, full of "style" in Derrida's sense, a skill no doubt cultivated by years of reading Kierkegaard. And certainly not after seeing what an excellent torment they have proven to Marsh who charged at them at once, mounting a mighty masculine assault on them, clad in full armor, high astride his Habermasian steed, full speed ahead (only to land you know where). No style, no way with women.

There are so many ways to catch the style of the saying and to avoid the sheer density of thinking it a simple *contraditio in adjecto* (as if the deconstructionists' mothers bore dumb children). The simplest way is to go back to what Yount calls the dispute between capitalized and un-

capitalized radical hermeneutics which he himself developed so felic-
itously in the concluding pages of his very sensitive reading of RH (*supra*, 40–41). The sentence should be read as a play of "capitals": the
*t*ruth (no capitals) is that there is no Truth (capitalized).[1] Originally in-
vested by Plato and gaining interest for thousands of years, Truth finally reached the fullness of its value in modernism from Descartes to
Husserl. Now it is against that capitalism, the over-accumulation of
capital, of which Marsh and I share a common suspicion, against all of
that inflation, that RH makes a protest. The hard hermeneutic truth
(uncapitalized), what I (speaking in my own name) called the *cold*
truth, is that there is no Truth, no Hot Truth, no Platonic solar energy
supply of capital Truth. We lack the authority to lay claim to such a
Truth—and that's the truth, if we own up to it (such "owning up" being the favored sense of "authenticity" in RH). The result of this owning up is not the hand-wringing despair of the sickness unto death but
a willingness to live within the limits of the hermeneutic situation, to
get by with our little presumptive truths which are meant to get us
through the day, and some of which are much better than others. Part
III of RH is devoted to sorting out which of our little uncapitalized
truths are better than others.

The famous eight words have been amply anticipated for some time
now: the dream is spent; the *cogito* is wounded; the point of undertaking the transcendental reduction is to see its impossibility; Dasein is
always factical being-in-the-world; *a-letheia*, with an un-capitalized,
hyphenated alpha-privative. The point has been made repeatedly in the
last one hundred years of European philosophy. It is surprising that the
Knight of Truth did not notice this before he charged.

Another way to give the remark some style is to go back to Nietzsche,
who is the horse's mouth for these famous eight words, which may not be,
as Westphal notes with considerable Kierkegaardian-Derridean circum-
spection, from Caputo's own mouth. Nietzsche said that morality perished
of its own truthfulness (*Wahrhaftigkeit*).[2] For truth is a moral virtue in the
Christian-Platonic scheme of things, and that hard will to truth, Nietzsche
thinks, finally led to unearthing the cold hard truth about Christian morality, the exposure of its origin in *ressentiment*. Now the interesting thing
about that remark, of course, is that it means that Nietzsche, too, is
marked by just this truthfulness, by the archi-morality of an archi-truth-
fulness. Such an archi-truth would mean the will to unearth the most
subterranean forces which flow beneath the most honored names of the

western tradition, e.g., God, Morality, the Ego—and, of course, Truth—
the will to find, as Deleuze puts it, *"what wills"* there, in these famous
European capitals. That means that Nietzsche too is held fast by the ascetic
ideal, the hardest and coldest ascetic ideal, that of the cold truth, the truth
that would kill you if you tried to face it four-square, the truth that we are
in quite a fix, that we have no cosmic assurances (cf. RH 189).[3]

It is in this radical-ascetical sense that RH proposes a radical-
hermeneutical notion of truth, which implies that the truth is that Truth
is always incised by *différance*, by the *es gibt*, which leaves us then
with our little, differentiated, mediated truths, some of which are better than others, none of which is uncontaminated by contingency and
ambiguity (enter: inside/outside). And the whole point of RH, Part III,
is to ask, given the impossibility of Truth-in-the-Inflated-Sense: how
are we to sort out the better from the worse? How are we to proceed
here and now in the concrete flow of life and science?

It is a completely unreconstructed modernism, a modernism which
is not *post*-Cartesian at all, a modernism to which Marsh is—I am
tempted to say, in all truthfulness—hopelessly addicted, a failure of
hermeneutical finesse, a breakdown in sensitivity to the style of ambiguity, to argue as Marsh does that, because there is no Truth in the inflated sense, anything goes. Westphal, who has the advantage of being
a Kierkegaardian, sees this clearly and says so nicely.

Still, Westphal must be fair. He is a diplomat who is trying to get
Marsh and me to sign a treaty; he cannot help this, he has been named
to do it. He is preparing a document to which we can both put our sig-
natures in which it will be stipulated that we are both right, both serious, equally serious. He wants to be fair both to the Knight of Truth
and to the veiling, feinting woman, to get them to reach an agreement
which will put an end to this strife which must seem as if it has been
going on for thirty years. Westphal is still worried about RH, still worried that she—for RH wants to be a woman—has at least been pricked
by the Knight of Truth, at least thus far, that RH is so obstinately, one-
sidedly negative about things that she is always telling us what we cannot do or cannot trust or cannot believe and why we cannot communicate. Which is, of course, cheating, the cheating of Cratylus, about
whom Plato has written well and communicated clearly, maybe even in
a "lively Eastern seaboard prose." Re-enter the performative contradiction, at least in a weaker sense, viz., that while RH does not deny
truth and communication, still RH can give no account of how truth

and communication, even in the decapitalized sense, are achieved, whereas we all know that *ab esse ad posse valet*.

But that is a bad rap and a kind of optical illusion induced by Derrida's and RH's rhetoric. For RH (which has allowed her pen to be filled by Derrida) has a deeply affirmative upshot. Allow me to cite RH:

> So the point of the Derridean stylus is not to dismember the theory of intentionality but to deflect Husserl's intentional arrow just a bit. . . . There is only one way to hit the mark of virtue but many ways to miss it (E.N. 1106 b 28ff.). Intentional marksmanship, like virtue, is hard, and the point of deconstruction is to restore the difficulty both to life and to intentionality.

> The point of all this—the Derridean, Heideggerian, Kierkegaardian, neo-Husserlian point—is to concede the elusiveness of the thing itself, to catch on to its play, not to jettison [N.B. all Knights of Truth] it (whatever that would mean). That is the cold, hermeneutic truth, the truth that there is no truth [the famous eight words spoken *now* in my own name], no master name which holds things captive. [RH 192]

That remark follows a discussion of what in the context of Westphal's objection we should call the "positive" theory of communication which Derrida is really getting at, or claiming that Husserl is getting at, in spite of himself (Husserl's self). Now here is the optical illusion: Derrida tends to emphasize Husserl's discovery of *empty* intentions, the *impossibility* of fulfillment, and he criticizes the teleology of full presence which governs Husserl's very acute and critical descriptions of intentional life. But the positive upshot of Derrida's Husserl—nay, of Husserl—is to show just how *powerful* empty intentions are, for they free us from the constraint of having constantly to redeem them intuitively, which would hopelessly bog down everything from simple telephone conversations to the history of geometry. It is precisely the power of signifiers to operate in the absence of intuitive fulfillment which was Husserl's greatest discovery and which explains how writing works and why we can still read about Cratylus although we will never meet the man.

That ability to operate in the absence of intuitive redemption is what constitutes *écriture* (which antedates the distinction between speech and writing-in-the-*empirical*-sense so that both telephone conversations and the history of geometry are subject to it). The productive power of empty intentions belongs to Husserl's greatest accomplishments, even though Husserl kept trying to push it back in the box in favor of his favorite examples of intuitive fulfillment. Hence, on the preceding page (RH 191) I argue that the textual chain is what *links* us to things, that without *différance* the thing itself slips away, that Derrida's point is indistinguishable from Heidegger's when the latter says that language is not a barrier between us and the world but rather the way the world is delivered to us. I commend a most careful reading of RH 191–92—in which I say that Derrida is "opening up a kind of grammatological phenomenology" (which is what RH means in part to be)—to all those who believe that RH suffers from the sickness unto death. Westphal seems to entertain the strange notion that Derrida (and hence RH) thinks that writing does not work, whereas Derrida's whole point was to show that it works just in virtue of those features which the metaphysical tradition kept trying to erase (which also explains why the metaphysical tradition thinks it can work perfectly, without ambiguity, at least as an ideal).

Furthermore, the fact that RH has, and means to have, a considerable amount to say about reason and truth in a positive sense (so long as you promise that you will not erect reason and truth into capitals), is clear from its (her) pronounced interest in the natural sciences, a point about which both Marsh and Westphal are singularly silent. It goes unnoticed by them that Kuhn's story of the history of scientific change is central to the "positive" account which RH is giving and that, in Kuhn's story, insisting on Habermasian criteria shifts you to the side of the old positivist accounts of scientific theory-making.

Pressed by Westphal to say something positive, not to be so depressing, I point, with opened-eyed amazement at such a demand, to the joyful wisdom defended in RH, at the whole account of what I call "metaphronesis," surely RH's most Gadamerian (or maybe meta-Gadamerian or meta-Aristotelian) moment (RH 262). RH is interested in those moments of rational life when reason is cast back on its own resources, when all of the stable guidelines that have governed our practices (in both science and ethics) tremble, when the established frameworks have come unstuck. RH tries to supply a grammatological hermeneutics of the life of reason in just those moments, "moments" which have taken on an interesting likeness to Kierkegaardian *Augenblicke*. Metaphronesis is to be distinguished from Aristotelian or Gadamerian *phronesis*, because the latter notion assumes the stability of what Aristotle called the *schema* which is to be appropriated. But the

postmodern situation is precisely defined by the wavering of the established schemata, by what Lyotard calls our "incredulity" toward them.

I argue that it is just such a moment — which in the case of the natural sciences is the moment of scientific "crisis" in Kuhn's sense —
which is *reason's finest hour*. In such times of crisis, when reason is on
its own, reason must make a certain cut into the flux, configure things
on its own, in relatively untried and originary ways. It must stay loose,
"be capable of unexpected moves, of paradigm switches, of following
up unorthodox suggestions" (RH 229). That is very much what
Aristotle meant by simple *nous*, by the first intuitive cut into the *Sache*,
the initial, stammering stabs we make at things, and it is the moment of
human intelligence which utterly baffles the advocates of AI, as Hubert
Dreyfus joyfully points out again and again. I would go so far as to call
this moment in the life of reason "pure reason," where "pure" means
"helpless" reason, reason without guardrail, reason on its own, *blosse
Vernunft* where *blosse* means it has been abandoned to its own
inventiveness.

Now it is true that there is a sense in which reason does have something to fall back on at this point, viz., certain "values" — like consistency, fruitfulness, predictability, simplicity, or the Habermasian canon
of sincerity, etc. But such criteria suffer from the severe disadvantage
of being utterly vacuous generalities which are useless, and this for two
reasons. First, we do not know what they *mean* in the *concrete*, which
is what we must find out, and for that — under pain of infinite regress —
there are no criteria. Furthermore, as Kuhn shows, we have no idea of
how much weight to give one value against the other in any given situation. Sometimes it is better to tolerate a high degree of inconsistency
and go for fruitfulness, sometimes the other way around, and sometimes better to forgo both for the sake of simplicity, and so on. As I said
in RH, such values or criteria are of no use because "everybody can
agree about them without agreeing about what to do" (RH 218). Such
"criteria" are either vacuous (and therefore of no help) or question-
begging, because they tell us what to do only after we have already
done it (and again are of no help, except in training apprentices in normal science). (PCM alert: that was a formal argument, and from a
man/woman in a state of formal self-contradiction. *Mirabile dictu!*)
RH is interested in a radical grammatological hermeneutics of an inventive reason (of the sort, e.g., one finds in Polanyi) which must learn
to find its way, must learn to be *unter-wegs, meta-odos*. After which

teams of epistemologists and (des)cartographers will swarm all over
the newly discovered regions, taking measurements and staking out
building lots, and in general strutting about like Knights of Scientific
Method (cf. RH 216ff).

In short, in a way that telescopes Aristotle, Gadamer, and Kuhn, RH
argues that the best formulation of the method of science is that there is
no Scientific Method, not if you take a cold hard look—in the spirit of
Nietzschean-Feyerabendian truthfulness—at the actual, factical history
of science, at the "facts" (of which there are none, only interpretations.) But what *there is* (*es gibt*) is the very fertile operations of scientific reason which, it turns out, does not look at all like its Modernist
caricature. RH is interested in giving a positive sketch (for it is only a
sketch) of the main lines of a quasi-hermeneutics of scientific life (reason). Scientific *nous* comes down to the metaphronesis of a scientific
intelligence, of one who has been apprenticed in scientific practices by
his/her elders, who has an "instinct for good science," a sense nur-
tured by a good deal of hands-on experience for what will work, a nose
for what will be fruitful and what will not, for what looks promising
and what does not. The best such minds will perform the experiments
that will get into the textbooks and be used to train the next generation
of apprentice scientists.

Now I thought science was the "hard case" (RH 214), but Marsh
and Westphal think ethics, or the ethico-political, is. The truth is, I suppose, that they are of comparable difficulty. The main difference is that
so long as scientists keep delivering superconductors and supercompu-
ters people do not care what philosophers say they are doing. But when
all this talk of play gets around to ethics, when it looks like it is going
to spill over into the streets, people get worried. Now it was actually in
connection with ethics that I used the expression "metaphronesis," by
which I meant a sense of civility we must cultivate for one another,
"we" who are having trouble saying "we," we who live in the midst
of often irreconcilable differences, we who live in the time of need, of
the breakdown of shared paradigms, of our incredulity toward commu-
nal beliefs, which is pretty much what the postmodern situation in ethics comes down to. Bataille calls "us" the "community of those who
have no community."[4]

RH defends an ethics which respects differences, which has turned
its attention to the exceptions, the abnormal, the marginalized, the excluded. In a way that parallels its Kuhnian taste for anomalies and the

moments of creative scientific energy which anomalies precipitate, RH is also interested in the ethico-political anomalous, those who have been ground under by the great ethico-political capitals—be they the Natural Law or the Categorical Imperative, the Social Contract or the Laws of Historical Materialism. (In my book, materialist dialectics is very Capitalistic.) RH thinks that totalizing tendencies cannot be closed except with violence and that this sound Kierkegaardian-Derridean point holds no less for structural linguistics than for ethics. That is why Westphal is misled to suppose that this ethics of the exceptional one, of the excluded and marginalized, is an *ad hoc* preference of mine or of Derrida which has nothing to do with "deconstruction," as if "marginalization" were not at once both a discursive and an ethical category.

As Julia Kristeva writes in "The Ethics of Linguistics," since the end of the nineteenth century "something quite new" has emerged, viz., ethics has turned its attention away from finding the universals that ensure the cohesiveness of a social group and toward the exceptions and the abnormal ones who tend to be ground under by cohesive social groups.[5] In a world which has been very profoundly grounded and stabilized by the lust for power, capital, and social control (by technology, capitalism, and socialism), which faces far greater dangers from totalizing forces than from anarchistic ones, the need arises to attend to the alienated, the dispossessed, the unempowered. If it were the other way around, if anarchistic forces were everywhere in the ascendancy, then RH would start to worry about what that was excluding. Like Derrida, RH always worries about what at any given moment is out of favor (which explains why, after two decades of giving very critical readings of Heidegger, Derrida is now defending him against a literally international multi-lingual attack).

Now that inspires the obvious objection from Marsh and Westphal that this brand of postmodernism is excessively formal and proceeds without regard to the substantive merits of what is in or out of favor. They raise the obvious question—and I think it is obvious, with all the advantages and shortcomings of obvious questions—of whether we should respect homocidal rapists and neo-Nazis and tolerate their "difference." Now since such folks as these do not respect others—viz., the ones whom they victimize—in the first place, I fail to see why they appear to win approval from the ethics I am defending, viz., an ethics of respect for the life and dignity of the other. But Westphal's and

Marsh's question does flush out the point, and this is the usefulness of the question, that the otherwise highly formal notion — "tolerating difference" — actually has a substantive content — "respecting the other, respecting his/her life and dignity," what Derrida has lately been calling the "call of the other" (a nice mesh of Heidegger and Levinas).[6] The question highlights the fact that RH does not tolerate (does not consider it a good, defendable, uncapitalized truth that we should tolerate) differences which do not respect others. RH does not consider the desire to rape the other (physically or economically) a difference to be respected but rather a failure to respect the different, i.e., the other, the vulnerable other, the other who cannot defend herself or himself. In RH others always come to us from "on high" (in an ethically commanding position) just because they have been laid low, to invoke the dynamics of Levinas's curved ethical space.

Still, the Knight of Truth and Westphalian diplomat might reply (as they do): But if you will not take a Habermasian oath, will not swear allegiance to some Universal, to some Criterion, if you will not apply for membership in the Ideal Speech Community, why ought you or we to respect others at all? Why not let others go to the devil?

Now that is either a foundationalist question or not (and I do not think that they are clear on this point, even to themselves). If it is, then it suffers from all the corruption of foundationalist questions. It arises from the dissolving, analytic frame of mind of the Enlightenment which simply melts down the bonds which tie us to the world, to one another, to the multiple traditions we inherit, and demands that such bonds be made totally transparent. But that cannot be done. That is why I trot out Nietzsche and the story of the little star, which is, I think, a vivid way of portraying our limits, of saying that we cannot get assurances that go all the way down.

But at this point a surprising thing happens. The Westphalian diplomat objects that this is cold-hearted, dogmatic atheism (*supra*, 177–78), whereas I thought it was just cold hermeneutics. Westphal, whom I took to be a skillful treaty maker, a man of quiet diplomacy and judicious mediation, now politely makes his excuses out the back door of the conference chambers, slips out of his business suit, and comes charging in the front door, to my utter surprise, clad in a full suit of armor, the shining valorous Knight of Faith. So now I have two knights on my hands, two spears aimed at my hide, I who do not even own a (high) horse! (This business of dodging valorous knights is getting dangerous. Besides, who ever heard of knights attacking maidens?)

Westphal writes that I should say not, "with Nietzsche, There is no God," but, "with Kierkegaard, We are not God" (*supra*, 178). Now first of all *Nietzsche never said* there is no God but rather that he found the God of Lutheran Christianity excessively gloomy, that he much preferred the gods of the Greeks, gods who laugh and celebrate life, and that, generally speaking, Christendom seemed to him a fraud—a line we might think he must have stolen from Kierkegaard were it not for the fact he had not read Kierkegaard. Secondly, *I never said* there is no God, but rather that we do not know if we believe in God, not if we are honest (RH 288), by which I meant to display cold hermeneutic truthfulness, my and Nietzsche's ascetic ideal, the faith of a postmodern. In RH such undecidability is not the abolition of faith but the condition under which faith labors, the condition of possibility for a faith which is anything more than a *dogmatism* (N.B. all Knights of Faith), even as in Derrida and Kierkegaard undecidability is the condition of authentic deciding, not its abolition. I do not conceive faith as a way to make the foundations stop trembling but as my response to the trembling, in which the fear and trembling keeps right on rumbling. I conceive faith as a hermeneutic move one makes, prompted by ambiguous motives, to construe the darkness in which we are all caught, which has a lot to do with the dark night of the soul, which I take to be a profound spiritual insight. There were times when Theresa was sure she was an atheist. Heaven save her from the spear of the Knight of Faith. The main thing to do, Climacus liked to say, is to remind the faithful that they still belong to the Church militant and have not as yet graduated to the Church triumphant.

Now if the question—about preferring the marginalized—is not a foundationalist question, then we are pretty much back to where we left the scientists in the time of scientific crises, back to what post-Kuhnians call "good reasons," or what post-Wittgensteinians call "assertability within a language game," by which they mean doing the best one can, where some approaches are a good deal more plausible than others. That is where a quasi-phenomenology, a grammatological hermeneutics, a hermeneutics of suffering comes into play, where it is hermeneutically situated. I am willing to say, defend, argue in public fora, even do battle with Knights (two of them!), that ethical beliefs and political arrangements which cause people to suffer, in body or in mind, in spirit or in the flesh, in terms of their physical health or sense of personal dignity, are to be rejected—even as we ought to be maximally tolerant of the differences that people exhibit when they are not injuring one another (which is the typically postmodern slant).

I think the starting point in ethico-political debates must always be a kind of hermeneutics of the injury we do one another. Such a hermeneutics makes the horror of useless suffering stand out. This is not a hermeneutics centered on beautiful bodies wrestling in the Games and shining with Greek glory. That was the model Heidegger finally settled for (which, in my view, leads to trouble ethically) after having originally set out on a more Kierkegaardian and Lutheran approach to phenomenology in *Being and Time*. RH pursues instead a hermeneutics of crucified and tormented bodies, rather a more Jewish than Greek hermeneutics, a hermeneutics which sides with all those who have been torn apart, in body or in mind. Its aim is to let the face of the victim lay claim to us.

Now most of the time, what we need to do is to figure out just what is causing suffering and what will fix it, and just what short-term sufferings should be endured for the sake of long-term gains. For that, we need people committed to the ethico-political good who have the same sort of instincts as the young scientists I described who have a nose for good science. If we try to come up with hard and fast universals which will guide our way through these stormy waters, such universals will be just as vacuous as the scientific values described by Kuhn. That is why Westphal is just bogging down in a Marsh(ianism) when he calls for "norms" and "an ideal speech situation" (*supra*, 180–82) which are vacuous and cannot possibly be translated into anything determinate except after the fact.[7] They are only good for repeating backwards and training apprentices, not for repeating forwards, as all good Kierkegaardians will appreciate. (The spears these two Knights aim at RH are made of clay and they go limp just when they are supposed to make a point.)

By the same token we ought to be equally cautious in supposing that there are usable norms that will flesh out what people should do when they are not causing one another injury but rather finding new ways to be and to be with one another. Homoerotic love is love, not war, and belongs to the legitimate sphere of preferences protected by (post)modern liberal freedoms. Homoeroticism is fast constituting a postmodern subcommunity of its own. It is not unnatural but a good example of just how flexible, undecidable, and ambient human "nature" is and how intolerable it can be to try to draw a clean line of decidability between the natural and the unnatural.

What I am saying is that all of the claims we make in ethics and politics "cash out" in terms of flourishing and suffering, and that the time has come for ethics to pay attention to the suffering that has been inflicted on so many people by our norms and universals. RH pursues an ethics which worries over the violence which is embedded in the binary oppositions which we are incessantly constructing, oppositions between normal and abnormal, natural and unnatural, male and female, believer and atheist, black and white—one could go on for a very long time making new entries in such a list. It wants to make these distinctions tremble, to make them waver in undecidability—which is not to say throw them out or "jettison" them altogether (N.B. all Knights of Truth). (The problem with knights is that they always think they have a royal commission while too often proving to be a royal pain.) I say tremble, which makes us wonder to what extent they are oppressive, exclusionary, unfair.

For there are victims everywhere—from the slums of large American cities to the killing fields. Indeed the killing fields are here, at home, and we have helped seed them.

Long before "racism is unjust" becomes a claim we make, upon which, like Judge Wilhelm, we can congratulate ourselves—more proof, thank God, that we are not like the rest of men; long before it is a valid claim which assures us—thank Habermas—that we are Men of Reason, Reason's appointed spokesmen; long before any of this, it is a claim which is made upon us, a claim that issues from the smiling face of a child who will never see the inside of a decent school. Otherwise it is the tinkle of sounding brass or, behind closed doors, an occasion for brutal, muffled laughter.

NOTES

1. The truth is, there never was even a formal contradiction because the sense of the word "truth" is different in each occurrence; the truth is, it is not the same thing which is affirmed and denied in the same way at the same time.

2. Friedrich Nietzsche, *The Will to Power*, trans. Walter Kaufmann and R. J. Hollingdale (New York: Vintage Books, 1967), #5, p. 10.

3. For Nietzsche's commitment to the ascetic ideal, see *The Twilight of the Idols* in *The Twilight of the Idols and the Anti-Christ*, trans. R. J. Hollingdale (Baltimore: Penguin Books, 1968), #2, p. 43. For Deleuze, see *Nietzsche and Philosophy*, pp. 75–78.

4. Cited by Maurice Blanchot, *The Unavowable Community*, trans. Pierre Joris (Barrytown, N.Y.: Station Hill Press, 1988), p. 1ff.

5. Julia Kristeva, *Desire in Language: A Semiotic Approach to Literature and Art*, trans. Leon S. Roudiez (New York: Columbia Univ. Press, 1980), p. 23.

6. See Jacques Derrida, "The Politics of Friendship," *The Journal of Philosophy*, 85 (1988), 632–44; and "Force of Law: 'The Mystical Foundations of Authority'," *Cardozo Law Review*, 11 (July–August, 1990): 919–1046.

7. In fact, Yount's criticism of RH is much closer to the mark (*supra*, 36–38). He criticizes RH not because it does not invoke an ideal speech situation but because it very nearly does. In its talk about ensuring that the game is fair (RH 261–62), RH is not sufficiently suspicious of such a notion, and indeed appears to defend a version of liberalism.

It may be there is a version of liberalism I would defend, but it would have to be a liberalism which conceded (1) that liberalism originates in a corrupt metaphysical atomism (does the metaphysical indigence of the English have something to do with their genius in devising progressive political instruments?); and (2) that liberalism tends to be blind to the deep structural inequities which systematically displace the efforts of liberal individuals to command their fates. One way to mend these inequities is open public debate in liberal democratic institutions and it would be extreme folly to want to throw these over. Another way is a massive ground swell from below of people who are sick of being manipulated. Hannah Arendt calls that "power" and it is the expressions of such very non-Foucauldian power that we are seeing in Eastern Europe in the late 1980s.

But in general I would rather have no "ism" to defend because I think that ethical and political metaphronesis is a matter of staying on our toes when opportunities to promote flourishing and diminish suffering present themselves. What political theory predicted the events that transpired in 1989 in Eastern Europe or in the Soviet Union in 1991, or is prepared to tell us what will happen next? As always, it is only after the fact that we are swarmed with explanations and political *sagesse*.

# The Gentle and Rigorous Cogency of Communicative Rationality

## James L. Marsh

As we approach the end of this tournament of Knights of Truth, Faith, and Infinite Evasiveness, let us briefly determine where we are and how far we have come. In my discussion of *Radical Hermeneutics* and in my "Ambiguity, Language, and Communicative Praxis," I articulated four different critical questions to postmodernism. Is it self-referentially inconsistent? Is it descriptively adequate? Is it hermeneutically fair to the tradition and to its modernist other, or guilty of one-sided negation and obliteration of difference and otherness? Is postmodernism politically inefficacious in its absence of criteria for critique, inability to identify positive leverage points of transcendence within the social system, and failure to systematically identify classes or groups capable of moving us forward?

The ensuing discussion has been devoted mainly to the issue of self-referentiality and criteria of critique, one aspect of my fourth question. Little or nothing has been said by Caputo about descriptive adequacy or hermeneutical fairness. I will, therefore, in my concluding remarks, focus on the issues of self-referentiality and criteria of critique. Under these two headings I will discuss some of Merold Westphal's very illuminating questions and insights.

### THE DOUBLE GESTURE

Suffice it to say that I do not think—and here I am really repeating and emphasizing earlier remarks—that the double gesture gets Derrida off the performative hook. Rather, it just *names* the problem; any contra-

diction, *A* simultaneously affirmed with *not A*, is as such a double gesture, but remains nonetheless a contradiction.

Now, I agree with Jack that there is a danger of taking Derrida too
simply here. He is not, and never has been, engaged in a "simple"
transcendence of metaphysics if by that phrase one means an attempt
and a claim to leap into a post-metaphysical beyond with no acknowledgement of the use of metaphysical themes and concepts. Even in
very early works such as *Grammatology* there is this double movement
or double gesture of somehow remaining within metaphysics while attempting to go beyond it.[1]

Consequently my use of the term "simply to be overcome" on page
261 of *Post-Cartesian Meditations* may be unintentionally misleading.
What I meant to indicate is the one gesture of transcending. I never
meant to deny—and indeed page 120 of PCM affirms—the other gesture of remaining within. What I argue in those pages, as I have argued
in this book, is that the strategy of the double gesture is self-referentially inconsistent, logically and hermeneutically, communicatively
and cognitively. Not only is Derrida more complex than my use of the
word "simply" might indicate, but my interpretation of Derrida is
more complex than Jack's characterization of my position might indicate. Here I would insist upon being read with as much fairness, sympathy, care, and attentiveness to nuance as Jack and Mark rightly insist
we read Derrida.[2] Critical modernist otherness and difference and
complexity need to be recognized and responded to also.

What Caputo would have to do here to get off the hermeneutical,
self-referential hook is to distinguish, more adequately than he does,
between the valid and invalid aspects of the metaphysical tradition.
Westphal's mention, in our three-way discussion, of Levinas's distinction between ontology (bad) and metaphysics (good) would be one example of a way to go, but Caputo does not generally take this route.
Metaphysics, as he characterizes it, includes the whole of tradition,
both ontology and metaphysics in Levinas's senses. One reason Caputo
resists such a path, I suspect, is that such nuanced, dialectical "yes"
and "no" to the tradition puts him in or close to the camp of critical
modernism, where he does not want to be. In his approach to the tradition he is up to something much more negative, totalizing, and
rejectionistic. As such, there is a tension between this negative, totalizing stance and his concrete, performative use of elements in the tradition. Like early Wittgenstein, he is trying to climb a broken ladder.

If Caputo, pushed by Westphal and me to modify or qualify his neg-atively totalizing stance, does on occasion concede that he is merely talking about a part or strand of the metaphysical tradition, then his stance approaches or equals that of critical modernism toward the tra-dition. The relevant distinction becomes that between good and bad metaphysics. The dilemma, then, for Caputo is the following: deny the validity of the metaphysical tradition as a whole at the price of perfor-mative contradiction (Caputo's dominant stance), or criticize only a part or aspect of metaphysics. In the latter case metaphysics, good meta-physics, remains legitimate, and postmodernism has to be given up.[3]

For this reason I do not think that merely quoting Caputo's claims that he is consciously operating inside as well as outside the tradition, rationality, and truth, as Westphal does, helps Caputo. Even in PCM, in my review of RH, and again in my first essay in this volume, I admit and recognize that point. What I am arguing is that such explicit rec-ognition just makes more explicit the performative contradiction of somehow negating or criticizing the tradition as a whole, and yet op-erating inside that tradition.[4]

Westphal's second line of defense for Caputo against the charge of performative contradiction, a defense centered on the claim "The truth is that there is no truth," deserves more comment. This is an ingenious defense/reconstruction of Caputo-Derrida that I think genuinely gets at something going on in their texts. As Westphal puts it, the import of "the only truth is that there is no truth" is a-thetic, not thetic; perlo-cutionary, not locutionary; performative, not constative. My first re-sponse is that, although such an a-thetic, aesthetical, ironical move is present in Caputo-Derrida, this kind of thing is not going on all the time. There is plenty of thetic positing and negating as well—for ex-ample, Derrida's description and critique of logocentrism and Caputo's description and critique of metaphysics. When thetic claims are made, there is the problem of performative contradiction. When there is a move to the a-thetic, a tension or inconsistency emerges in the text be-tween thetic positing or negating and a-thetic playing and performing.[5]

A second point is that although such an a-thetic move may help Caputo off the performative hook at times, it can only do so at an enor-mous cost: the critique of logocentrism has to be softened or given up. For such an ironical-aesthetic gesture can only manifest difference, not superiority—like Joyce writing *Ulysses* after Meredith has written *The Egoist*. Such a move can *suggest* or imply superiority, but whether its suggested alternative genuinely is superior would require a reasoned, thetic form of reflection and argumentation. At this point another dilemma arises: make the critique of logocentrism at the price of performative contradiction, or avoid performative contradiction through a-thesis at the price of giving up or softening the critique.[6]

Another way of making this point is to say that critical modernists can make their own a-thetic gestures as well. A poem or play by Brecht, for example, suggests the superiority of a critical modernist praxis and discourse over other forms. In confronting a postmodernist gesture, the Brechtian is merely different, not superior; superiority would have to emerge through a form of reasoned discourse — literary, aesthetic, political, philosophical. The critical modernist has no problem with such discourse; she can carry it out in a performatively and contextually consistent way. The postmodernist, however, is faced with another dilemma: defending the superiority of his gesture with meta-aesthetic, thetic argumentation at the price of self-contradiction, or not defending, merely gesturing in an a-thetic manner, at the price of being merely different.[7]

Oddly enough, and ironically enough, Westphal's proffered help to Caputo is no help at all; indeed, it is of greater help to me. In weakening directly or by implication the critique of logocentrism, the a-thetic gesture leaves the doing of metaphysics quite in order. As merely different but not necessarily inferior to the postmodernist gesture, it is quite legitimate for me to continue doing metaphysics. The postmodernist may wish to assert the superiority of the a-thetic–aesthetic–literary mode of expression over the rational, reflective, metaphysical, but this superiority can be demonstrated only through a meta-athetic rational form of reflection. Another contradiction arises between postmodernist intention and result, the intention to overcome metaphysics and the result of leaving metaphysics perfectly in place as merely different but not illegitimate. Like the choice of apple pie over cherry, the choice becomes one of personal taste.[8]

It is difficult, however, not to sense or suspect in this current presentation of Jack's an unacknowledged softening of earlier, more apocalyptic, extreme stands. Here he sounds at times, if not friendly to metaphysics, at least willing to accept his status as a player within it. The gesture of transcendence is so played down that we can easily forget that this is the author of an earlier book subtitled *An Essay in the Overcoming of Metaphysics*, and "overcoming" here is obviously intended in the strong sense of *"Überwindung"* and not *"Verwindung"*; or that even in RH, Caputo II, metaphysics is presented as necessarily an attempt to escape the flux. It is hard to square these texts with his quoting of earlier Heidegger's claim that *Dasein* is in the truth, especially since Caputo claims not only to have gone beyond early Heidegger but also later Heidegger; that "the only truth is that there is no truth," and that the truth is merely a useful fiction.

I sense a problem here not only of performative but of textual and existential inconsistency, which renders dialogue difficult or impossible. The postmodernist at one point says A and the next *non-A* in such a way that he cannot be pinned down—he is a moving target. Where does legitimate playfulness end and the responsibility to the conditions of a dialogue begin? Where does legitimate linking of rhetoric to argument end and illegitimate obfuscation of argument with rhetoric begin? These are not accusations but questions occasioned by the encounter between postmodernist and critical modernist. What responsibility does the postmodernist have to the conditions of a philosophical dialogue rooted in a tradition that he claims in some way to transcend? If he violates those conditions at one point and obeys them at another or argues against them *explicitly* while employing them implicitly *in actu*, can we not talk about the possibility of existential, dialogal self-contradiction or inconsistency violating the minimal conditions of conversation? The postmodernist pretends to play the game of philosophical conversation, but he is not really bound by its rules or committed to it the way the other participants are. Consequently, he can tacitly slip out of the conversation and play by different rules. In developing the notions on comprehensibility, truth, sincerity, and rightness; openness to the other in dialogue, and the four transcendental precepts in my book, I articulated my own version of such minimal conditions for dialogue.[9]

In this respect the charge of triviality or irrelevance that Caputo directs against the self-referential argument fails. Rather, the question of self-referential consistency bears upon the *authenticity* and *integrity* of my praxis of philosophizing. Is my communicative and cognitive praxis at odds with or in harmony with the validity claims and transcendental precepts? In this respect, Caputo's own charge that I have misinterpreted him and Derrida bears reluctant, inconsistent witness to the presence of the validity claims in his own philosophizing. Is postmodernism in its communicative praxis at odds with the conditions of its own philosophizing or antiphilosophizing?[10]

One question that reflection on such praxis raises is that of unity versus pluralism, a question that emerged in the three-way discussion among Caputo, Westphal, and myself. I do not arbitrarily presuppose unity in my dialogue with Caputo; rather, we both presuppose unity insofar as we engage in any dialogue: the unity of transcendental precepts, validity claims, a common language, a common philosophical tradition. We also presuppose difference insofar as the heremeneutical, transcendental precept to be responsible implies respect for the otherness and difference of one's dialogue partner and willingness to learn. Such unity and difference as essential to a situation of dialogal, communicative praxis are presupposed by Derridean disruptions. Such disruption would not be understandable but for the shared understanding and recognized differences of a shared praxis. As Gadamer argues, even ''irony'' presupposes a set of common, mutually understood, cultural meanings in light of which something is seen as ironical. An a-thetic, ironical understanding of ''the only truth is that there is no truth'' presupposes a shared understanding of what ''truth'' has meant in the western philosophical tradition.[11]

Nonetheless I sense something new emerging in Jack's position that needs to be addressed and that I think has some positive merit. Thinkers should not be tied or held down to past claims, even recent past claims. ''What is he saying now?'' is the important question. In what I now perceive to be a softening, qualifying, and backing off from earlier, more extreme stands, there are at least four possibilities that need to be considered.

First, in the shift from *Überwindung* to *Verwindung*—a weaker sense of overcoming—there is a sense of metaphysics as a sickness from which one cannot escape. The relationship of the thinker to metaphysics is that of man to wife in a bad marriage; there is a lot of playing around, infidelity, one-night stands, late nights at the office. The husband, for reasons that are emotional, moral, legal, or religious, cannot escape from the marriage, but he is fooling around as much as possible on the margins outside of it, trying to find loopholes in the marriage. *The Margins of Marriage.*[12]

As I see it there are four problems even with this weakened sense of ''overcoming.'' A) The performative problem is still present. Even if metaphysics remains merely a sickness with which I deal but from which I cannot escape, the critic of metaphysics uses elements of that sickness to criticize it and to ''get well.''

B) Another problem that arises is the antinomy between necessity and freedom. The postmodernist aspires to a freedom outside of the bad marriage to metaphysics and makes moves to achieve that, but is continually called back to necessity; eventually he has to go home to the woman and give an accounting. In a way analogous to the disagreement between Leibniz and Spinoza, there is a postmodern antinomy between freedom and necessity. Like Sisyphus, he rolls the rock up the hill, but it continually rolls back down. The postmodernist never reaches the top of the hill, he never reaches the freedom to which he aspires. A contradiction emerges between the freedom aspired to and the limited freedom attained, between freedom and necessity.

C) Another problem with the idea of metaphysics as a necessary sickness is an issue discussed in my reflection on RH.[13] Such a claim is descriptively inadequate as an account of experience insofar as it may not do justice to the distinction between good and bad metaphysics, appeal and coercion, liberation and domination. Also, what is the standard of health in the light of which metaphysics is sick? If such a standard is merely assumed and unthematized, then we have a problem of dogmatism; if it is argued for, then the standard is not outside of but within the metaphysical tradition it claims to be criticizing.

We see here that Caputo cannot avoid the problem of a "criterion" simply by ascribing the demand for a criterion to a strong foundationalism or transcendentalism. Not only does such a claim miss my distinction between a triumphalistic and fallibilistic modernism, but Jack's own position requires such a criterion. Without some standard of health, how can he call metaphysics "sick"?

D) Another issue is the question of hermeneutical adequacy of this description of metaphysics as a sickness; again, I discuss this issue in my reflection on RH.[14] Is all metaphysics an attempt to escape the flux or only some versions of bad metaphysics? When we think of Aristotle's critique of Plato for not doing sufficient justice to the reality of change or Hegel's critique of Kant for being too tender with reality, being unwilling to ascribe contradiction to it, or Merleau-Ponty's critique of Husserl for his lack of attention to the lived body in the life world, are not Aristotle, Hegel, and Merleau-Ponty thinking the flux from within the metaphysical tradition?

A second move is to insist, as Caputo does following Yount's suggestion, that "the only truth is that there is no truth" means that "the only *truth* is that there is no *Truth*." Even though I do not think this is the most obvious or even the most plausible way to read either Caputo's or Derrida's text, Caputo, like the woman he claims to be (a notion of women that many feminists would find objectionable), is enormously inventive in finding strategies of evasion, ways off the performative hook. Caputo becomes a Knight of Infinite Evasiveness. Like other strategies, however, this one also fails.

There are three related and overlapping dilemmas to which the above move leads: critical modernism or postmodernism, self-contradiction or arbitrariness, performative or textual inconsistency. The move to a small "truth," to a fallibilistic, chastened conception of rationality and criticism of "Truth" is a kind that critical modernists like Merleau-Ponty and Ricoeur made also; were Caputo interested in giving a positive, reflective account of such truth, then his position would be indistinguishable from the modernism he is trying to transcend.

If, on the other hand, Caputo's small truths are postmodernist, then there is little or no positive account and justification for his preferences, and they become arbitrary. The norms and criteria used in either ethics or science, for example, are either empty or redundant and after the fact; Caputo here escapes the pole of self-contradiction by moving to the pole of arbitrariness. There are truths, he says, but he can give no positive metaaccount of those truths (*supra*, 129–30). Fair play and respect are desirable, but he gives no reason for preferring these to other accounts such as those of Rawls, Walzer, or Nozick. Capitalism and socialism are apparently bad, but no positive argument or systematic account is given to justify these claims. In this respect, "small truths" probably cohere more easily with Rorty's complacent acceptance of capitalism than with the "big critiques" of Baudrillard or Foucault or Caputo himself. Certain groups of marginalized are to be preferred and others rejected, but there is little or no justification for this distinction. This Prometheus nailed to the rock of his revolt against western rationality twists back and forth between the nail of self-contradiction and that of decisionism.

Caputo's claims and preferences and criticisms, even though I agree with many of them, remain curiously external to his theory. The odd result of such decisionism is to risk a theory as aggressive and willful and "pushy" as the western rationality he is criticizing and trying to transcend. Why and how is reason "in its finest hour" distinguishable from willfulness? Here aggressive masculinity conflicts with the stance of femininity; like any male on Saturday night insisting on having his way, something is true because he says it is true. An adequate phenomenology of human thinking and willing, such as I try to develop on pages 92–106 of PCM, shows that leaps and changes of paradigm, whether in individual human life, science, or politics, are not sheer blind jumps from nowhere to nowhere, but are motivated by reasons that are criticizable. The change from Newton's theory to Einstein's theory of relativity, for example, was motivated by such newly discovered phenomena as the constant speed of light. Relativity theory accounted for such phenomena in a way that Newton could not, while retaining Newton's law as valid for normal speeds, distances, and velocities. In this way criteria such as parsimony and comprehensiveness are operative in the "leap" itself, not merely in some *post-hoc* reflection on it.

Here I do not wish to deny the value and importance of the question, preconceptual insight, hermeneutical ambiguity making multiple readings possible, judgment, and *phronesis* in moral, aesthetic, and scientific spheres. Principles, norms, and criteria are necessary but they do not dispense us from the necessity of thinking "on our own" in a sense. They are not substitutes for but rather expressions of inquiring intelligence and reasonableness. Caputo moves from this legitimate and insightful point to denial or de-emphasis of the *positive* role that method, concept, principle, and norm can play. "Reason in its finest hour . . . ": yes indeed, but positively linked to method, concept, definition, principle. The full life of reason encompasses the play between both of these aspects, not simply one or the other. Such play implies neither that "anything goes" nor that principles, norms, and criteria are to be embraced in a dogmatic, totally unquestioning manner. They also are or can be up for discussion. Caputo is as phenomenologically one-sided in *his* denial and emphasis as defenders of a strong version of rationality such as Popper and Lakatos are in theirs.

The externality of Caputo's ethical and political choices to his theory, the "in-difference" of his leftist politics to Derridean *différance*, is the real meaning, I think, of the recent revelations concerning De Man and Heidegger. Because the theory is so weak and thin—indeed, so anti-theoretical in many respects—one can just as easily be right-wing as left-wing, just as easily march with the storm troopers as with comrades singing the *Internationale*. The putative advantage of critical modernism, as I have argued for it here and in PCM, is that in making such distinctions as those between coercion and appeal, alienating and non-alienating objectification, monologal and dialogal rationality, a technocratic rationality linked to a class and group domination and a dialectical, phenomenological, hermeneutical rationality linked to liberation, there is a clear critique of and alternative to western domination. In its capacity to make such critique, to lay out its positive ground and to present a clear, distinguishable alternative, dialectical phenomenology may be the more radical position.

Again there is a tension between self-contradiction and textual inconsistency. In moving to small truths, Caputo is textually inconsistent with big claims that he makes concerning logocentrism, metaphysics, the western tradition, and modern industrial society. The critique of western reason is a big truth, incompatible with the epistemic localism and particularism Caputo chooses to escape performative contradiction. If, on the other hand, he were to give up such a critique in order to be sufficiently and consistently small-minded, then western reason remains clearly in place and legitimate. Caputo's postmodernism is compromised by his attempt to escape performative inconsistency and the movement to small truths. Contradictions emerge between postmodern particularism and universalism, its intention to criticize or transcend western reason and the result of leaving it intact. In spite of its animus against totalization, postmodernism engages in a one-sided negative totalization of western reason at odds with its commitment to "small truths."

A third possibility in the qualifications Jack has introduced (*supra*, 56) is that the questioning of metaphysics is not a hard-and-fast rejection of metaphysics, which would be performatively inconsistent in its strong or weak versions. To question $A$ while using the resources of $A$ does not have the same performative problems as the rejection of $A$ while using the resources of $A$. There is, however, another kind of performative relation involved, in the sense that the conditions necessary for asking the question are an implied answer to the question, or part of the answer. Just as an implied positive answer to the question "Should one seek the truth?" is implied in seeking the true answer to that question, so also an implied answer to the question "Should one do metaphysics?" is partially contained in the performance of asking this question within the metaphysical tradition. Questioning metaphysics has metaphysical presuppositions that cannot be evaded.

Now a fourth possibility related to and overlapping with the third is contained in Caputo and Derrida: a questioning of metaphysics that is friendly to metaphysics, that sees the necessary marriage to metaphysics as a good marriage. This friendliness to metaphysics is much more obvious in such late Derridean texts as *Limited Inc.*, in which Derrida refers to himself as a classical philosopher and advocates traditional logics and hermeneutical methods. Such friendliness is sometimes hinted at by Jack but left undeveloped. For the most part, even in his very late work as I read him, the rhetoric and logic of his position is that of an unsatisfied spouse in a bad marriage.[15]

Nonetheless, I find real philosophical value and validity in some of the implications of this latter possibility—the emphasis on and restoration of a Socratic moment to philosophy. Here we have a questioning of metaphysics that forbids premature closure or certainty, a twentieth-century "I am wise because I know nothing." Such a questioning would occur for the sake of metaphysics itself. Bad metaphysics would forbid or eliminate or minimize this Socratic moment; good metaphysics would involve a movement back and forth, a dialectic if you like, between ignorance and knowledge, question and answer, insight and concept, uncertainty and certainty, unsystematic and systematic. Such dialectical play is present in PCM when I argue for the movement back and forth between ambiguity and objectivity. Such play is my own metaphysical alternative to Derridean, Caputean dissemination.[16]

At this point Jack's position would approximate, but not equal, the critical modernism I am defending here. Both of us insist on the Socratic moment, the necessity of metaphysics, the reality of dissemination or ambiguity, the pathology of bad metaphysics, the legitimacy and necessity of suspicion and critique. We would still have some other differences concerning the legitimacy of the transcendental and the reality of the self. But our positions would have come a lot closer. The price Jack would have to pay for such an approximation is that the logic and rhetoric of overcoming metaphysics is given up. He would have to overcome overcoming metaphysics. The price I would have to pay is to be careful that I give sufficient play and value to moments of uncertainty, ambiguity, and questioning. I would have to own up to and accept a necessary and legitimate hermeneutical anxiety. I would have to admit "that there is no quick or final fix."[17]

## CRITERIA FOR CRITIQUE

All of these myriad difficulties postmodernism has on self-referential, descriptive, and hermeneutical levels come home to roost on the most concrete, political level. Postmodernism is so indeterminate and negative on these first three levels that it can offer no positive, constructive ethics or politics. Critical modernism, on the other hand, can and does. To drive this point home, I would like to turn my attention to some of Jack's comments toward the end of "On Being Inside/Outside Truth." He says that "I doubt that Marsh has any better reasons for preferring the marginalized than I do," and further on, "we are both impressed by western ideas about democracy and justice. . . . We find these ideas more reasonable, fairer, better, more persuasive."[18]

I find these to be interesting claims that bring many of the differences between us to a head and focus. Jack's positive recourse to the western tradition, I think, still has the logical and self-referential problems mentioned above, unless the fourth friendly version is adopted. Also, the claim that I do not have any better reasons than he does for preferring the marginalized would have to confront arguments in my book concerning the four validity claims, the transcendental precepts, the ideal speech situation, and the use of Marxist immanent critique to evaluate capitalism. To the extent that capitalism as a class society violates the demands of the ideal speech situation in a way that leads or can lead to a legitimation crisis, those on the margin—the poor, women, blacks, and homosexuals—are there unjustly and irrationally.[19]

Because capitalism violates and contradicts its own ideals of equality and freedom and property and happiness, people on the margins because of such violations are unjustly marginalized in a way that Wallace and Barnett are not. The advantage here of a *dialectical* as opposed to a *deconstructive* critique is that dialectic can draw on positive norms and values within capitalism in order to criticize it from within; capitalism and modernity are not totally bankrupt as a deconstructive critique tends to say, but are a contradictory unity of truth and error. Deconstruction in either the strong or the weak versions developed above does not have such positive values and criteria available to it; it cannot generate a positive ethics or politics. For this reason there are the problems developed in my reflection on RH of distinguishing between legitimate and illegitimate marginalization. The only way deconstruction can supply such criteria is by drawing on the liberal tradition, as Jack does in his remarks here; in making such a move he has to give up the totalizing critique of the western tradition that includes liberalism as a part.[20]

Again, in my reflection on RH, I mention a whole tradition of ethical and political theory, including such thinkers as Habermas and Rawls, that claim to go beyond and avoid the extremes of a naive, triumphalistic modernism and a skeptical postmodernism. Telling postmodernist arguments against triumphalistic modernism are not cogent against such a fallibilistic modernism. For these reasons such criteria as Rawls's two principles of justice are available to distinguish between legitimate and illegitimate marginalization. In a sequel to PCM, I am working on my own version of such a theory of justice.[21]

In this respect, I think Merold Westphal's comments in his essay are insightful. In the fallibilism built into Habermas's ideal speech situation, which is defended and incorporated into PCM, there is already a safeguard against the kind of thing Caputo is worried about: arrogant, totalitarian, repressive theory. On this issue PCM already stakes a claim to the "Hegelian" middle ground, which Westphal also very persuasively claims to occupy, between fear of dogmatism and fear of arbitrariness, undecidability and determinacy, ambiguity and objectivity. In the light of my account of rationality, totalitarian abuse, even or especially that carried out in the name of reason, can be criticized as irrational and unjustified. The problem with such repressive rationality is not too *much* but too *little* rationality. Thus, technocracy or capitalism or state socialism, inadequate forms of rationality and politics, can be criticized in light of a more adequate, comprehensive, nuanced conception of rationality. We do not need to move to a postmodernist "beyond," a transcendence of western rationality, to criticize and overcome such inadequate forms of rationality.[22]

Here I like and accept Westphal's suggestion that the genuinely adventurous, radical stance is not either harmonious mediation or postmodern disjunction between poles of ambiguity and objectivity, but living in the existential tension between the two poles. It is failing to be radical in my sense simply to absolutize either one of the two poles or to opt either for simple mediation or simple disruption. In living and thinking this existential tension, however, I think that ambiguity in some limited sense can be thought, as we reflect on its kinds or aspects, its relationship to thought (for example the relation of implicit to explicit, unthematized to thematized, lived body to reflection, ground to figure), and the limits it poses to thought. Such thinking, "media-tion" in a qualified sense, is never total or absolute, because there is more in heaven and earth than is dreamt of in our philosophy. The play of language always overflows its boundaries, rendering mediation not null and void, but limited. This insight, present in different ways in both Derrida and Merleau-Ponty, is *incontestible*. Another tension, therefore, that emerges is that between ambiguity as thought and as lived. As the examples of Merleau-Ponty and Ricoeur, Gadamer and Habermas show, western, evidential rationality emerges at its best in living and thinking such a tension—the kind, gentle, capacious, non-vio-lent appeal and call of a committed, dialogal, fallibilistic rationality.[23]

Jack's phenomenology of suffering in RH was quite powerful and illuminating, and I did not give it the attention it deserved in my initial reflection on RH. I would say such a description was a good *beginning* but is inadequate because it does not distinguish between justified and unjustified suffering. Barnett and Wallace and Hefner shoved to the margin in a fully liberated society suffer also. Why do we give less credence and attention to their suffering than that of the poor, women, blacks, gays, exploited laborers, victims of American imperialism? Why ought we to do anything about such suffering, or should we do anything at all? Thinkers such as Nozick, confronted with the fact of such suffering, say that we are not obligated to do anything at all. He would presumably be moved by Jack's description, but would not think he *had* to do anything. What would Jack have to say to such thinkers who mirror and reflect and legitimize very prevalent attitudes in the United States?[24]

Now I am wary of seeming to be unfair. The suffering described by Jack in RH obviously is different in depth, extent, and seriousness from that experienced by a Wallace, a Barnett, or a Hefner. It is already obvious that the persons Jack describes are oppressed rather than the oppressors, victims rather than the victimizers, exploited rather than exploiting. In this way Jack, in his very description, is already select-ing out people who are not only on the margin but on the margin un-justifiably. Jack here is drawing, explicitly and implicitly, on the resources of the western philosophical and Christian tradition. In such selectivity he has to presuppose and presume as valid the resources of this tradition to which he has such a problematic relation. Thus we con-front, once again, the performative issue.

A final question concerns the risk of dogmatism concealed beneath Caputo's quite skeptical approach to these questions. In saying that he and I both know, drawing in a rough way on the liberal and Christian traditions, that one should prefer the margin to the center and certain kinds of marginalized people to others, Jack offers a phenomenology of suffering and a sense of being called by those on the margin. There are reasons for being against Apartheid, he tells us, but what are they? What makes one account of being "called" better than another? Botha in defending the status quo of Apartheid could also appeal to being called.

In being unwilling to push justification beyond a certain point, Caputo runs the risk of a dogmatic as opposed to a reflective justification. "We do not need to reflectively justify through argument our sense of being right because we already know that we are right and what right is"—many pernicious political systems and policies, from Stalinism through American policy in Central Ameria, have flourished on just such avoidance of further reflection. Short of reflective justification, Jack's preference for the liberal tradition as what he and I know already to be right runs the risk of being dogmatic; his postmodernist skepticism seems not to be opposed to dogmatism, but to imply it. Ironically, a stance animated by the fear of dogmatism is itself dogmatic—deconstruction deconstructs itself, self-destructs. One of the reasons Habermas, within the Marxist tradition, is at such pains to undertake such reflection is that the biases within institutionalized Marxism flow from such avoidance of reflective justification—the Stalinist party did not need to undertake such reflection because it already knew what the truth was. Jack appeals to commonly held liberal beliefs within our culture; but what if liberalism itself is suspect, as thinkers such as Unger and Sandel have tried to show?[25]

Now Caputo, when pushed, at times does approach giving such a justification (*supra*, 190–91); the criterion offered is one of respecting difference. Barnett and Wallace violate this criterion in a way that King and Steinem do not. The problems with Caputo's answer here are, first, that he is offering something close to a criterion in contrast to his general reluctance. Second, how does one get from the formal hermeneutics of deconstruction to the substantive ethics of "respecting the other"? There is a gap between form and content that Caputo does not bridge; the ethics remains external to the deconstructive hermeneutics and methodology. Third, as the starting point and basis for his ethics, why is not "tolerating difference" as formal, empty, vacuous, and metaphysical as Habermas's validity claims? Caputo's critique of critical modernism conflicts with his own formalism here. Fourth, what counts as a justified and unjustified toleration of difference? The distinction requires a theory of justice. Fifth, as Yount has already pointed out (*supra*, 36–37), such a liberal ethical criterion contradicts Caputo's radical politics. Why not just be a disciple of Rorty? Finally, one is left with the question, "Why respect difference?" I agree that we should, but since neither a deconstructive hermeneutics nor a phenomenology of suffering answers the question, the account remains decisionistic and arbitrary.

For these reasons, and also because Caputo has not eliminated the possibility of a third, fallibilistic way of providing such justification that evades the postmodernist critique, it is too facile to say that the cosmos yawns in the face of such appeals to reflection. After Auschwitz, Dachau, Vietnam, and Central America, such skeptical-dogmatic sleepiness is a luxury we cannot afford.

In the face of the totalitarianism, terrorism, exploitation, and imperialism of the twentieth century, the postmodernist can give us no positive, constructive ethics or politics, offers no account of human dignity, human rights, or justice, and invites us to opt for its own dogmatic, arbitrary preferences.

The cosmos trembles.

## NOTES

1. Derrida, *Grammatology*, pp. 3–93.

2. PCM, pp. 118–22.

3. For Westphal's comment, see the three-way discussion among himself, myself, and Caputo, pp. 137–39. Caputo's momentary concession occurs on p. 140. For Levinas's distinction between ontology and metaphysics, see *Totality and Infinity*, trans. Alphonso Lingis (Pittsburgh: Duquesne University Press, 1969), pp. 33–52. For examples of Caputo's negative totalizing tendencies, see note 9 of this essay.

4. See PCM, pp. 19, and pp. 93–94, 152 of this volume.

5. On Derrida's critique of logocentrism, see the discussion in this volume on pp. 116–17, and *Grammatology*, pp. 1–93. There is one passage especially that is quite revelatory on pp. 110-11.

The "rationality"—but perhaps that word should be abandoned for reasons that will appear at the end of this sentence—which governs a writing thus enlarged and radicalized, no longer issues from a logos. Further, it inaugurates the de-struction, not the demolition but the de-sedimentation, the de-construction of all the significations that have their source in that of the logos. Particularly the sig-nification of *truth*. All the metaphysical determinations of truth, and even the one beyond metaphysical onto-theology that Heidegger reminds us of, are more or less immediately inseparable from the instance of the logos, or of a reason thought within the lineage of the logos in whatever sense it is understood: in the pre-Socratic or the philosophical sense, in the sense of God's innate understand-ing or in the anthropological sense, in the pre-Hegelian or the post-Hegelian sense. Within this logos, the original and essential link to the *phone* has never been broken.

Notice here the questioning of rationality and truth, the characterization of the philosophical tradition as a whole centered on the logos is logo-centric, the connection of logocentrism with phonocentrism. On the next page, p. 12, logocentrism and phono-centrism are linked to presence: "Logocentrism would thus support the determina-tion of the being of the entity as presence." Here is one basis in the Derridean text for Caputo's negative characterization of metaphysics. The orientation to presence is what enables metaphysics to launch "an all-out assault upon things," which is a "power play," an attempt to "capture things in its net," to insure that "Things are subdued by the will to know" (RH, p. 185).

For a more extended discussion of this a-thetic, aesthetic move in Derrida, see my "Strategies of Evasion," 339–49.

Since writing this piece I have concluded that the double gesture, not aesthetic re-ductionism, is the main strategy of evasion in Derrida, and I would emphasize more strongly the point I made that aesthetic, a-thetic reductionism is just part of the story, not the whole story about Derrida. There is also a strong, argumentative, philosophical side that Caputo and Gasché, in *The Tain of the Mirror*, pick up. I would disagree with Habermas's interpretation and critique of Derrida as an aesthetic reductionist to the extent that he makes it the whole story. See Jürgen Habermas, *The Philosophical Dis-course of Modernity*, trans. Frederick Lawrence (Cambridge: MIT Press, 1987), pp. 185–210. Such reductionism, as Westphal's comments indicate, is, however, part of the story. As a critique of that part, Habermas is right on the money.

6. "Strategies of Evasion," pp. 344–45.

7. *Ibid*, pp. 345–46.

8. *Ibid*.

9. See *Heidegger and Aquinas: An Essay in Overcoming Metaphysics* (New York: Fordham University Press, 1982), pp. 149–50, 153–54, 176–81, 185–86. For an ex-ample of a text justifying an interpretation that overcoming is present in the strong sense, consider "but the task of thought is to go one step farther than metaphysics" (p. 150). Or "On the contrary these thinkers [the pre-Socratics—the brackets are mine], whom philosophy considers to be semi-philosophic and still encumbered by the old myths, are in fact non-metaphysical thinkers who were not yet victimized by Western *ratio*" (p. 185). In RH, consider "Hermeneutics thus is for the hardy. It is a radical thinking which is suspicious of the easy way out, which is especially suspicious that

philosophy, which is metaphysics, is always doing just that'' (p. 3), or ''The truth is that there is no truth'' (p. 85). Or,

> metaphysics launches an all-out assault on things; it is a power play on the part of human conceptuality, and the critique of humanism was meant to counter its pretentiousness and will-to-power. The history of metaphysics is the story of so many attempts on the part of metaphysics to capture things in its net, to see to it that things are subdued by the will-to-know. [p. 185]

What is interesting about these quotations is the negative, unfriendly attitude towards metaphysics — it is not just some metaphysics but all metaphysics that is guilty. Again, since radical hermeneutics is presumably not guilty of the same sins, then it is beyond metaphysics in some sense. It is not hard to read even the claims of RH as pointing toward a strong sense of ''overcoming metaphysics.''

On my articulations and defense of the conditions for dialogue, see PCM, pp. 148–57, 161–69.

10. See Caputo's essay in this volume, ''On Being Inside/Outside Truth,'' pp. 54–55.

11. See *supra*, pp. 157–61; also Gadamer's comments in *Dialogue and Deconstruction*, pp. 37–51. I must also register a disagreement here with Westphal's comment in his essay in this volume, p. 180, that I am as closed to Derrida as Caputo is to Habermas. Whatever Caputo's stance toward Habermas is or may be, I have maintained, or tried to maintain, a stance of critical sympathetic openness to Derrida. I have disagreements with him, of course, but in his method of deconstruction, his discussion of dissemination, his concept of writing, his insistence on the mediated character of human existence, and his sympathy for the marginalized, I find much that is positively valuable and insightful. See PCM, pp. 117–22, 162–64, 245, 260 note 11, and ''Ambiguity, Language and Communicative Praxis,'' pp. 95–96, 98–99, 101, 105–107.

12. The sense of metaphysics as basically a sick enterprise is certainly present with greater or lesser explicitness in much of Caputo's work, including the quotations of note 9. Caputo becomes explicit on this issue in the discussion on pp. 117–18. I owe the metaphor of the bad marriage to Martin De Nys.

13. See ''Marsh Reads Caputo: In Defense of Modernist Rationality,'' pp. 11–12.

14. *Ibid.*

15. Derrida, *Limited Inc.*, pp. 125–27, 143–44. On Caputo's unfriendliness to metaphysics, see the quotations listed in note 9.

16. See PCM, pp. 121–22. See Caputo's' talk of ''loosening up the tradition,'' *supra*, 136–37.

17. See ''On Being Inside/Outside Truth,'' p. 52.

18. *Ibid.*, p. 59.

19. See PCM, pp. 148–57, 165–66, 212–30.

20. Marsh, ''Marsh Reads Caputo,'' pp. 19–20.

21. *Ibid.*

22. For Westphal's comment, see his essay in this volume, pp. 180–81. For my account of rationality as critical of technocracy, capitalism, and state socialism, see

PCM, pp. 200–58, 232 note 21; and "Ambiguity, Language, and Communicative Praxis," in this volume, pp. 104–105.

23. For Westphal's comment in this volume, see *supra*, p. 175.

24. Robert Nozick, *Anarchy, State and Utopia* (New York: Basic Books, 1974), pp. 149–175.

25. Michael Sandel, *Liberalism and the Limits of Justice* (New York: Cambridge University Press, 1982). Roberto Mangabeira Unger, *Knowledge and Politics* (New York: The Free Press, 1984).

# Index

Ambiguity, critical modernist vs. post-modernist responses to, 3–4; triumph of, in postmodernism, 4; triumph over, in critical modernism, 4–6, 9–10, 142–45; as part of a performative contradiction in Marsh, 8; Marsh's response to Caputo's critique, 99–104; as in a lived existential tension with objectivity, 164, 175, 209

Augustine, Saint, 65, 83

Caputo, John, similarities with Marsh, 12, 59, 88; critique of Heidegger, 13–14; politicizing of reason, 14; his Derridizing of Heidegger, 23; as rational, contrary to Derrida, 32–34; his line of argument in RH, 88; his misinterpretation of Marsh, 98, 101; Marsh's response to, 99–105, 203–206, 211–12; denying the implications of making a truth claim, 100–101, 143–44; having no meta-account of rationality, 129–31; Humean meta-account in, vs. Marsh's Kantian meta-account, 133–35; relationship to the tradition, 135–42; his attempt to justify a preference for the marginalized, 176–80; his dogmatism, 177–78; his allergy to Habermas, 180; as a Knight of Infinite Evasiveness, 197, 204

Communicative praxis, 202

Consistency, 18. *See also* Performative self-contradiction; Self-referentiality

Cratylus, 173–81, 185

Critical modernism, xii–xiii, 1, 106–107, 131, 133, 143, 148–49, 153, 159–61, 214*n*11; its confrontation with radical hermeneutics in Caputo, 58–62

*Dasein*, as being in the truth, 46–47, 54, 184; as being in untruth, 48–49

Deconstruction, 28, 56–67, 93, 95, 138, 208–209

De Nys, Martin, 93, 97–99

Derrida, Jacques, his theory of *différance*, xii–xiii, 51–52; as the left wing of hermeneutics, 13; as the source of the radicalism of radical hermeneutics, 27–28; as rational, contrary to Marsh's reading, 29–32; Marsh's interpretation of as rational, 93–94, 198; his relationship to the philosophical tradition, 135–42; his a-thetic discourse as a way of avoiding self-contradiction, 169–74; his use of Levinas, 176–77; the value of empty intentions in, 186–87; critical modernism's critique of his a-thetic move, 199–200; as friendly to metaphysics in his late work, 207

Descartes, René, 2, 88, 147–48

Descriptive adequacy of postmodern claims, 92–93, 197

Dialectical phenomenology, 4, 6–11, 30, 66–83, 122–14; critique of capitalism and state socialism, 94–96, 104–105, 116

*Différance*, its role in human understanding, xii–xiii; compared with Ha-